SAVED BY
HER ENEMY

SAVED BY HER ENEMY

An Iraqi Woman's Journey
from the Heart of War
to the Heartland of America

Don Teague
Rafraf Barrak

HOWARD BOOKS
A Division of Simon & Schuster, Inc.
New York Nashville London Toronto Sydney

Published by Howard Books, a division of Simon & Schuster, Inc.
1230 Avenue of the Americas, New York, NY 10020
www.howardpublishing.com

For information about special discounts for bulk purchases, please contact Simon & Schuster Special Sales at 1-866-506-1949 or business@simonandschuster.com.

The Simon & Schuster Speakers Bureau can bring authors to your live event. For more information or to book an event contact the Simon & Schuster Speakers Bureau at 1-866-248-3049 or visit our website at www.simonspeakers.com.

Published in association with Ambassador Literary Agency, Nashville, Tennessee

Library of Congress Control Number: 2009029974

ISBN 978-1-4767-8645-2

Designed by Jaime Putorti

AUTHOR'S NOTE

Saved by Her Enemy is a true story, but it is not a work of "journalism" in the strict sense of the word.

Rafraf and I didn't plan to write a book as we lived through the events on the following pages. As such, we weren't taking notes or recording conversations with others. This work reflects our present recollections of our experiences over a period of years.

The names and some identifying characteristics of certain people in this book have been changed (in most cases for their protection). Dialogue between characters has been reconstructed from memory—Rafraf's or mine—or, in limited cases, imagined based on our best understanding of events. Certain events have been compressed and some individuals are composites. There are a few scenes within the book that are re-creations of events of which Rafraf and I had no firsthand experience. In those instances the scenes are imagined based on the best information we could gather.

With that understanding, the goal of this book is to tell our story as accurately and truthfully as possible.

To my father, who always believed in me,
and my mother, who believed in him.

CONTENTS

FOREWORD

Mother Teresa once said, "If we have no peace, it is because we have forgotten that we belong to each other."

She could have been describing this book by Don Teague and Rafraf Barrak, two people who can teach us a thing or two about how much more connects than separates us.

Rafraf I met through her story, which reveals courage, compassion, and a stunning willingness to stand against injustice. She is just the kind of person the United States needs and can be proud to call one of its own.

Don I know personally as a colleague and a friend. He's the guy who doesn't just call 911 if he sees someone in trouble; he jumps right in to help. At NBC News he earned a reputation for being a dependable reporter and a strong and honest writer who could be trusted to get it right, with poignancy and intelligence.

Still, despite the years and war zones we've shared, I suspect I did not fully know Don's depths until this book. Who among us has the quality of character to do what Don has done for Rafraf?

Saved by Her Enemy is a kind of road map to the future, when, inevitably, I think, we will know that no matter whether we are American or Arab, Christian or Muslim, man or woman, we are actually not enemies at all, but brethren.

This glimpse of war is instructive. May it help you find peace.

Ann Curry
NBC News Anchor, Correspondent

EYE CONTACT

I brahim looked at me through the rearview mirror. We both expected a burst of gunfire to riddle the beat-up Suburban at any second, but it never came. Instead there was a moment of eerie silence as our SUV careened down the dirt road . . . trying to put as much distance between us and the school as possible. Our army convoy had left us to fend for ourselves; the protection of their turret-mounted machine guns was nowhere in sight.

How many were dead? We had no idea, but seconds before the explosion, the street had been filled with children. Now there was only chaos and rage. We were completely unable to defend ourselves, two SUVs carrying a half dozen frightened journalists and our British security adviser, Rupert.

Young Iraqi men lined the road, some running toward the still smoking aftermath of the blast, some watching us race away in stunned silence, others shouting and raising their fists in anger.

Rupert rode shotgun. His pistol would be worthless in the expected ambush. It never left his holster.

"They bombed the bloody school," Rupert shouted into a hand-held radio. "Repeat! They bombed the school!"

There was no answer.

"Don't slow down," I told Ibrahim, "no matter what."

"Go!"

The Iraqi driver floored the accelerator.

The Suburban bounced and bucked as our makeshift convoy roared down the dirt road past the squatty concrete homes that dotted the landscape of western Baghdad. The residents knew enough to stay inside; the roads were empty save for a few stray dogs and goats.

Somewhere ahead was a left turn that would lead us to a busy road. The risk of ambush would be smaller if we could just make that road, but our chances of getting there seemed remote. We managed to put half a mile between the school and us, but none of us could relax. Not yet.

In recent weeks, insurgents had modified their tactics. No longer content with simply bombing foreigners, they had begun ambushing survivors with AK-47s as they tried to run. And we were running for our lives. Our unarmored vehicles would be no match for bullets, much less another bomb.

I turned and looked out the back window. The school was receding into the distance, the crowd outside still visible even through the dust cloud left hanging in the air by our racing convoy.

For the first time in the last—what had it been, three minutes?—I caught my breath, the adrenaline replaced by a sudden wave of nausea. I recognized the feeling from the last time I was almost killed; it would pass. That's when I noticed Ibrahim, looking at me in the rearview mirror. He was telling me something with his eyes.

I suddenly became acutely aware of Rafraf. She was sitting on my right, closest to the door. But she wasn't sitting as much as lying down half across my body. She seemed tiny and frail, even wrapped in what was supposed to be my body armor. I could feel her body rise and fall with each breath. I could feel her tears on my arm.

And there was Ibrahim again, looking at me in the rearview mirror.

Rafraf was twenty-three years old. She should have been in school, but Baghdad University had been closed for more than a year. So instead of enjoying her last semester as a college student, Rafraf was putting her English skills to work doing the most dangerous job in the most dangerous city on earth. She was working as a translator for NBC News, which currently meant trying to survive the ride back to our hotel.

"What about all the children?" she asked, her voice barely above a whimper. "There were children everywhere. Don't they care?"

"Maybe the children knew in advance," I said. "Maybe they had warning. I didn't see any bodies." It was the most I could offer, but I wasn't convinced.

Rafraf sobbed, "There were so many children." I felt her body shudder.

I squeezed her hand, and for the first time realized I was holding her hand, my right arm draped around her for protection. I loosened my grip to allow her to sit up, but she didn't move. I became aware of the scarf that covered her head and most of her face, aware, in fact, of all that meant.

Rafraf was a Muslim woman in a culture that demanded separation between men and women. In the weeks I had worked with Rafraf I had never actually touched her . . . not even a handshake. Now here I was with my arm wrapped around her body.

Ibrahim spoke little English, but in this case he didn't have to. He had been sending me a message with his eyes . . . perhaps a warning: RAFRAF IS ONE OF US, NOT ONE OF YOU. DON'T TOUCH OUR WOMEN.

I gently nudged Rafraf back to her upright position and let her go.

"It'll be okay," I said weakly. But I knew it wouldn't. I also knew deep down this wouldn't be the last time I tried to save Rafraf.

ONE

CHILD OF WAR

There's absolutely no similarity between English and Arabic. To me, as an American, a conversation in Arabic sounds like a song that has forgotten its melody. The words are soft and lilting, even when the subject matter is life and death. I can't imagine what Americans sound like to Iraqis. I'm often told our language is harsh and generally unpleasant to listen to. Easy to believe.

Dogs, on the other hand, speak the universal language of . . . "dog." Sure, no one would confuse the bark of a rottweiler with that of a Chihuahua, but walk up to any kid in the world and go "Ruff ruff," and that kid will know you're speaking canine. Which explains why Rafraf has mercilessly been teased about her name since her father plucked it from the Koran.

Loosely translated, *rafraf* means "the green carpet." As used in the Koran, it's the beautiful meadow that Allah has waiting for his followers in heaven. It's a beautiful image, but the word is rarely used as a proper name for a person. Even for native speakers of Arabic, it's difficult to ignore that *rafraf* sounds like a barking dog.

Do a Google search for *rafraf* and you'll get thousands of hits, but only a handful will point you to actual people, none like Rafraf Barrak.

Rafraf was literally a child of war. She was born in Baghdad during the fall of 1980, just two months after Iraq invaded Iran, beginning eight bloody years of fighting. For the first few weeks of her life, she had no name at all . . . her mother simply called her "baby." The baby's name would have to wait until her father came home from the war.

When Kamal Barrak returned on leave, he opened the Koran, ran his finger through the pages, and stopped on *rafraf.*

"Please, no," her mother begged. "It's not even a real name. The other children will make fun of her."

But Kamal would hear none of it. "Rafraf," he said again. He had made up his mind. This girl, the fifth child in a family that would grow to ten children, would be named after one of Allah's greatest gifts—the promise of paradise to come. With that, he went back to war, where he would serve for another five years.

For Rafraf, the teasing would last a lifetime.

Still, she led a normal life by Iraqi standards. Through most of her childhood, the family lived in a small house in what was considered a middle-class Baghdad neighborhood. The homes on her street were solidly built; many were even two stories, although the tiny Barrak home had just a single level. The roads were paved, the sewers worked, and most yards were big enough for a small garden or fruit tree.

The neighborhood was mostly populated by Shiite Muslims, the largest religious sect in Iraq. Kamal was a Shiite, which meant Rafraf and the other members of the family were Shiites as well.

During the rule of Saddam Hussein, Shiites were, in large part, second-class citizens. Saddam was a Sunni Muslim, as was about 20 percent of the Iraqi population. The Sunnis, despite being in the minority, enjoyed favored status: better homes, better jobs, better military assignments, and better lives.

It made it all the more remarkable that Kamal Barrak was able to succeed at all. He had been stricken with an unknown illness in childhood that left him partially disfigured. But despite his handicap, and his second-class status, Kamal always found a way to succeed.

Before the war with Iran, Kamal worked as an accountant in a government ministry. He saved enough of his small salary to buy a home for his growing family. The house was tiny, with just two bedrooms, but it was in a safe neighborhood where the electricity usually worked.

By the time Rafraf was born, the bedroom set aside for children was woefully too small. So her parents converted the living room into a bedroom and turned the bedroom into a tiny living room. As a result, until she was sixteen years old, Rafraf slept in the same room with every one of her brothers and sisters. Privacy was unheard of.

As with any house, the walls of Rafraf's home were covered with photographs: children's birthdays, school graduations, and family gatherings. But no matter where you looked in the house, the one thing you wouldn't find was a picture of her parents' wedding. It was not a joyous occasion.

Jamila was barely more than a girl, a teenager who hoped to meet a man someday and fall in love. Kamal, a distant cousin, was a few years older, and already engaged to the love of his young life, a girl he had met in school.

A chance encounter changed everything.

Jamila's mother, Allaya, and Kamal's mother, Lela, bumped into each other one day in 1970 while shopping in a Baghdad street market. Casual conversation between the two cousins led to a discussion about their children.

"All of my children have married," said Allaya, "except my youngest, Jamila."

"How old is she?" asked Lela.

"Seventeen, and beginning to attract the wrong kind of attention. She was seen walking with a boy from her class last week. Zaid punished her when he heard about the boy, but she's so strong-willed. If she sees him again, I fear her father will kill them both. You should thank Allah that all of your children are married."

"All except Kamal," Lela corrected. "He's engaged to a girl from university."

"But not yet married?" asked Allaya.

"Not yet."

And with that, the fate of two cousins was sealed. The women determined that their children, who had never even met, would marry.

Kamal was heartbroken. He was forced to end the engagement to a woman he truly loved, one who had chosen him despite his physical handicap. But there was no choice in the matter.

Marriage for many Iraqi families was about tribal alliance, money, political relationships, and influence. Love was too far down the list of priorities to really make a difference. And in Iraq, you didn't question such decisions.

So, no wedding pictures are on the walls of Rafraf's family home. There is no trunk with cherished tokens, no veil or wedding dress passed down to daughters. Kamal and Jamila created a family, and a life together, based on respect for their parents. It was a hard fact of life in a culture that demanded obedience.

Which was why Rafraf never really fit in. She had a disobedient streak that always caused her, and her parents, trouble.

She figured her name was at least part of the problem. She couldn't begin to count the number of jokes she heard whispered just within earshot. But Rafraf stood out for other reasons.

She was a stunning beauty, even as a child, with long black hair, an oval face, and brown eyes that hinted at Asian ancestry. Her eyes, she knew, were her best feature, conveying the subtlest idea of mystery and mischief.

She was also extremely smart, with a near-photographic memory, and an uncanny ability to recall mundane bits of information. This may sound like a gift, but as a child, Rafraf's intelligence and independence got her into a lot of trouble at school.

Iraqi schools, at least during Saddam's reign, were somewhat similar to American schools. Rafraf attended a public school, with classes of both boys and girls. Teachers were good or bad, doting or authoritarian, and principals were respected and feared. There were lockers, lunch periods, recesses, and homework.

Except Rafraf rarely did her homework. To the frustration of her teachers and her parents, she did the absolute minimum required of her to get by. It's a common trademark among intelligent kids. If unchallenged, they simply cruise along waiting for something to come along that actually interests them.

"You have to study," her mother would scold. "You're not even trying."

"Why should I?" was the frequent response. "It's just a waste of time. Everything is too easy, why should I bother?"

And it was easy for Rafraf. Through six years of elementary school, Rafraf had perfect scores on every test, perfect grades in every class . . . all without cracking a book, or giving any of it a second thought. Her academic success would have continued through university if not for two major changes that threw her life into complete disarray.

The first sounds innocent enough: she discovered boys. To be sure, most girls start showing some interest in boys somewhere between the ages of twelve and fifteen, but in Rafraf's strictly religious neighborhood, even the slightest contact with the opposite sex was considered sinful, and cause for a severe beating.

Not just by parents. If a father wasn't available to beat his daughter for disgracing the family, then his brothers or sons would beat her. If family members weren't up to the task, men from the neighborhood would beat a woman who had behaved badly.

And punishable contact wasn't limited to kissing, holding hands, or even touching. Premarital sex could literally be fatal, but simply talking to a member of the opposite sex in public or, worse, being caught alone in a room together was an affront to Allah himself.

But Rafraf found it almost impossible to resist attention from boys, not that she didn't try.

Under the secular rule of Saddam, women in Iraq weren't required to cover up as they were in many other Islamic countries. Still, it was expected that at the very least proper women would wear traditional Muslim head scarves that covered their hair and partially concealed their faces. When she was fourteen years old, Rafraf told her mother she wanted to start wearing the scarf.

"You're kidding," snipped Laila, Rafraf's older sister. "Nobody will believe you're doing it for Allah. You just want to wear a scarf because I wear a scarf."

Laila was right. The primary reason Rafraf wanted the scarf was because her big sister wore it, but she would never admit that to her mother.

"I'm not going to buy you a scarf," her mother said. "You'll wear it for a little while, then take it off, and then people will talk."

"I promise," said Rafraf, "I'll wear it forever. I'm a woman now."

"No, you're not," said Laila. "You're just an annoying little brat. You follow me around, do everything I do, and get everything I got before I did. It's not fair."

"Enough, both of you," their mother demanded.

"Please."

"The rules change with the scarf, Rafraf," her mother said, "whether you actually are a woman or not. From the moment you put on that scarf, you're held to the standard of a woman who knows how to act, not a child."

"I know."

"And you're absolutely sure?"

"Yes, absolutely."

And with that, Rafraf the child became a woman.

The second event that changed Rafraf's life was entirely out of her control. Her father, Kamal, had resumed his civilian career after returning from the war. For the first few years, he worked as a cashier in Baghdad's water purification department. The pay wasn't much, but it was enough for Kamal to provide for his rapidly growing family.

In 1993, Kamal left the government payroll and went to work for a private company as an accountant. The pay was better, and the job held some prestige. Kamal was moving up in the world. At least, that's the way it seemed.

Then came the fall of 1996.

Rafraf was sixteen years old. The turmoil of what we now call Gulf War One had settled down. American warplanes regularly patrolled the "no-fly zones" established over areas of northern and southern Iraq. But in Baghdad, Saddam Hussein's power was unquestioned. The city's 5 million residents lived in relative peace, and in the case of Kamal Barrak, obscurity. The quiet father of ten plodded away at his accounting job, with no hint of trouble on the horizon.

So, it was a big surprise for Kamal when the Iraqi police burst into his office one day. His boss, it seemed, was a cheat—stealing from his own company. A substantial amount of money was missing, powerful people were offended, and Iraqi authorities were determined to set things right.

Surely the company accountant was in on it.

Surely Kamal knew where the money was.

He didn't.

Rafraf was at school that day. When she came home, her sister was crying.

"What's wrong?" Rafraf asked. "Why are you crying?"

Nala was known for her overly dramatic displays, but this wasn't an act.

"They took him away," her sister sobbed.

"Who, not Rami?"

Rami, Rafraf's little brother, was five years her junior. She loved him dearly and had doted on him from the day he was born.

"Not Rami," cried Nala, "Baba, our father. They've taken him to jail."

"Why? For what?" Rafraf was horrified, well aware that being taken away by Iraqi police could mean never being seen or heard from again.

"I don't know. They just took him from work. Mama is going to the police station to talk to him."

But Jamila wasn't allowed to see her husband. He wasn't allowed to see anyone, even a lawyer, for weeks.

Kamal was never charged with or even accused of a crime. He

was held because police hoped to use him for information and leverage against his employer. He remained behind bars, locked up in a holding cell of a giant Baghdad police station for nearly a year.

It was a difficult year for Rafraf. She had been raised to believe the police were infallible. Her mother wouldn't talk about what was happening . . . for weeks not even acknowledging that her husband was in jail. Rafraf took this to mean her father must have done something terrible . . . why else would the police have taken him away?

She was shamed at school, embarrassed for her family, and afraid of what the future might bring.

Then, just as suddenly as the whole episode began, it ended. Kamal, after the better part of a year in jail, was simply let go. He wasn't the only employee the police had been pressuring, and they finally got the answers they wanted.

Kamal was innocent after all, but the months locked in a cramped cell with twenty other men had taken their toll.

Sanitary conditions were horrific. By the time Kamal was released, his body was covered with seeping sores. There had been no medical attention, no showers, no fresh clothes, and no real facilities. But leaving the jail didn't end the suffering.

Kamal was released with no job and no money. He had borrowed money to pay for a useless attorney and debts were due. Within days of returning, Kamal was forced to sell his home, moving his family into a slum southwest of Baghdad.

The neighborhood had broken underground pipes that gushed raw sewage. It flowed down the unpaved road in front of Kamal's house, digging a channel of waste that made it impossible for cars to pass. On most days, the road was little more than a septic mud pit. City officials knew about the sewage and pledged to fix it, but never did.

Still, the new house was bigger, with multiple bedrooms and room for a vegetable garden in the backyard. When the wind blew from the south or east, the smell of sewage baking under the hot sun drifted over the neighbor's house, away from Kamal's. In Baghdad, good news came in small gusts.

By then, Rafraf was in high school, and even a head scarf couldn't hide her beauty. The move to the new neighborhood, which was strictly Shiite, was potentially dangerous for her. The rules of her religion were expected to be followed closely. The new neighbors were unlikely to approve of Rafraf's growing rebellious streak.

Rafraf had strong moral values. She respected herself, loved Allah, and tried to live a sin-free life. But Islam placed high demands on behavior. For Rafraf, the standards were difficult to live up to.

At an age when most American girls were dating, she was forbidden from talking to a member of the opposite sex without a male family member present. Of course, she wanted to, and so did her friends. They were teenage girls who hoped to someday marry a man of their choosing—not some stranger chosen by their parents, or worse yet, a cousin. But how could they make that happen?

In the case of Rafraf and her friends, getting to know a boy required an elaborate system of sneaking around. Seriously. Lookouts, ruses, lies, and deceptions, all in an effort to spend, say, thirty seconds flirting with the boy from the next block. This time-consuming operation ultimately affected her schoolwork just enough to change the course of her life.

In Saddam's Iraq, college was free to anyone with the grades to get in. Anyone. Men, women, Sunni, Shia . . . you get the grades, you get the education. What you didn't get was a lot of say in the matter. While there was an application process, the government ultimately decided which college you got into, and what you majored in. It was all based on grades.

And Rafraf's grades were slipping. She had hoped to attend Iraq's top school, Baghdad University, and get a law degree. But just as in this country, law school and medical school were reserved for the top achievers, and Rafraf, despite her intelligence, just missed the top cut.

Initially she was devastated when she opened the letter from the Ministry of Education. Law school was out. She would still attend Baghdad University, but her major would be English literature.

"What on earth will I do with that?" she asked her mother, tears filling her eyes.

"You could teach school," Jamila offered, "you're so good with children."

"I don't want to be a teacher. I want to be special. I want to be respected, not just another teacher."

"You can take that up with Saddam," her mother quipped.

"I'll get right on that," Rafraf replied, forcing a smile.

That night, she cried herself to sleep, convinced that the path of her life had veered wildly off course. She was, of course, right.

TWO

HIGH FLIGHT

A Tuesday morning changed my life forever. Not in the devastating way it did for those who lost family and friends on that September day, but in the same way it changed the lives of millions of Americans. Our collective innocence was lost.

"The world will never be the same." That's what we said then. Some of us believed it.

I was working in San Diego, anchoring and reporting for the number one TV station in the city. Times were good.

My wife, Kiki, was taking our two girls to school that morning. I had the day off and was sleeping in.

Suddenly, the door to the bedroom burst open. To this day I believe she kicked it open, but Kiki swears she didn't.

"Get up," she said, "now." She had a phone to her ear and disappeared into the living room.

"What?" I sat up in bed.

"Get up!" She repeated, using her I'm-not-kidding-around voice. I noticed a hint of sadness.

"This can't be good," I said to myself, figuring I had managed to screw something up, big-time. I walked into the living room just in time to see the second tower fall.

We cried, all four of us, then we held hands and prayed. We prayed for the people in those planes and buildings, and prayed for their families. We prayed for protection. We thanked God that we were safe, and that our girls were too young to fully comprehend what was happening.

"What do we do now?" Kiki asked.

How the hell am I supposed to know? I thought, but didn't say.

My heart told me that my girls were never going to leave my sight again. The world was just too dangerous, and I couldn't risk losing them. My brain eventually took over and found something to say.

"I think Rachael and Maddie can be late today. Let's give it a couple of hours and see if they still have classes. Maybe we'll take them in around noon."

It wasn't much, but it was a plan. In those first hours, even baby steps were so hard to take.

By one o'clock the girls were at school, and I was on my way to work. I should have noticed there were no airplanes in the sky— everyone else seemed to—but I was lost in thought.

I was thinking about my army uniform, still hanging in the closet. It had been more than four years since I last wore it, but I knew it still fit. The truth was, for the first time in my life, I wanted to kill someone. Really and truly kill someone.

I had served eleven years in the Army Reserve and National Guard, all the while working my way up the local TV news ranks.

Thankfully, killing people really wasn't my thing. I was a captain when I left the service, and a helicopter pilot. My last job in the Guard was commanding an air-assault helicopter company. In times of war, that means leading one hundred men and women, flying troops into battle. But most of my time was spent training . . . endlessly training.

For eleven years, I never took a vacation from my civilian job. The demands of the army, even part-time, took all of my free time, and since most TV stations don't pay you when you don't work, I used my vacation time to cover my two weeks of annual military training.

Throughout the year, I averaged six to eight days every month in uniform . . . staff meetings, training meetings, inspections, and flight training just to stay safe and meet minimum flight times.

When I took the job in San Diego in 1998, I knew it was time to give up the army. I missed the smell of jet fuel, missed the camaraderie of the men and women who shared the danger and excitement of army aviation . . . but I owed Kiki more than a decade of quality time and missed vacations.

We vacationed in Europe, we renewed our wedding vows, we loved life. Times were good . . . or at least they were until that awful Tuesday morning in September.

By four o'clock on the afternoon of September 11, I had made my way to the parking lot of a mosque in the San Diego neighborhood of Clairemont Mesa. Police said shots had been fired at the mosque earlier that day. I interviewed one of the imams from the mosque, who expressed his sympathy for the victims. He asked that people not hold Islam responsible for the criminal actions of a few. I did a live report asking people not to shoot at the building as they drove by.

It was weeks before we learned that two of the hijackers, Nawaf al-Hazmi and Khalid al-Mihdhar, had been members of that very mosque.

IT WAS LATE AFTERNOON IN Baghdad when the footage of planes crashing into the World Trade Center first appeared on television. Rafraf's family, like millions around the world, watched the images in stunned disbelief. Jamila couldn't stop crying, but couldn't stop watching either.

"Oh my God," she sobbed, "those are people jumping from the buildings. They're burning."

Jamila turned to her children with pleading eyes, as if they could help her understand. They of course had no answers either.

By early evening, the first pictures appeared of Palestinians dancing in the streets. They were celebrating the attack, clapping their hands, laughing, and flashing victory signs. The scene infuriated Jamila, who scolded her oldest boys.

"I don't care whom they think they're doing this for," she demanded, "but there's no way to justify burning people alive."

She turned to Rami.

"Go get the Koran," she demanded. "Now tell me where it justifies murdering innocent people. Or killing yourself? Even in the name of Allah! If you commit suicide, you will go to hell. If you kill innocent people, you will go to hell. This is not justified."

Still, the dancing on television continued. While celebrations were isolated, the view among many in the Arab world that "America got what it deserved" was widespread.

But, such words, or even thoughts, were not allowed in Rafraf's house.

"You can't take pleasure in another's pain," Jamila reminded her children at the end of that terrible day. "It will always come back to you."

TELEVISION NETWORKS, INCLUDING THE ONE I worked for, have since stopped showing the video of the World Trade Center falling. The images, they reasoned, were simply too painful for those who lost loved ones. I respectfully disagree.

Remember back in the days before we had six hundred television channels to choose from? When I was growing up in Los Angeles, there were a half dozen or so VHF (very high frequency) stations, and about the same number of stations on UHF (ultra high frequency), and that was it. Their broadcast days had an actual beginning, and end. When the stations signed off after midnight, they played a short film of a fighter jet soaring across the sky.

"Oh! I have slipped the surly bonds of earth and danced the skies on laughter-silvered wings," the narrator would say, reading from a poem called "High Flight." "Sunward I've climbed and joined the tumbling mirth of sun-split clouds, and done a hundred things you have not dreamed of. Wheeled and soared and swung high in the sunlit silence."

If it were up to me, I would have reinstituted the sign-off tradition at every television station and broadcast network in America. But instead of "High Flight," I would have ended the day with a memorial to the victims of September 11—including images.

What would the narrator say? I have no idea. Maybe nothing. But the events of that day dramatically changed the world and America's place in it. It's important to remember. I believed that with all my heart.

THE NEXT EIGHT MONTHS OF my life were a whirlwind of change. I know this sounds clichéd, but I have an agent. A true-to-life, Beverly Hills, hybrid-driving agent who says things like "Love ya, babe" and "Let's do lunch when you're in town." David Ahrendts gets 10 percent of my every paycheck, but he has earned his pay over the years by giving sound advice and always looking out for my best interests.

Several months before the terrorist attacks, David suggested I send a résumé and some samples of my work to the major networks.

"Yeah, I'll get right on that," I said skeptically.

"I'm serious, Don," he encouraged. "I think it's time to take the next step in your career."

I was happy working in local news. The last thing I wanted was to start living out of a suitcase, which is a fact of life for network correspondents. Besides, the odds of making it to the "big leagues" for any reporter are about a million to one.

Television news is an incredibly competitive business. An on-air opening at any station will result in literally hundreds of applications, all from reporters in smaller cities hoping to move their way up to bigger cities. Bigger populations mean more viewers, which means more money from advertisers. All of this translates to higher pay in bigger cities.

And there's nothing bigger than network. The broadcast networks of ABC, NBC, and CBS are the holy grail for the thousands of reporters doing important work covering crime, traffic accidents, house fires, and city council meetings in more than 210 news markets in the United States. It's what seemingly every reporter aspires to. Except me.

"Knock yourself out, David," I said. "But I'm not holding my breath."

"You won't have to" was his confident reply. It turns out, he was right again.

A few weeks after September 11, David started getting phone calls. A major cable network and two broadcast networks were interested in my work. They all seemed to have the same need.

"They're intrigued by your military experience," David said. "Most of their reporters don't know anything about the military."

That made sense to me. Army officer to TV reporter isn't a common career path. Although many media outlets work hard to honor military service members in times of war, some journalists seem to loathe the military or, at best, distrust it. They believe America uses the military to project ideology onto the rest of the world and are unsettled by the notion.

I'm not that guy.

My father was an army officer. Not a career soldier, but a guy who was proud to do his time, then move on with his life. He served during the Vietnam War and repeatedly volunteered to go. Instead the army sent him to Germany, where he and the combat-engineer company he eventually commanded prepared to save Western Europe from a Russian invasion.

The invasion never happened, but I consider his time in Germany pretty important, because that's where I was born, at a U.S. military hospital in Heidelberg.

My dad never pushed me to join the army, but from watching his example, I figured that's what you do when you grow up.

So when I started college at San Diego State University, I enrolled in army ROTC. I minored in military science, while getting a bachelor's degree in broadcast journalism.

I was a good cadet (that's what they call you in ROTC) and an okay student. But I achieved an extremely high score on a standardized military test called the Flight Aptitude Selection Test. The FAST is like a cross between an IQ test and a personality profile. Apparently I had whatever it was the army looks for in a combat helicopter pilot. I was also blessed with good health and the ability to pass a military flight physical . . . which only a fraction of the population can do.

So, three months after graduating from college in 1987, I began flight school at the United States Army Aviation Center at Fort Rucker, Alabama.

I guess the aptitude test had me pegged, because I found it pretty easy. Several hours every day in a UH-1 "Huey" helicopter, followed by several hours of classroom work and periodic tests called check rides. Military flight training is intensive and covers everything from physics to meteorology. There are emergency procedures to learn, combat tactics to practice, and on weekends . . . beer to be consumed.

Some struggle, and others don't make it through, but for me it was thirteen months of great fun. The shared dangers helped forge relationships that I cherish to this day.

Still, I was young and foolish, so against all good judgment, I also enrolled in night classes at a nearby branch of Troy State University. I earned a master's degree in international relations while I was in flight school . . . a feat made possible by coffee and a fear of failure. It added considerably to my stress level and workload, but that entry on my résumé also caught the eye of network executives.

"CNN is looking for a reporter to cover the military beat," David told me.

"CNN has a military beat?"

"They do now, or at least they will. It's not at the Pentagon. They're looking for someone who's willing to get dirty. Are you interested?"

My contract was nearing its end in San Diego, and my news director had made it painfully clear to me that I was overpaid, despite strong ratings for the shows I anchored. It was time to find a new job.

"I'm interested," I said, "but I don't really want to get pigeonholed as a military reporter. And I certainly don't want to spend the rest of my life in Afghanistan."

"I couldn't agree more, Don, but this could be a good opportunity for you."

"Well, obviously I'll talk to them. What else is out there?"

"I've heard good things about you from NBC News. They like your writing style, but I'm not sure how quickly they're going to move."

That was an understatement. NBC News had only about forty correspondents. As the network had the top-rated *Today* show and *NBC Nightly News,* joining the team was sort of like making the starting lineup of the New York Yankees. There's not a lot of "up" left, so correspondents tend to stay in place for a long time.

With such low turnover, the network can afford to put potential hires through a lengthy process . . . several rounds of interviews, from the executive producers of each show, to the network president, and more vice presidents than you can count. They want to know about your news philosophy, why you're in the business, if you understand how stressful network news really is. There's even a writing test that's graded by the network president himself. I'm not kidding. They also watch your work, for months.

"They need to see more tape," David would tell me.

"How could they possibly need to see more stories?" I'd ask. "They've seen more of me than my wife has."

"This is how they work, Don. They want your last five stories, beginning with last night."

Ah. A pop quiz. That made sense . . . make sure I was not just sending them stories that I liked.

"Okay, I'll get it to them by tomorrow. Any idea how long this torture is going to last?" I asked, not really expecting an answer.

It was now April 2002. One month before the end of my contract in San Diego, and seven months after 9/11. It had been four months since my first trip to "30 Rock"—NBC's headquarters at Rockefeller Center—in New York.

The first series of interviews convinced me that NBC would be the right fit for me. They weren't looking to turn me into a war correspondent. Yes, they liked the military experience, and yes, they would send me to Iraq if the talk of war proved more than a saber rattling by the Bush administration. But they needed a "storyteller," whether it was a feature about feuding beauty queens or the aftermath of a hurricane.

Thankfully, NBC quit torturing me in June 2002 and hired me as their newest correspondent. After thirteen years of working in television news every day, I was a rookie again.

THREE

SHOCK AND AWE

H e was dangerous. That much Rafraf had been sure of since childhood. He lurked in the darkened shadows of buildings, or sometimes on empty streets at night. She had been warned of his cunning, deceptiveness, and murderous appetite.

Everyone had stories of encounters. Rafraf's friends, cousins, and especially her older siblings told awful tales of their run-ins with Mr. John. It was only a matter of time before he would come for her too.

What Rafraf wasn't sure of was who or even what Mr. John actually was. Was he a demon? A beast whose features only made him look human? Or was Mr. John simply a madman bent on the destruction of all things good and moral?

The truth, she learned, was even worse.

He was an American. More to the point, Mr. John was all Americans.

Just as children in the United States are raised to fear a common enemy, the bogeyman, the children in Rafraf's family were told Mr. John might be hiding under the bed or stalking them from behind the backyard shed.

What made these stories so frightening was that unlike the mythical bogeyman, Americans clearly do exist. In Rafraf's limited view of the world, the danger was no myth.

It was, she thought, Americans who had needlessly meddled in Iraqi matters during the first Gulf War. What business was it of theirs that Saddam had taken back the oil fields from the Kuwaitis? The Kuwaitis were getting rich by drilling under Iraqi soil, thus stealing what rightfully belonged to Iraq.

In the years following Operation Desert Storm, America had used its warplanes to enforce "no fly" zones over Iraq. American pilots, she was told, casually murdered Iraqi soldiers by dropping bombs on barracks as the soldiers slept.

America used its influence with the United Nations to impose crippling economic sanctions, causing Iraqi children to starve and suffer needlessly.

And it was America, Rafraf thought, that coddled the Jews in Israel. Like those in many Arab countries, she believed the Israeli government was wholly to blame for the continued conflict with the Palestinians. Arab solidarity with Palestine was a source of both pride and a shared sense of suffering. Without American support, she believed, the Palestinians wouldn't have to face murder, humiliation, and Israeli oppression.

All of this, Rafraf accepted without question, because there was no alternative.

So, it's not surprising that when a thunderous explosion shook her out of bed early on the morning of March 20, 2003, Rafraf's first thoughts were of the murderous Mr. John.

By then she was twenty-two years old, just a semester short of receiving her degree from Baghdad University. The school had, however, been closed for several days. It was thought of as merely a precaution. Surely the American president wouldn't really attack. Would he?

* * *

THERE HAD, OF COURSE, BEEN warnings. The first drum-beats . . . a staccato outburst on a Tuesday morning just over eighteen months before. Four beats out of rhythm that still reverberated in the broken hearts of 300 million Americans.

"Either you are with us, or you are with the terrorists," President George Bush famously told the U.S. Congress just nine days after September 11.

His words echoed those spoken by the junior senator from New York on September 13.

"Every nation has to be either with us or against us," said Hillary Clinton. "Those who harbor terrorists or who finance them are going to pay a price."

At the time, it seemed that the Bush administration was convinced Saddam Hussein had weapons of mass destruction. Evidently, so were the governments of Russia, China, Germany, France, Great Britain, and many other countries. Some of those countries had close ties with Iraq. Though they opposed the decision to disarm Saddam, they expressed no doubts, based on their own intelligence, that he had WMDs.

Saddam Hussein encouraged these beliefs by openly defying UN weapons inspectors. Saddam himself told FBI interrogators after his capture that he purposefully deceived the world into believing that he had WMDs in an effort to prevent Iran from invading his country.

While it was later determined that he had no nuclear, chemical, or biological weapons, to the United States he posed other problems. The Bush administration had spent months laying out the case against Saddam Hussein:

- His antiaircraft guns routinely shot at American warplanes, which were operating under UN authority enforcing the no-fly zones.
- He had attempted to assassinate former president George H. W. Bush, seeking revenge for U.S. intervention in Kuwait.

- He was financially supporting Palestinian suicide bombers in the ongoing intifada against Israel, paying surviving family members $25,000 to reward the bombers' acts of terror.
- While he wasn't responsible for September 11, he did offer "safe haven" to known terrorists.

In a world where "you're either with us or against us," the American president put Saddam Hussein at the top of the list of those not with us.

All of which I tried to remind myself while standing on the rooftop of the Kuwait City Sheraton hotel as the bombs began falling on Baghdad.

I had been in Kuwait for more than two months, reporting on the preparations for war. American troops were gathering by the tens of thousands in the desert near the Iraq border, and there were stories to be told.

To tell those stories, reporters from all over the world were gathering in Kuwait in what sometimes seemed like greater numbers than the army itself.

When I arrived in the first week of January 2003, the entire NBC News contingent could ride to dinner in a single van. We consisted of two producers, a cameraman, soundman, broadcast engineer, and security consultant.

Security was a serious concern, despite the decidedly "pro-American" views of most Kuwaitis. In October 2002, a group of marines was attacked by an alleged Al Qaeda sympathizer while training in Kuwait. One marine was killed, and another seriously wounded.

Shortly after my arrival, terrorists ambushed an SUV carrying two civilian contractors near the shipping port where U.S. military gear was being unloaded. Both men were killed in a barrage of bullets from AK-47s. By chance, we had been scheduled to drive that same stretch of road, in a similar vehicle, within minutes of the attack.

The Kuwaiti government even arrested one of its own National Guard soldiers, who confessed to passing information to the Iraqi government. He also had detailed plans to bomb Kuwait's utilities and assassinate government officials.

The U.S. State Department warned Americans in Kuwait that terrorists would strike civilian targets, including shopping malls, hotels, and restaurants.

Against this backdrop, NBC's own preparations for war were under way. By March 2003, the NBC News bureau in Kuwait had grown exponentially. There seemed to be hundreds of us, though the actual number was probably closer to sixty or seventy. Technicians prepared "fly away" satellite transmitters that would be taken into battle.

Correspondents and producers who would cross into Iraq were inoculated by military doctors against an array of diseases, from malaria to diphtheria. The anthrax vaccine was controversial and caused a terrible itchy sore. Doctors told us it was voluntary, but with the memory of the anthrax attacks in America still vivid, most of us decided it was worth the discomfort to get inoculated.

I reported dozens of stories for the *Nightly News* and the *Today* show during that time and did hundreds of live shots for our cable network, MSNBC. In between broadcasts our security consultants, who now numbered about a dozen, drilled us on performing first aid, donning our gas masks and chemical suits, and reacting to bomb blasts or kidnapping attempts.

The correspondents and camera crews who would "embed" with military units spent time getting to know the men and women they would go into battle with.

Those of us who would travel in the war zone without the protection of military units were called unilateral. We practiced driving over sand dunes and made plans to move our operation into southern Iraq once the shooting started. All of us worked twenty-hour days, seven days a week.

It was, in a word, surreal. A dizzying time of nervous anticipation and sleep deprivation. We had great meals at any number of excellent restaurants scattered throughout the city. The country's strict Muslim code didn't allow alcohol, so gourmet meals were washed down with Diet Coke instead of wine. We debated until late into the night the pros and cons of the war we all knew was coming.

And a few of us prayed.

David Bloom's arrival in Kuwait City was humbling. Not because of his reputation as one of the network's top journalists. Not because of his rising-star status at NBC News. His arrival was humbling to me because of his faith.

I didn't know David before he walked into our workspace at the Sheraton in February 2003. I expected him to be a driven, hardworking, likable guy . . . which he was. What I didn't expect was the question he asked me shortly after we met.

"Is there a church nearby?" he asked.

"I think so," I answered, unsure why he wanted to know. "It's about two blocks away. I don't know what the security situation is there."

"I'm sure it's fine."

But I wasn't sure at all.

I worried that despite Kuwait's tolerance of Christianity, it would be unsafe to actually attend a church there. Our security consultants urged us to keep a low profile, avoid sitting near windows in restaurants, and travel in groups. Why tempt fate or terrorists by openly worshipping at a Christian church in an overwhelmingly Muslim land?

So I didn't. I brought a Bible with me and read it often, but always made sure to tuck it out of sight and back in the suitcase before leaving my room. I prayed silently and generally kept my faith to myself.

But not David. He was incredibly busy readying the "Bloom Mobile" for war. He spent days at a time in the remote desert near the Iraqi border, coordinating with military officials and the troops with whom he would ride to Baghdad once the shooting started. But he found time twice a week to walk to that church, seemingly unconcerned by any risks.

So, I was humbled to see a man who seemed so completely devoted to God and the mission he was undertaking. David Bloom crossed into Iraq on the first day the shooting started, carried by faith and the army's Third Infantry Division. I knew that within days I too would cross that border and face unknown perils. I took strength from watching David go first.

THREE HUNDRED AND FIFTY MILES away, the danger Rafraf faced was much closer to home.

Boom!

"What was that?" she half shouted to her sister, suddenly awake, but not knowing why.

Boom. Boom. A low rumble came from distant explosions.

"That's just thunder, right? It's a storm," Rafraf pleaded.

"No," Alaa answered grimly, "it's started."

Then the house shook violently as bombs fell much closer. American fighter jets streaked high overhead, their pilots dropping laser-guided bombs on military targets across the city. Cruise missiles roared above the neighborhood, so low it seemed they were using street signs to navigate.

Rafraf's house, of course, was not a target, but she had no way of knowing that. It seemed the sky was simply raining bombs. The house, a sturdy structure built from concrete block, offered some protection, but a direct hit would have obliterated it and everyone inside.

At the time, the "bedroom" for Rafraf and her older sister was still the living room. They slept on mats, barely thicker than throw rugs, placed directly on the cold tile floor. The effect was a very real connection to the earth itself. Rafraf felt each explosion vibrating up from the ground and, it seemed, shaking every cell in her body.

Rafraf was terrified, at first unable to function at all. On that first morning, with the city bathed in darkness, and fury falling from the sky, she never got up from the floor. She curled into a fetal ball, pulled the covers over her head, and went back to sleep. The first hours of "shock and awe" faded into a far-off dream, with Mr. John hiding in the shadows.

Then, the sun came up, and something unthinkable happened. The bombs stopped falling. Rafraf saw no point in hiding inside, so with her sister and little brother in tow, she headed to the roof.

"What are you doing?" her mother asked.

"We have to see what's happening," Rafraf answered seriously. "We're going up."

Her mother threw up her arms in exasperation, but knew it was pointless to argue.

Even before the war, electricity was scarce in Baghdad. Priority for service was given first to Saddam's numerous palaces and government buildings, followed by well-to-do Sunni neighborhoods. That left the rest of the city facing daily blackouts. Most homes could count on no more than four to six hours of electricity per day. With summertime temperatures often reaching 120 degrees Fahrenheit, the last place Iraqis without electricity wanted to be was indoors in dark, sweltering homes. As a result, houses are built with flat roofs that serve as out-door living areas. During the hottest months, many families drag their beds onto the roof at night to escape the stifling heat trapped inside.

There was nothing particularly special about Rafraf's house. Like the others in her neighborhood, it was built of concrete block, with a low wall surrounding the rooftop. The entire house was painted the color of sand. The house, just four miles from the center of the city, afforded a remarkable view of the war.

Since most of the houses in the neighborhood stood the same height, nothing obstructed her view of the surrounding city. To the northeast she could see the large clusters of high-rise buildings, an-tenna towers, and mosques that marked downtown. To the west she could see Baghdad's airport, which was also about four miles away. A few hundred feet south of her house was a busy highway, which was often clogged with traffic. All around were her neighbors, most of whom spent hot summer nights sleeping on their roofs too.

But in March, temperatures are mild, at times even cold. Rafraf ignored the slight chill as she bounded up the stairs that led to the roof. She emerged into sunlight, and yet another surprise.

The city wasn't awash in flame. Some fires were burning in the distance; black smoke billowed from unseen buildings; but the inferno she expected to see simply wasn't. What's more, the houses in her neighborhood were still standing. All of them.

"Why did they stop bombing?" she asked, as much to herself as her sister.

"I don't know," Alaa answered. "Maybe we won."

"Yeah, right," said Rafraf grimly.

Like many Iraqis, Rafraf and Alaa knew little about the capabilities of the U.S. military. They had no idea, for example, that pilots have night-vision equipment that allows them to see in near total darkness. They were also unaware that the majority of munitions being dropped on the city were precision-guided, each aimed at a specific military or strategic target. Nor did they know that the U.S. military fights by rules designed to limit civilian casualties.

In Rafraf's mind, this war was about America killing as many Iraqis as possible. That her house was still standing was probably just luck. Eventually, her neighborhood and her home would be reduced to little more than rubble. Everyone she loved would be killed. Of this she was certain.

But for the time being, Rafraf and her family were still alive. She stood on the roof, watching the far-off smoke, and wondered when the bombs would start falling again. She didn't have to wait long.

Shortly after sunset, the air-raid sirens began to wail, and a new wave of explosions rolled across the city. The terror of the first night of bombings returned, but this time Rafraf was determined to see the battle for herself.

From her vantage point on the roof, it was an awe-inspiring sight. Tracer fire rose from hundreds of antiaircraft guns positioned all around the city. The gunfire came from the rooftops of government buildings, private homes, schools, and mosques. The antiaircraft rounds rose into the sky looking like flaming tennis balls, most to little effect.

Rafraf couldn't see the jets over the darkened city. But she could hear their engines roar. Sometimes she would catch a glimpse of blue flame when pilots kicked in their afterburners. She cheered when Iraqi air defenses shot back and prayed to Allah the fighter planes would be shot down. She imagined them burning and falling from the sky in pieces.

But the bombs continued to fall. American warplanes, with stealth technology and countermeasures designed to defeat antiaircraft missiles, owned the skies over Baghdad.

On the third night of bombing, Rafraf was in her usual spot on the roof when she heard the distinctive, jetlike sound of a Tomahawk cruise missile. The U.S. military launched more than five hundred cruise missiles at targets in Baghdad during the first few days of the war. The Tomahawk, which can be fired from fifteen hundred miles away, flies to its target at about 550 miles per hour. It's kept aloft by stubby wings and pushed through the air by a small turbojet engine that produces 660 pounds of thrust. It flies low to the ground and uses a combination of GPS technology, terrain mapping, and other high-tech systems to strike fixed or moving targets with pinpoint accuracy. At least, that's how it's supposed to work.

The missile that flew over Rafraf's house on the third night of shock and awe was so close she felt she could reach up and touch it. But instead of continuing on to destroy a distant target, as other missiles had, this missile didn't. The engine propelling the Tomahawk simply quit, and in a moment of eerie silence the projectile, with its thousand-pound warhead, fell from the sky.

It's unclear where the missile was supposed to go, but it certainly wasn't intended to land where it did. The missile skidded along the street just two blocks from Rafraf's house, then exploded with a thunderous blast. The Tomahawk left a giant crater in the street and destroyed the nearest house. The shock wave from the blast knocked Rafraf and her little brother off their feet, but the house stood strong.

The pattern—bombs by night, silence by day—would continue for weeks. All the while American ground forces were racing toward Baghdad at unheard of speed. Rafraf didn't know it, but the city would soon fall, and Saddam Hussein, who had sworn to fight to the death, would go into hiding.

IN THE MEANTIME, SHE HAD a life to live. Even as the air war continued, citizens of Baghdad had certain things expected of them. Rafraf, like just about everyone else she knew, was officially a member of Iraq's Baath Party.

In the simplest of terms, the Baath Party, which also exists in other Arab countries beyond Iraq, is a political organization founded on principles of socialism and nationalism. It is the party of Saddam Hussein, and for those living in Saddam's Iraq, membership was seen as an important step for getting ahead. With its secular roots, membership in the party was open to Sunni and Shia Muslims, as well as Christians. As a result, many who were members of Iraq's religious minorities saw Baath membership as an equalizer . . . a place to gain some degree of status normally reserved for Saddam's favored Sunnis.

Rafraf's parents saw membership simply as a matter of survival. Their neighbors were members, their friends and relatives were members, so Kamal and Jamila were also members. Nearby schools had membership drives to see which could reach 100 percent membership among teachers and students. A school that reached that goal was considered to be "locked up" . . . a good thing. Incredible pressure came from all sides to join the party.

Rafraf was a member too, and as such she had responsibilities. First and foremost, she was required to attend regular Baath Party meetings in her neighborhood.

Rafraf's neighborhood, like most others in Baghdad, had a government informant who monitored every move. Do or say the wrong thing, and the consequences could be dire.

Shortly before the war, a sixteen-year-old boy she knew was with a group of four or five boys . . . one of whom told a joke about Saddam. The headmaster of the school was passing by and heard the joke, but didn't hear which of the boys told it. Not taking any chances that he was being tested by the government, the headmaster reported the joke to the neighborhood informant along with the names of all of the boys present. A few days later, a car arrived at the school, and all of the boys were summoned. Nobody knows exactly who came for them, or where they were taken, but the boys were never seen again. The family of the boy Rafraf knew refused to have a funeral . . . holding out hope that he had been imprisoned and would be released after being punished. But everyone else in the neighborhood knew the truth. The boy and his friends were executed. Jokes about Saddam would not be tolerated.

Jamila was so frightened of the government, she wouldn't even allow the word *Saddam* to be spoken in the house. If one of her children mistakenly mentioned his name in passing, she would immediately interrupt and begin singing, "Saddam is great, Saddam is great." Even the walls of her home, she feared, had ears.

"Walk in the shadows and don't say anything," Jamila reminded her children. "If you don't mess with the government, you won't get hurt."

Majida, a student with Rafraf at Baghdad University, had her own strategy for staying out of trouble. Rafraf discovered this after noticing bruises on the young woman's arms.

"What happened?" Rafraf asked, gesturing to Majida's arms.

Like Rafraf, Majida was a beautiful young woman. She always dressed fashionably and, in Rafraf's view, not modestly enough.

"It's nothing," Majida answered.

"Nothing, sure," Rafraf said, clearly not convinced. "Did your father do that?"

Instead of answering directly, Majida pulled Rafraf aside.

"Always keep your enemies close," Majida whispered in a conspiratorial tone. "You're so pretty. I can help you."

Until that moment, Rafraf had only suspected what Majida had been up to. She knew the young woman was well connected and, Rafraf suspected, dangerous. The previous semester at school, Majida had been caught cheating on a test. That would ordinarily have brought severe punishment, but she wasn't punished at all. Instead, the professor who caught her was transferred to a different university the very next day.

"Uday likes girls like us," Majida began. "Sometimes he gets mad, but he's very powerful. He also pays very well."

Rafraf was shocked.

Uday was Saddam Hussein's eldest son . . . at one time considered the heir apparent to Saddam. Although he was no longer favored as the successor to his father, he was indeed powerful and brutal.

In 1988, a then twenty-four-year-old Uday murdered his father's personal valet by beating him with a cane, then carving him up with an electric knife. This happened at a party in front of dozens of terrified guests. More recently, he was head of Iraq's Olympic committee and reportedly tortured athletes who failed to live up to his expectations. He had survived prison (sent there by his father), and an assassination attempt in which he had been shot no less than eight times.

And Majida was having sex with him in exchange for money and protection.

"He pays me more if I bring friends with me," she told Rafraf. "He'll pay you too. He'll like you, I'm sure of it."

Rafraf was horrified.

"No!" was all she could blurt out before practically running away from Majida. She did her best to avoid the woman from that point on.

But she couldn't avoid the weekly Baath Party meetings, and even bombs falling from the sky offered no respite.

"You have to go," her mother scolded on the fourth day of the American bombing.

"But it's so stupid, and boring," Rafraf answered.

"This won't last," Jamila said, pointing toward the sky. "The Americans won't kill Saddam. Nothing will change." She whispered the last part, violating her own rule of not saying Saddam's name out loud.

"You know you'll get reported if you don't go," Jamila continued. "We don't need any more trouble than we already have."

"Do you know what they taught me at the last meeting?" Rafraf asked seriously.

Jamila shrugged.

"They taught me how to put out the flames if I get too close to the stove and catch on fire."

"Seriously?" Jamila asked.

Rafraf nodded.

"Well, that really is stupid," her mother said, stifling a laugh.

"I know."

After a brief moment of silence, both women broke out laughing. It was a rare moment of levity in a trying week.

"You still have to go," Jamila said when the laughing had stopped.

"I will."

And she did. But this time she didn't learn about kitchen fires. This time local Baath Party officials taught her how to field strip, clean, and shoot an AK-47 assault rifle.

Rafraf told her mother about the training at breakfast the following day. Jamila's reaction was a nervous laugh.

"When the Americans come," Jamila said to the rest of the children, "everyone hide behind Rafraf."

Nobody else thought it was funny.

AS RAFRAF'S FAMILY WAITED OUT the bombing in Baghdad, I was reporting on the war from Kuwait City and southern Iraq. U.S. ground forces had breached the border between Kuwait and Iraq within hours of the start of the air war and were still pouring into Iraq. A number of my colleagues at NBC News were embedded with military units and also racing toward Baghdad.

David Bloom's live broadcasts from the Bloom Mobile captivated the nation. Kerry Sanders and Chip Reid were on the move with the marines, and both found themselves in the middle of serious combat.

My job was to drive into Iraq for specific stories of interest, then bring the footage back to Kuwait in time for the *Nightly News* broadcast each evening. It was more dangerous than I expected it to be.

Before the war began, I had an unrealistic vision of how things would go. Once U.S. or other coalition troops had moved through an area, I assumed that area would be somewhat secure. Surely a large contingent of troops would be left behind for security, right?

Wrong.

U.S. forces were moving at lightning speed toward Baghdad. That's where the real focus was. There simply weren't enough of them to leave large numbers in rear areas for security. As a result, when I first entered southern Iraq a couple of days after the initial push, I was shocked at how few friendly forces I actually saw.

One of my first assignments was to have a look at Iraq's oil fields just across the border from Kuwait. During the first Iraq War, Saddam's forces set Kuwait's oil wells on fire as they retreated. It was an environmental and economic disaster that took years to clean up. The U.S. military feared Saddam would do the same to his own oil fields this time . . . blowing them up rather than surrendering them to the advancing Americans.

The army and marines had made saving Iraq's oil infrastructure a top priority. They were eager to show the world they had succeeded, so a hasty media event was arranged, and journalists from the networks and major newspapers were invited to see for themselves.

We were asked to meet at the army's media headquarters in Kuwait City, where, we were told, soldiers in armored vehicles would meet us. Our convoy of civilian Dodge Durangos and Chevy Suburbans would be perfectly safe, escorted through the war zone by heavily armed soldiers. At least that was the plan.

But somehow none of it materialized. We were met instead by an exhausted army captain who told us he hadn't slept in two days. A public affairs officer, he would be our escort. He also wanted to know if he could ride with us . . . because he didn't have a vehicle. Nor did he have a map, radio, or satellite phone. He did, however, have a 9 mm handgun and GPS coordinates for where we were supposed to go. So as long as one of us had a GPS, we should be fine. The captain climbed into our already crowded vehicle.

"You do have a GPS, don't you?" he asked.

We did.

Since our vehicle had the GPS and the 9 mm (the captain fell asleep as soon as we started moving), we took the lead in a "convoy" that consisted of a handful of shiny SUVs and zero armed escorts. The army had insisted we limit the number of vehicles in the convoy, so a CBS News correspondent and camera crew crammed into the third-row seats of our Durango. Seven or eight people, with camera gear sitting on their laps, were stuffed into the SUV.

We found the designated dirt road that took us through a hole in what used to be a fortified border. We continued for a couple of hours until, amazingly, we found ourselves in the middle of a giant oil field.

A handful of drilling rigs were on fire, but as promised, the vast majority of the infrastructure was still intact.

Following the GPS coordinates, we eventually arrived at a small building in the center of the oil field. In the dirt parking lot was a brigadier general, a couple of his aides, and the promised briefing. After showing us some before and after satellite photographs of the oil field, the general turned us loose to have a look around for ourselves.

We drove a couple of miles down yet another dirt road to get a closer look at a rig that was burning. Just as we stopped on the road to take pictures of the rig, I noticed a white Toyota pickup coming toward us.

"Who do you suppose is in that truck?" I asked nobody in particular.

"Iraqis for sure" was the response from someone sitting behind me.

As the truck drew closer, we could see it was full of men. Three men in white robes and kaffiyehs on their heads sat in the front seat. The bed of the truck had at least half a dozen men in it. Some of them were standing. Was one of them manning a mounted machine gun? It was hard to tell for sure, but if so, we were in big trouble.

"Hey, Captain," I said, "you might want to have a look at this."

"At what?" he asked, more asleep than not.

"That truck!" I said, pointing to the rapidly approaching vehicle. "It's full of Iraqis. Don't military units and police drive trucks like that?"

"I'm sure they're friendly. They wouldn't be here if they're not friendly." He turned his attention back to whatever he had been doing. He seemed uninterested in the truckload of Iraqis.

I never took my eyes off the truck. The hairs on the back of my neck stood on end as the vehicle came to a stop next to us on the dirt road. I expected the robes to fly open and guns to come out, blasting us all to bits in our now dust-covered Dodge Durango.

Even if we had wanted to hide, we couldn't have. We were in the middle of a vast desert. The nearest American troops were a dot in the distance, still gathered around the brigadier general who had given the press conference. The only sound I heard was from the roaring, fuel-fed flames burning from the nearest oil rig.

As we all locked eyes with the men in the truck, the occupants of both vehicles wondered what would happen next.

Then, the Iraqis did something I didn't expect.

They surrendered. Seriously.

The men threw their arms in the air and began speaking all at once, clearly hoping to turn themselves in.

I shook my head and pointed toward the troops and the general.

"Over there," I said. "The army is over there."

The driver of the pickup nodded his appreciation and took off in the direction of the troops.

"That was weird," someone behind me said.

We all piled out of the vehicle and went about the business of taking pictures. All, of course, except the captain, who was again fast asleep.

As my camera crew shot the burning oil rig, I brought out my DV camera and used the telephoto lens to watch the Iraqi pickup. Through the shimmering heat waves rising up from the desert, I saw the men get out of their vehicle with arms in the air and surrender to the U.S. troops.

At that moment I told myself I should be ready for anything. It was good advice.

We later learned that another Iraqi pickup approached the same group of soldiers just before sunset that evening and opened fire with automatic weapons. Perhaps that first pickup was just a test run to evaluate security.

On the trip back from the oil fields, our army captain decided he should navigate. It was a bad idea, but he was allegedly in charge, so we let him. We quickly became hopelessly lost, unable to find the hole in the fortified border that would take us back to Kuwait.

Instead, we followed a nameless dirt road south across the desert toward the Iraqi border town of Safwan. We arrived in the middle of a battle between British military forces and either the Iraqi army or insurgent fighters.

Artillery pounded an area of town less than a mile from our SUVs. British attack helicopters flew overhead. Several fires burned in the village.

It's a miracle we weren't killed. The British soldiers saw us coming long before we saw their fortified position. When we rolled up on their flank, a soldier motioned for us to stop. He was tense and obviously annoyed.

"Who are you, and what are you doing here?" he asked incredulously.

The captain was already out of our vehicle and approaching the soldier. He pulled the irate man out of earshot, and the two had what seemed to be an animated conversation. I don't know what was actually said, but based on the body language, here's my interpretation:

"Excuse me, but would you happen to know the way back to Kuwait City?" asks the captain.

"You can't be serious!" responds the soldier. "Are you daft?"

"I'm Captain Smith with public affairs."

"Well, Captain, do you see that man?" The soldier points to a man behind the trigger of a .50-caliber machine gun mounted on an armored vehicle.

"Yeah."

"Well, that's Sergeant Hill, and I had to talk him out of shooting the lot of you."

"That was nice of you. Thank you. Now, about those directions?"

"Well, for starters, how about going across the border and getting off my bloody battlefield."

"And the border is which way again?"

A moment later, the captain was back in the vehicle, looking ashen. We were just a few hundred yards from the border. We made it home safely, and I resolved to find a good map of Iraq.

I should point out that *safe* was a relative term. Shortly after the United States began raining bombs on Baghdad, Saddam Hussein retaliated by firing missiles at Kuwait. It was feared that those missiles would contain chemical or possibly biological weapons, so each time the air-raid sirens sounded in Kuwait City, we all put on our gas masks and headed for the roof of the hotel. The roof was the least safe place to be. It was particularly unsafe during a missile attack. But our camera positions were on the roof, thus creating the somewhat comical chaos of producers, camera operators, and correspondents rushing to the roof while everyone else was looking for a safe place to hide.

The missiles came daily. Sometimes, the sirens would wail several times a day throughout the city. We never heard the missile impacts. Instead, we would hear a few hours later about a missile either being intercepted and destroyed by a U.S. Patriot missile, or exploding somewhere in the desert far from its intended target. Still, it's a bit unnerving knowing that missiles are being fired at you.

Only one missile that I recall came close to our hotel.

It was after midnight, and I had just hung up the phone after my nightly call home. I assured Kiki that I wasn't going into Iraq the next day, and she shouldn't worry about me. Minutes later, there was a thunderous explosion. The Sheraton hotel vibrated with the impact.

I put on my gas mask and ran to the roof. Within minutes we were broadcasting pictures as flames rose into the air from the point of impact. A missile with a five-hundred-pound warhead had slammed into a mall less than a mile from the hotel. There were no injuries, but the blast was a reminder that war with Iraq was indeed a dangerous proposition.

Still, the threat of missiles beat the heck out of driving around in Iraq looking for stories. In a dozen or so trips as far north as Nasiriyah, we were attacked by looters hurling rocks at our vehicle, robbed by a deranged man wielding a knife, chased by an enraged mob, and on one occasion stumbled into an Iraqi paramilitary unit with more than a hundred armed men.

Some reporters enjoy working in war zones. I'm not one of them. Still, I went to war by choice. Rafraf had it thrust upon her.

ABOUT A WEEK AFTER THE bombing of Baghdad began, Rafraf's brother Ayser came home. Ayser was four years older than Rafraf and had just finished his training as a Baghdad police officer. He wore a gun and a uniform, but as a rookie cop he was relegated to pushing paperwork. He processed criminals at a police station near the city center.

Ayser is self-confident. So much so that some think he's arrogant. But the day he came home, he was anything but confident.

"Why are you here?" Jamila asked hopefully. "Are you staying?"

"No," he said, hurrying past his mother and up the stairs. He came down a moment later, wearing civilian clothes and stuffing more clothing into a bag.

"They told us to get our clothes. And we're moving. The police station has been compromised."

"I don't understand," Jamila pleaded. "Did you get bombed?"

Ayser stopped long enough to look his mother in the eyes. "It's not safe at the police station. The people . . ." He paused, looking for the right words. "The people want revenge. Against Saddam, against the government. That means me now. Anyone in a uniform isn't safe."

He headed for the door.

"But where are you going?" Jamila asked. "How will I know you're okay?"

"We're going to a bigger police station. It has a wall. We can defend it."

Ayser gave his mother a hug, and a kiss on the cheek.

"It's near grandmother's house in the north of the city," he said. "If things go bad, I'll go to her house. Look for me there."

He left without another word.

The police weren't the only government workers in Iraq making plans to hide. Rafraf's house was just a few hundred yards from an Iraqi military installation. The small base consisted of a few buildings, some barracks, and a few hundred acres of barren, sandy land used for training.

On the ninth day of the war, one of Rafraf's brothers was on look-out on the roof of the house.

"Hey, come up here and see this!" Samir shouted down the stairs.

Rafraf and Rami immediately ran up to the roof.

"Look at what they're doing." Samir pointed across to the base.

A military transport truck was parked in the middle of the sandy training area. Several large missiles had been unloaded from the truck and were being piled into a shallow hole. The Iraqi flag was painted boldly on the nose of each missile.

"They're burying the missiles," Rafraf observed.

Their mother joined them on the roof.

"That's not safe. That's too close," Jamila cautioned.

The family watched in somber silence as the military continued burying missiles in the sand. Any hope that Iraq might still find a way to win the war was quickly fading away.

"We should go now," Jamila told her children. They followed her downstairs without another word.

That night, the wind began blowing. Within two days, it had blown away so much sand that the missiles were completely exposed again. The Iraqi flags now marked the target from above. Nobody bothered to cover them up again.

BY THE FIRST WEEK OF April, U.S. troops were closing in on Baghdad. Ordinary Iraqis didn't have that information. Most still believed the United States lacked the will to launch a ground war in Iraq.

Even during the air war, Saddam Hussein was a fixture on Iraq's nightly news. He said Iraq's army would defeat the Americans in a bloody battle for Baghdad's streets.

But what Rafraf saw around her hardly matched the rhetoric. She could hear the battle as it moved up the main highway that runs into Baghdad from the south. The Iraqi army was dug in south of the city, but taking a pounding from the advancing Americans.

By late in the first week of April, Rafraf could actually see the battle from her rooftop. Tracer fire and artillery explosions were visible in the distance. Most of the munitions were directed at Iraqi positions.

From both sides, as it turns out.

One of Rafraf's brothers was on the lookout one evening near sunset.

"Hey, everybody, come see this!" Samir shouted down the stairs. Rafraf, Jamila, and Rami ran to the roof.

"Look what they're doing," Samir said, pointing to the nearby military installation. "Who are they shooting at?"

Three people, a man and two women, were in the field. They were civilians, but just a few yards from the spot where the missiles had been buried in the sand. The missiles were still visible in the rapidly dwindling light of evening. But where the people were wasn't as disturbing as what they were doing.

The trio had set up an 81 mm mortar tube—basically a portable artillery system—and they were firing mortars. While not as powerful as the larger artillery shells fired from howitzers, mortars are dangerously accurate and deadly in the right hands. A properly trained mortar team can fire fifteen rounds per minute, dropping high-explosive charges on targets more than three miles away.

The man with the mortar must have been a supporter of the United States and was hoping to aid the Americans in battle. One of the women was helping him load, handing him the next round after the last had left the tube. The other woman seemed to be a lookout. The target of their attack was clear to everyone on the roof. They were shooting at the Iraqi military.

"Can't they understand?" Jamila asked incredulously. She shouted from the rooftop toward the man firing the mortar. "You're not fighting Saddam, you idiot! These are your sons! You're killing your own kids!"

Others also saw what was happening and tried to stop the slaughter. Four men from the neighborhood finally ran toward the mortar position. Rafraf could see everyone was shouting, but she was too far away to hear what was said. The shouting escalated into a scuffle, the neighborhood men trying to drag the man away from the mortar. But they failed to account for the women. Both of them jumped into the fight and a brawl ensued.

It might have been funny had the stakes not been so high. From the roof of Rafraf's house, it seemed the entire fabric of Iraqi life was unraveling.

Eventually, the man and his accomplices escaped the fight, but they didn't get far. A car carrying high-ranking Baath Party members raced to the scene, followed by an Iraqi police car with its lights flashing. Guns were drawn, arrests were made, and the mortar crew was finally dragged away.

Jamila and her children cheered. It would be their last opportunity to celebrate a victory.

ABOUT 350 MILES TO THE south, in Kuwait City, the phone in my hotel room rang. The sun was up, but I had no idea what time it was. I thought about not answering it.

My dad once told me that the U.S. army considered three hours a full night's sleep in combat. Three hours, he said, is all your brain needs to recharge itself, and it's really the brain that needs the rest. I don't know if that's true, but I do know three hours a day was all the sleep anyone at NBC News was getting . . . and we were lucky to have that.

As I was one of just a handful of nonembedded NBC reporters in the war region, my base of operations in Kuwait was critical to providing live reports to the *Nightly News*, the *Today* show, MSNBC, and NBC affiliates around the country. Because of the difference in time zones, the highest demand for live shots came throughout the night. Most of our days were spent in Iraq, shooting stories and trying not to get killed, so there was simply no time to sleep . . . ever.

Still, I answered the phone on April 6 and knew immediately it was bad news.

"Don, dear, come to the workspace right now," said Heather Allen, the bureau chief for our operation. Heather has covered conflicts around the world and has seen about all there is to see. She's one of the toughest women I know and is highly respected at NBC News. Her real job, when not in a war zone, was running the network's Los Angeles bureau. She calls everyone dear.

"What's up?" I asked, trying to get my bearings.

"Not on the phone, dear," she said gravely, "just come in here now."

Two minutes later I walked into the workspace and found a place to half-sit on the edge of a desk. The room was quickly filling up with other staffers who'd all received the same call.

Heather didn't look good at all. Her eyes were red, her skin was flushed, and her blond hair was a mess. She surveyed the faces gathered around her. Probably twenty people were in the room.

"Is this everyone?" she asked nobody in particular. We all shrugged.

"David Bloom is dead," she said with a shaky voice.

Someone in the room audibly gasped. I couldn't tell who was saying what. My brain couldn't process the words I had just heard, let alone provide me with detailed information such as who was speaking. I sat numbly.

Someone else screamed, "No."

"I just received a call from Paul," she continued, referring to the producer who was traveling with David in the Bloom Mobile. "They think it was a thrombosis or an embolism."

"It wasn't combat?" someone asked, clearly in shock.

"No," Heather replied, "his leg had been hurting, and something happened. The medics tried to save him."

David was just thirty-nine years old, two years older than me at the time. He had a beautiful wife and three young daughters. He was gone, and the grief among those in the room was enormous.

A cameraman was sitting on the desk next to me. He was a big, strong guy with a kind heart. He had worked with David many times over the years and counted him as a close friend. He put his hand on my shoulder to steady himself. His whole body shook, and he sobbed uncontrollably.

"How can that be?" he asked. He looked me in the eyes pleading for an answer that would make sense and take away the pain. Tears streamed down his cheeks. "Not David. How can that be?"

I didn't have an answer, at least not one that made sense. In fact, what I did say made absolutely no sense. It came out before I could stop it.

"It'll be okay," I said, embracing him. "It'll be okay."

"No, it won't, it won't."

"I'm so sorry."

I had only met David for the first time a few weeks earlier, but the day he died was one of the saddest experiences I had ever been a part of. My heart broke for his family, and for all of my colleagues who had worked with him for years. Many of the people in the room didn't just like David, they clearly loved him.

But I also knew David and his wife were close to God and had drawn even closer in recent weeks. I drew comfort from that, but not nearly enough.

David's death did not shake my faith, but it did remind me that nothing in life is guaranteed. If a man who seemed so in tune with God could be taken away from his family in such a senseless way, what did it mean for the rest of us? I felt selfish for even considering the question.

ON APRIL 7, RAFRAF WAS once again watching the world from the roof of her house. She saw Iraqi soldiers running down a nearby road. They were stripping off their uniforms as they ran and changing into civilian clothes. Some of the soldiers didn't have civilian clothes. They pounded desperately on doors and begged those inside to give them clothes to change into. Rafraf knew that the war was about to take a turn for the worse.

The sky was dark and overcast on April 9. Rafraf couldn't see anything from the roof of her house. Instead, she grabbed her transistor radio and sat on the step near the front door where reception was clearest.

Ordinarily she listened to Iraqi radio stations, but she couldn't find any broadcasting on April 9. She managed to tune in Radio Monte Carlo, a French network with an Arabic-language channel.

The network had an Iraqi correspondent reporting from downtown Baghdad. He described the scene in detail as U.S. forces rolled into the city. He was there when Iraqis helped by U.S. troops tore down the statue of Saddam Hussein. The television images mesmerized the world, but Rafraf never saw them. She could only listen, her mind imagining the scene of Mr. John destroying everything she loved.

Saddam Hussein, who had promised to fight the Americans to the death, was nowhere in sight.

Just a few miles away, Rafraf's brother Ayser was running for his life. When it became clear that Saddam was no longer in power, Iraqis, as his commanders predicted, attacked the police stations.

Ayser's unit was massively outnumbered and unable to defend even their new police station. So he and nineteen of his fellow officers ran out the building's back door. They hoped to make it to a large estate nearby. The house was owned by a man of considerable wealth and was well fortified. The officers knew the owner had fled in advance of the war. If the men could only get inside the walls of the estate, perhaps they could mount a stand and survive.

But as they approached the home, they were met with gunfire. The owner had left a security detail behind to combat looters, and the last thing the guards wanted was for the police to bring trouble to the boss's house. Ayser and his unit were pinned between the mob of rioters on one side, and armed security guards shooting at them on the other.

The only chance for survival was to drop their weapons and try to blend in with the crowd. That was no easy task because all police officers carried identification that marked them as cops.

During the turbulent hours after the fall of Baghdad, armed mobs challenged any person they met on the street. Men who showed government ID were shot on sight. Men with no ID were suspected of being cops, so they were also shot on sight. Many others were shot for apparently no reason, or because they tried to defend their homes, shops, or families. In some neighborhoods, blood literally ran in the streets on the night of April 9.

Ayser was in one of those neighborhoods. He was on foot, unarmed, and had no identification. He had one chance of making it to safety, and it was a long shot.

Many of the dead men lying on the street were about his age and looked somewhat like him. He went from body to body, searching for identification that he could pass off as his own, that would not mark him as a cop. He finally found one.

Ali Hassan's unfortunate murder saved Ayser's life. Ayser carried the dead man's identification with him and tried his best to stay in the darkest shadows as he walked from the neighborhood police station to his grandmother's house. The walk took all night.

Of the twenty police officers who ran from the police station on the night of April 9, only Ayser and four others survived to see the sun rise on April 10.

RAFRAF WAS AWAKENED THAT MORNING not by the rising sun, but by an unfamiliar noise. It began as a rumble and built to an overwhelming screech. A high-pitched metallic clanking soon followed, sending Rafraf rushing upstairs.

She arrived at the rooftop just in time to see the first M1A1 Abrams tank rounding the corner. A hatch was open on top, and the tank commander stood in the opening.

The man wore a helmet with a darkened visor, giving him the menacing look of Darth Vader in desert camouflage. Rafraf's mind raced back to childhood. Mr. John from her worst nightmares was not only real; he was here. He scanned the rooftops for trouble. If he spotted it, a .50-caliber machine gun was at the ready.

Rafraf reflexively ducked behind the low wall surrounding her rooftop. A moment later, she cautiously peered back over the wall toward the road.

She saw the first tank was followed by a second. Neither tank had any interest in her or her neighborhood. Both were coming from the west near the airport and barreling toward the center of the city.

The Abrams is powered by a fifteen-hundred-horsepower turbine engine and roars like a jet airplane. The sound of two tanks together, moving between buildings and over asphalt, is deafening.

"What's that flag?" she asked as Rami joined her on the roof. She had to shout for him to hear her over the noise. The house shook beneath them.

Rami shrugged.

Both tanks were proudly flying the same scarlet colors. On the face of each flag was a picture of what looked like a globe rotated to show North and South America. An anchor seemed to pass through the globe from right to left, and standing on top of the north pole was an eagle.

"I've never seen it before," Rami said. "That's not the American flag, is it?"

"It says something on the bottom," Rafraf said, "but I can't read it from here."

Had she been closer, she would have seen writing above and below the globe. A small banner above the eagle reads SEMPER FIDELIS.

A larger banner waves across the bottom of the flag, the letters practically jumping from the fabric. It reads UNITED STATES MARINE CORPS.

Rafraf didn't need to read the words to know the news she had heard on Radio Monte Carlo the night before was true. Her body shook . . . not from the rumbling tanks now leaving her view . . . but from somewhere deep inside.

For the first time in her life, Rafraf had seen an American fighting man. Perhaps it was better she didn't see his eyes. To her he was simply a machine, every bit as deadly as the screeching monster he rode in on.

Baghdad was lost.

Rafraf crumbled to the floor behind the roof wall and cried.

FOUR

OCCUPATION

I t's often said that opportunity knocks, but rarely is the saying literal. Still, a knock on the front door set a new direction in Rafraf's life.

The hands doing the knocking, like every other bit of Susu Ali, looked as if they belonged to a man. Standing over six feet tall, with hulking, muscular features, Susu was an imposing figure. That the thirty-six-year-old Susu was actually a woman amplified the effect.

On that afternoon in May, she stood knocking on the door.

"What do you want, Susu?" Jamila asked, answering the door.

"Rafraf speaks good English," Susu said. "Right?"

"Very good," Jamila answered proudly.

"Well, she should go to the Republican Palace. Haithem went there yesterday to file a claim with the Americans."

"And?" said Jamila, suspicion creeping into her voice.

"And he heard the Americans need translators who speak English," Susu said excitedly. "And you'll never guess how much they're paying."

"No, I won't."

"Five U.S. dollars a day," Susu said.

"He must have heard wrong; that's too much."

"Maybe, but it doesn't hurt to check." Susu looked around the house with a hint of concern in her eyes. "And it seems you could use the money."

"It would seem," Jamila said, aware of the slight. "Thanks for your concern, Susu." Jamila closed the door, leaving Susu on the step.

BY THE FIRST WEEK OF May, the shock of war had begun to wear off. Rafraf's family had stockpiled at least three months' worth of food in a storage room in preparation for war, but it would eventually run out.

Under Saddam Hussein, Iraqi citizens were issued government ration cards to buy food. The cards provided staples such as flour, sugar, rice, cooking oil, and beans. The ration card was meant to keep families alive. Extras such as beef, fish, chicken, or lamb had to be purchased out of hard-earned dinars (the Iraqi currency).

But when the war began and the government disintegrated, so temporarily did the ration program. That presented an immediate problem, especially for large families such as Rafraf's.

When the Iraqi government fell, unemployment skyrocketed nationwide. In Baghdad, some 70 percent of the population of 5 million was out of work. Schools were closed, police stations were empty, the security situation was worsening, and the population was idle.

For more than a month, Rafraf didn't leave the house at all. With most of the stores closed and Baghdad University shut down, there was simply no place to go.

To make matters worse, the family was broke. Their primary source of income had been Kamal's job as an accountant for a wholesale farmers' market. His salary, including a commission on sales, amounted to about sixty U.S. dollars per month. The family also owned a small stationery shop where Rafraf worked without pay. The shop earned about $15 per month. So even during the good times, $75 per month was all there was to support the family, which barely got by.

In postwar Iraq, times were anything but good.

The deteriorating security situation had forced the farmers' market to close. With looting and killings on the rise, Jamila and Kamal decided it was best to close the stationery store, too, and move the inventory into the house where it could be protected.

The family's income stopped.

If Rafraf really could make $5 a day working for the Americans, it would go a long way.

RAFRAF WAS STIR-CRAZY AFTER WEEKS of sitting at home. Her sisters were driving her nuts. The university had announced that it would resume classes in the last week of May, but Rafraf couldn't wait to get out of the house. If nothing else, she figured, applying for a job with the Americans would at least give her something to do for the day. Besides, she wanted to have a look at what was left of her city.

So on a hot, sunny day in mid-May, Rafraf walked the short dirt road from her house to the main highway. She flagged a private bus, paid the driver, and had him drop her off at the Republican Palace, which the Americans had begun calling Assassins Gate.

Actually, she didn't quite get to the gate because a line of Iraqis stretched all the way up the street and around the block. The line, she learned, was just to get a number. Those who got numbers before noon would be given an appointment and allowed to speak with someone from the U.S. military or one of its contractors. If you didn't get a number by noon, you had to try again the next day.

With a little planning, the Americans could have provided shade for the hundreds standing in line, but they didn't. Temperatures had already soared above ninety degrees, and tensions began running high.

An elderly man waiting in the line was in a wheelchair and in poor health. In an effort to ease his suffering, he rolled his chair toward a tree-shaded sidewalk about fifty feet from where the line was. He had planned to rejoin the line in his old place after cooling down, but he didn't get the chance.

An American soldier saw the man out of line and grew angry.

"Who told you to sit there?" he shouted. "Get back in line." The soldier was carrying a rifle and pointing with it, first at the man, then at the line. He walked aggressively toward the old man.

The man responded in Arabic and Rafraf heard him pleading, "Just a few moments. I need to cool down, please."

The soldier obviously didn't understand Arabic. He grew even angrier when he noticed others from the line were following the old man's lead. Now a dozen or more people were leaving their places in line and moving to the shade.

Clearly, the soldier's orders were to keep the people in line. He flew into a profanity-laced rage.

"I said get back in line!" he shouted. "Now!" He swung his weapon around toward the line. "All of you, get back into the line and stay there!"

The old man got the picture. He rolled his wheelchair out of the shade and back into the hot sun. The others who had moved to the shade followed, mumbling curses in Arabic as they went.

If the intent of the U.S. military was to win hearts and minds, thought Rafraf, they were off to a bad start.

Sure, Iraqis live in a blazing desert, but they cope with it by staying out of the heat of day. Who thinks it's a good idea to have people stand in the hot sun?

Still, that line had some benefit beyond its potential for Rafraf's finding a job. Her annoying sisters and older brother were nowhere to be seen. And her mom wasn't telling her what to do. It was as much independence as she had ever enjoyed. She also had exotic new people to look at . . . specifically, American soldiers.

Most of them were young men, about her age. They had chiseled features and an air of confidence. Many had fair skin and hair and blue or green eyes. Sure, the soldier monitoring the line seemed to have serious mental problems, but Rafraf had seen others doing their jobs with little conflict.

Perhaps the most striking visible difference between the soldiers and Iraqi men, the thing that Rafraf noticed the most, was the Americans' lack of facial hair.

Most Iraqi men wore thick black mustaches, some in the style of Saddam Hussein. Many also had heavy beards. Neither held any sway for Rafraf.

But she was also afraid of the Americans. Weren't these the same men who had unjustly invaded Afghanistan? The Afghan people had nothing to do with September 11, but the United States had bombed them. Now they were moving on to Iraq to steal the oil, and here they were in Baghdad. And they're hiring? Nothing made sense.

On the other hand, her family needed money. And what if the Americans were here to stay? It would be best to get in the good graces of this new government as soon as possible. Wouldn't it?

Rafraf figured she had come this far; why waste the day? She found her place at the end of the massive line and waited with the others in the hot sun.

Not everyone in line with her was looking for a job. Many had claims for damaged property or lost relatives to file with U.S. officials. Reparations would be paid to those who could prove their losses.

The man standing directly in front of Rafraf hoped to be paid for a damaged car; in front of him, another man was looking for a job as a translator. They waited under a scorching sun with no shade for more than three hours.

As Rafraf moved toward the front of the line, she grew increasingly nervous. She was excited about the possibility of finding work, and eager to show off her language skills. But she was also terrified. Her heart pounded in her chest; she could actually hear it in her ears. She silently prayed it would quiet when her turn came.

She finally made it near the front of the line just before noon. She strained to hear as the man two places in front of her approached the soldier, an army specialist, who was standing at the gate. His name tag said West, and he stood with a Jordanian translator by his side. When the Iraqi approached, the translator greeted him in Arabic.

"Is this where I come for a job?" asked the Iraqi.

"What kind of job are you looking for?"

"Translation. I speak English."

The translator turned to Specialist West and said in broken English, "He look to make translation."

"He speaks English?" asked West. "Like you?"

"Yes, he speak like me," the Jordanian replied.

West tried not to laugh. "Tell him I'm sorry, but we've filled our translator positions for now. He can try back in a few weeks."

The Iraqi walked away dejected, and West motioned for the next man in line to step forward.

The man looking for payment for his car was given a number and told where to go next.

Specialist West motioned next for Rafraf. Her fear grew, but so did her resolve. She stood to her full height of five feet three inches and flashed a nervous smile at the soldier. She tried to look into his eyes, but West was wearing wraparound sunglasses. Rafraf saw only herself, trying to look tall and brave, in the reflective lenses.

"Can I talk to you without the translator?" she asked.

"Of course," West responded.

"My name is Rafraf Barrak," she said boldly, "and I am a student at Baghdad University. I speak English."

"Obviously," West said, smiling.

The Jordanian translator was shocked. Rafraf assumed it was because of her boldness. He started to speak, but West cut him off.

"Tell the guy who was just looking for a job to come back here."

The Jordanian gave West a confused look.

"Tell him this woman just saved him," West continued. "If I hire her after saying we're not hiring, that makes me a liar. And I'm not a liar." West handed Rafraf a piece of paper. "Take this to the other gate around the block. Tell the soldiers there dressed like me that Specialist West sent you, hand them the paper, and tell them I'll be there in fifteen minutes. Do you understand?"

"Yes, of course," Rafraf answered nonchalantly. Her heart was still pounding in her chest. She silently thanked Allah that she didn't throw up.

"Of course you do," West said. He never stopped smiling.

As Rafraf walked toward the next gate, she thought about the exchange with West. He was the first American soldier she'd ever seen up close, certainly the first she'd spoken to. What was it about him that was so different? She was still trying to figure it out when she reached the second gate.

"Specialist West told me to come here and wait for him," she told the soldier.

"Okay," he said, "you can wait over there in the shade."

There it was again. He had only uttered nine words, but something about the way the American spoke to her was different. What was it? She was still trying to put her finger on it when Specialist West arrived.

West had Rafraf and the other man seeking work as a translator searched. An Iraqi woman searched the contents of Rafraf's bag, while a soldier waved a handheld metal detector around her to make sure she wasn't armed. She and the other man were then escorted through the gate into the area that would soon be known as the Green Zone.

"Hey, Sergeant Frank," West called to his squad leader, "can you help me with these two? They need to go to the translator's office, but I've gotta see the platoon sergeant about that other thing."

"That's cool," said Frank. "I'll run them to the bus stop."

He motioned for Rafraf and the man to follow him. When they caught up to him, Sergeant Frank asked Rafraf, "So you speak English?"

"Yes. I learned in school. We all have to take English classes."

"Really?" Frank said with genuine surprise.

"Of course," Rafraf replied, proud of the new phrase she had casually lifted from West. "And we watch American films."

"No kidding?"

"No. I have *The Little Mermaid* at home, and the green-genie movie . . . *Aladdin*. My brother's favorites is *Rocky* and *The Terminator*."

"So you know Ah-nuld," Frank said, doing his best Schwarzenegger impression.

"Uh-huh," Rafraf said, suddenly realizing the sergeant might be flirting with her.

"Imagine that," Frank said.

Rafraf began to feel more comfortable walking toward the bus with the sergeant. She was finally getting her nerves under control. The Iraqi man was still with them, but he never said a word. He shot a discreet yet disapproving look in her direction.

"Then how come y'all don't all speak English?" asked Frank as they reached the bus.

"Most people thought it was a waste of time. But I thought I might need it someday. And I don't like reading subtitles."

The three arrived at the bus.

"Take this bus to the second stop, then get off." Frank pointed up the road. "Cross the street, and you'll see an office building there. Go inside for your interview."

"Thank you," Rafraf answered while climbing onto the bus.

"You're welcome, ma'am. And good luck."

The doors closed, and the bus started down the road.

Rafraf thought about both of the soldiers that she had met as the bus bounced toward the first stop. What was it about them? She looked around at the other Iraqis in the bus, and the answer hit her.

For all of her life, Rafraf felt she had been treated like a second-class citizen. Not just because she was a Shiite in a nation that favored Sunnis. She was second-class because she was a woman.

She knew, of course, that men looked *at* her. But she always felt that Iraqi men looked down at her. She felt scrutinized, judged, evaluated, intimidated, even threatened by the way men looked at her. That Jordanian translator had done the same thing, hadn't he? He'd tried to put Rafraf in her place with a look.

Rafraf's place in society had everything to do with men. What they told her to do, where they told her to go, who they told her she was.

Despite her belief in Allah, and strong desire to do his will, she had stepped foot in a mosque only once in her entire life. She'd read the Koran many times from cover to cover and could recite numerous passages at will. But was she welcome in the main room of a mosque?

Rafraf didn't think so.

The call for prayer that blared from loudspeakers every day at sunset, in Rafraf's view, was a call for men to come to the mosque, not women. As men gathered in the great room to pray, the few women who did show up were sent into a small room in the back. It didn't even have a proper floor. It was dirty and of much lower quality than the floor men prayed on.

It is common in Islamic societies for men and women to be segregated during worship. Different Islamic communities apply the practice in varied ways. Some encourage women to pray at home, while others have a separate part of the mosque set aside for women. Rafraf knew that the separation was intended to show respect for women and to protect their purity, but she never saw it that way. She felt she was being treated as something less than a man.

Why should women be treated like second-class citizens?

She often felt the rules of her religion and society designed to protect her had the real effect of minimizing her.

She knew well the verse from the Koran that says, "Tell the believing men to lower their gaze and to be mindful of their chastity: this will be most conducive to their purity."*

The problem was that Rafraf interpreted the refusal of most men to look her in the eye as a sign of disrespect, not honor.

That, she realized, was why she was so interested in how these Americans looked at her.

Frank and West both looked Rafraf in the eye when they spoke to her. She interpreted that as a sign of respect. Perhaps they even

---

* 24:30

thought of her as an equal? She couldn't know for sure, but that's how it made her feel.

By the time the bus made it to the second stop, Rafraf had decided it would be a good idea to get to know more Americans.

Things seemed to be moving so quickly. From the bus stop, Rafraf found the correct office and, within minutes, was speaking to an Iraqi woman named Rasha, who had authority to hire her on the spot.

She asked Rafraf to speak some English for her, and she did. The two women exchanged a few words, and Rafraf clearly saw that her own English skills were superior to the other woman's.

But instead of giving her a job, the woman handed her a piece of paper.

"You need to work on your English," the woman said. "This is an appointment for you to come back in a month. If you do better that time, maybe there will be some work for you."

Rafraf was too stunned to argue. The woman pointed toward the door, then waved dismissively.

A dejected Rafraf left the office. She resolved to work on her English, but she knew she was good enough to do the job. Because while her experience with soldiers was new, Rafraf had met and conversed with at least one American in the past. An American woman.

Journalists stationed in Baghdad had learned years ago that the best place to find English-speaking Iraqis to interview for stories was at the university. It was common to see television news crews or newspaper reporters hanging around the front of the building where English literature was taught.

Rafraf had encountered such a crew shortly after beginning her first year of college. She remembers the day, November 16, 1998, because it was the day before her eighteenth birthday.

For the previous three months, Saddam Hussein had toyed with the United Nations and the Clinton administration by refusing to allow UN weapons inspectors access to Iraq. Tensions had risen to the level where American-led military action seemed imminent. But at what seemed to be the last possible moment, Saddam relented and allowed the inspectors back in. The world's press called it "an exercise in brinkmanship."

NBC News, of course, was also reporting the story. A Baghdad-based producer named Carol Grisanti went to the university with a camera crew looking for someone willing to comment on the situation. The camera crew headed to the front of the school to shoot pictures of students, while Carol looked for someone to interview. She spotted Rafraf and introduced herself.

"Would you be interested in speaking to us?" Carol asked. She was accompanied by an Iraqi interpreter.

"About what?" Rafraf was flattered, but suspicious.

"About the weapons inspectors being allowed back into the country? It will just take a moment."

"Sure." As always, Rafraf was eager to speak English to people who would actually understand her.

"Great. I have to go grab my camera crew and I'll be right back." Carol left to find her crew, but the translator stayed with Rafraf.

"What do you think you're doing?" the translator demanded as soon as Carol was out of earshot.

"I'm going to answer their questions." Rafraf knew the translator worked for the government. He would report every word she said to his superiors.

"Don't say anything bad about Saddam. Just praise the government and say the U.S. is hurting Iraqi children."

"I know. Nothing but praise." Rafraf knew it was potentially dangerous to speak to the journalist, but she was too excited about the prospect of using her English to worry about it.

"Nothing," the man reminded her as Carol and the camera crew returned.

Rafraf answered the questions Carol asked her, making sure to praise her president, her country, and the Iraqi people at every turn. Carol, of course, knew Rafraf couldn't speak freely. She wanted to know how Rafraf really felt, even if the answers weren't on camera.

She also thought Rafraf's parents might be interested in being interviewed.

"Are you finished with classes for the day?" Carol asked.

"Yes. I'm just going to the bus stop and going home."

"Well, we can give you a ride. It's the least we could do."

The translator immediately stepped in. "I have to be in the car with you. You can't speak to her without me."

"Fine with me," Carol said, though it really wasn't.

"Me too," said Rafraf, and they all drove together to Rafraf's house.

It was a terrible mistake.

Before Rafraf could tell her parents what was happening, the translator barged through the front door and angrily confronted Kamal. "Do you know what your stupid daughter has done? She's brought American reporters to your house!"

Kamal stole an angry look at his daughter. Her excitement had turned to fear. The camera crew and Carol walked through the door into the living room.

"I thought you wouldn't mind," Rafraf pleaded to her father. "They seem nice."

"*La!*" said Kamal, practically shouting the Arabic word for "no." "*La, la, la.*"

He began herding the Americans toward the door.

"He doesn't want to speak to you," the translator told Carol. "You must go."

"Okay, okay," Carol said, backpedaling out of the house. "It was nice to meet you, Rafraf. Can we talk to you again?"

Rafraf tried to answer, but her father cut her off.

"*La,*" he said again, and slammed the door on the Americans.

"What did you do, stupid girl?" he shouted. "This is how people die! Don't you think we have enough trouble?"

"I'm sorry," Rafraf replied with tears streaming down her face. "I thought you'd be proud of me. They wanted to hear what I had to say."

"Enough," Kamal practically screamed. "Nobody wants to hear what you have to say."

He waved Rafraf away without another word. Her first encounter with Americans hadn't gone well.

But the next day, something strange happened. A friend from school came by the house and gave Rafraf an envelope. Inside was a birthday card, which Rafraf opened immediately.

The card wasn't from her friend, but from Carol Grisanti. Along with wishing Rafraf a happy birthday, Carol thanked her for the time and apologized for causing her any trouble at home. She also included her home address in London and encouraged Rafraf to write to her. Rafraf did write a few weeks later and was surprised to receive a prompt return letter.

It was a risk. Rafraf knew her father might discover the correspondence, but she was more excited about having a new friend than fearful of her father's potential reaction.

The two wrote back and forth over the next few months. They wrote about their families and jobs and generally exchanged pleasantries. They didn't write about government or politics . . . as it was widely suspected that mail coming and going from Iraq was monitored by the government.

Another surprise came the following year. One of the Iraqi drivers who worked at NBC's Baghdad bureau stopped by the house with a message for Rafraf. Carol would be back in town soon and wondered if Rafraf and her little brother might like to join her for lunch . . . a secret lunch without the nosy government translator.

The meeting would be an even bigger risk for Rafraf than the letters. What if the American brought a government spy with her anyway? Rafraf's father would be furious if he found out. Should she really bring her little brother? Was she putting him in danger too?

Rafraf knew she should have declined the lunch meeting, but her curiosity got the best of her. A few weeks later she and Rami met Carol for *schwarma* sandwiches and tea.

Carol now had a friend in Baghdad, and Rafraf had an American ally. Neither of the women knew where the relationship might eventually lead.

A MONTH AFTER BEING TURNED away by the Iraqi woman in the translation office, Rafraf returned to try again. She had, as directed, been practicing her English. She knew friends from the university who had been hired by the Americans . . . friends with English skills inferior to hers. She was optimistic about getting hired this time.

Her heart sank when she approached Assassins Gate. There was a long line again, and she would have to stand in it despite having a designated appointment time. That was the system. At least she wouldn't have to talk her way onto the bus this time. She held a paper from the office that would ensure her a place.

It was mid-June and even hotter than during her first trip to see the Americans in May. The relentless sun blazed, and temperatures soared well above a hundred degrees. The line was again exposed to the sun. She took her place at the end and began to sweat. After a few minutes she heard a soldier shouting but couldn't hear what he was saying.

The man was standing on a rooftop across the street. He was pointing his rifle at Rafraf and yelling. He kept waving the rifle and pointing toward the sidewalk. Rafraf wondered what she had done wrong. Still, she stood her ground.

A moment later, the soldier was in the street and walking toward Rafraf. He was wearing wraparound sunglasses and held his rifle tightly to his chest with both hands.

"Hey, Rafraf," the man said happily when he was about fifty feet away, "don't you remember me?" He took off the sunglasses. It was Sergeant Frank.

"Oh, yes, of course," she said, smiling with relief. "I didn't recognize you from so far away."

Frank smiled too and asked, "Why are you back? Didn't you already get a job?"

Rafraf felt self-conscious speaking so openly to the American within view and earshot of the other Iraqis. Despite that most were there also looking for jobs, she felt they would judge her for doing the same. She made a point of speaking loudly, so others wouldn't think she was saying something she shouldn't, even if they didn't speak English.

"They told me to work on my English and try again," Rafraf said, somewhat embarrassed. "So here I am."

"Oh," Frank said. "You must have met with a woman named Rasha?"

Rafraf nodded.

"She's afraid she'll get replaced if she hires someone smarter than her, so apparently she turns the best candidates away. It's sort of a big problem, but she's convinced someone that she's too important to let go, so she's still there."

"I see," said Rafraf, unsure if Frank was telling the truth or just trying to make her feel better.

"And why are you guys all standing in the sun?" Frank asked. "I keep pointing to the sidewalk where there's shade and telling people to move over, but nobody does."

Well, that explained the yelling and gun-waving, thought Rafraf. The Americans were learning after all . . . sort of.

"Anyway, come with me," said Frank. "I'll take you to the bus."

Minutes later, Rafraf was once again standing in the translation office. She was disappointed to see sitting at the desk the same woman who had turned her away before. Rasha obviously recognized Rafraf too and immediately acted superior.

"You came back?" Rasha said in Arabic. Perhaps, thought Rafraf, the woman knew her English was not strong.

"You told me to," Rafraf answered. "Here's my appointment slip."

The woman took the paper but didn't read it and snapped, "Speak some English."

"My name is Rafraf Barrak, and I'm a student at Baghdad University. I am pursuing a degree in English literature, and I've been speaking and reading English since the fourth grade. I also know the city very well and—"

"Enough," Rasha said, cutting her off. "It's not good enough. You need more practice."

She wrote a date down on a piece of paper and shoved it across the desk to Rafraf. "Come back in a month," she said, and waved Rafraf out the door.

Rafraf left the office, dejected once again. She would come back as directed in July. But in the meantime, she decided, she'd have to work on a plan B.

"HOW ABOUT THE PEOPLE AT NBC?" her sister suggested later that day. "You know that woman over there, don't you?"

That woman was, of course, Carol. Carol and Rafraf had stayed in touch in the five years since their first meeting. Rafraf's father had eventually approved of the friendship and had even allowed Carol to come to the house for a family dinner.

In fact, Rafraf had just seen Carol again in May 2003.

A few weeks after the fall of Baghdad, Carol, a camera crew, and correspondent Ron Allen had shown up at the door of Rafraf's house. Ron was assigned to report on how Iraqis were getting by in the aftermath of the bombing, and Rafraf's family seemed an obvious choice. With Saddam Hussein no longer in power, the danger to the family seemed much less.

Kamal reluctantly agreed to allow cameras in his home. *NBC Nightly News* later aired footage of Rafraf and her mother baking bread and even included a sound bite from Jamila, translated by her daughter.

Carol was no longer simply a producer at NBC. She was now the Baghdad bureau chief. Maybe she needed more translators? Rafraf decided to call her and ask for a job.

"I'm sorry," Carol said from her office phone. "With the war winding down, my budget is being cut. I can't hire anybody new."

At the time, in June 2003, Iraq was in limbo. The insurgency was still in its early stages, and optimism was high that the country would soon become a stable, self-governing democracy.

Just two weeks earlier, on June 5, President Bush had flown what *USA Today* called a "victory lap" around Iraq in Air Force One. He addressed U.S. troops in Doha, Qatar, later that day.

"America sent you on a mission to remove a grave threat and to liberate an oppressed people," said Bush, "and that mission has been accomplished."

Interest by Americans in news from Iraq was waning. Millions were war weary after months of round-the-clock coverage.

"Thank you anyway," said a disappointed Rafraf. "Can you please keep me in mind if something does come up?"

"I will." Carol didn't sound very convincing.

But things change fast in the news business. The next day, a driver from NBC showed up once again at Rafraf's house.

"Be ready," he said, "for work tomorrow morning. I'll pick you up and take you to the hotel."

Rafraf was confused. "What's happening?"

"Tom Brokaw is coming to Baghdad tonight," he answered. Rafraf had no idea who Brokaw was, but he was obviously important. "Apparently they need your help."

When Rafraf arrived at work the next day, Carol filled in the details. Tom Brokaw was the anchor and managing editor of *NBC Nightly News*. He was arguably one of the most recognized faces on American television. He would be in Baghdad for a week, and the *Nightly News* would be live from the city. That meant a platoon of producers and camera crews were also in town and would need to generate a large number of stories. Another translator, especially a smart one such as Rafraf, would be needed after all.

Rafraf thought she had misheard Carol when Carol told her how much she would be paid for the week's work.

"Three hundred fifty dollars for the week," Carol said. "If you impress the right people, we might find something longer term for you. It's up to you to prove yourself."

It would be enough money for Rafraf's family to live for nearly five months. More money than Rafraf had ever hoped to make. She told Carol she would accept the job and do her best . . . and she did.

The week was a blur to her, and she honestly knew nothing about how TV news, especially American network TV, worked. But she eagerly accompanied producers and correspondents on their assignments.

One of the first stories she worked on took her farther away from home than she'd ever been in her life. Richard Engel, NBC's correspondent based in Baghdad, was preparing a story on a former Iraqi military officer. Interviewing the man meant traveling by car to Diwaniyah, about three hours south of Baghdad.

During that time on the road, Rafraf saw things she'd never seen before. She looked out the window, fascinated by the vastness of the desert. When she noticed several odd-looking creatures lumbering along near the road, she said excitedly, hardly able to believe her eyes, "Look, camels!"

"Haven't you seen camels before?" replied Rich Latour, a producer who had made the trip with Brokaw. Rich lived in New York, but even he had seen camels.

"No. Never." Rafraf held up a small digital camera and took a blurry picture as the camels passed.

"Aren't they all over the desert?" Rich asked.

"I've never seen the desert either."

"Seriously? But it's all around the city."

"I've never been outside of Baghdad," Rafraf said matter-of-factly.

Rich laughed good-naturedly. Rafraf decided he was a nice guy.

Rafraf wanted to work hard, and it showed. In the following days she was often the first Iraqi to show up for work in the morning and the last to leave. She did, indeed, know the city and always seemed able to find people willing to be interviewed. What's more, people were more open when she translated the questions, which seemed to please the journalists.

But Rafraf also learned how emotionally demanding the work of a reporter can be. One of the stories she worked on during that first week was about a Baghdad hospital. She, Richard Engel, a producer, and a camera crew spent hours at the hospital, watching as patients were brought in from around the city.

"What happened to this man?" Rafraf asked the nurses in Arabic as a new patient was brought in for surgery. She would listen to the answer, then follow up with other questions, explaining to the Americans what was being said. She didn't know at the time that Richard spoke fluent Arabic. He listened to make sure she was passing on the important information.

Near the end of the day, a two-year-old child was brought into the hospital suffering from a gunshot wound. Rafraf learned the child's parents had been fighting. His father tried to shoot the mother during the fight, but the bullet hit the toddler instead. The child died from the wound.

"He was just a baby," Rafraf sobbed after returning to the bureau. She was on the verge of a complete breakdown. "How do you do this?" she asked Richard. He explained to Rafraf that death was part of war, that she would see it every day if she continued working for NBC. She should think hard about whether she had the emotional strength to do the job.

She composed herself and decided, "I can do it."

AT THE END OF THE week, Rafraf collected her money and went home. Carol thanked her for her hard work, but gave no indication whether she had indeed earned herself a regular job.

That question was answered the following morning when an NBC driver again showed up at Rafraf's house. Rafraf was, apparently, already late for a job she didn't even know she had. When she arrived at the office, she discovered Carol had left the country and wouldn't return for at least a month. But Rafraf's name was on the schedule to work . . . and it would remain that way for the foreseeable future.

And there was more money too: $750 a month, followed quickly by a raise to $1,000 per month. It was, for Rafraf and her family, all the money in the world.

Within weeks of her beginning the job, Kamal closed his stationery shop for good. Why work so hard for $15 a month when his daughter made that much in three hours? The farmers' market where he worked as an accountant had recently reopened, and Kamal was back on the job there. He no longer needed the money, but it wouldn't be right in his view not to work at all, so he continued working there.

But everyone else in the family was unemployed, so Rafraf's newfound wealth was a welcome blessing.

On payday each month, Rafraf would come home and start handing out money. First, she would set aside money for the house to continue operating. She would purchase groceries, water, gas for the generator, and other necessities. She would then set aside about $300 for herself, then split the remaining money equally among every member of the family.

And she shopped.

Rafraf had worn hand-me-downs her whole life. School uniforms and other outfits were well worn by her three older sisters long before they were passed on to Rafraf. She had two "housedresses" that she wore at home, and a precious few other articles of clothing that she had been given as gifts over the years. But that all changed when Rafraf started getting paid.

She discovered fashion . . . new blouses, sweaters, jeans, tops, and scarves.

One of the advantages of living in Baghdad, in Rafraf's opinion, was the availability of "Western" clothing for women. In certain areas in Iraq most of the women wore the abaya—a traditional garment similar to a burka but which didn't obscure the face. In some neighborhoods in Baghdad the abaya was also worn, but Western fashion was common in most of the city. Rafraf had always been allowed to wear Western clothes, though her wardrobe was limited entirely to hand-me-downs from her older sisters. Her new job changed that.

Rafraf bought new shoes—more than one pair—and had money for her favorite indulgence: pastries from the bakery on the first floor of the hotel. She was also generous to her siblings. She would often take her sisters or younger brothers to a store or market and say, "Anything you want." It was good to have a job.

But beyond the financial benefit, the job expanded her horizons significantly. At twenty-two years old, along with having never left the city or seen a camel, Rafraf had never driven a car, ridden on an escalator or a bicycle, and certainly hadn't flown on an airplane. She was soon crisscrossing the country. Diwaniyah, Baqubah, Fallujah, and Najaf . . . exotic cities that she had only seen on a map, she was now seeing with her own eyes.

IN THOSE EARLY DAYS WITH NBC—in the summer of 2003—the job was all about learning what journalists do and making money. The potential danger rarely crossed Rafraf's mind. But that would soon change.

As the "shock" began to fade following shock and awe and the fall of Baghdad, the Iraqi insurgency started to gain strength. The initial targets of insurgent attacks were military, either U.S. or Coalition troops, but civilians increasingly found themselves in the crosshairs.

Suicide bombings targeted restaurants, marketplaces, funerals, and mosques. Any opportunity to horrify the populace and weaken resolve was taken. Many of the bombers wore vests packed with explosives. Debate raged about whether the insurgents were Iraqis or foreign fighters who flooded into the country for jihad against the Americans. Al Qaeda in Iraq, a militant group that pledged its allegiance to Osama bin Laden, began to wage its own war.

On August 7, 2003, a cement truck filled with explosives detonated in front of the Jordanian embassy. The blast killed seventeen people and injured more than three dozen others.

Twelve days later, a flatbed truck pulled to the front of the Canal Hotel in Baghdad and detonated a five-hundred-pound bomb. The Canal was the headquarters for the UN operation in Iraq. The explosion killed twenty-two people and injured more than one hundred others. The toll was enough to convince the United Nations to pull its people out of Iraq and drop any plans to send in peacekeepers until there was a peace to keep.

Insurgents had their proof that the will of those seeking peace could be broken through acts of terror. The age of the car bomb had arrived in Iraq.

Rafraf accompanied NBC crews to the scenes of both bombings. She saw bodies and body parts on the streets and tangled within the wreckage of the buildings. She saw blood on the ground, fear and grief in the eyes of survivors. But she still felt somewhat insulated from the violence. The danger was in being accidentally caught in the cross fire of a battle or in the wrong place when a suicide bomber detonated, but she never considered herself, or the people she worked with, to be actual targets.

The insurgents thought otherwise. Journalists were, in fact, easy targets. They traveled without the protection of military troops. They went to dangerous places and asked questions of dangerous people. What's more, kidnapping or killing a journalist, particularly one working for a Western news organization, was a sure way to make worldwide headlines.

More reporters have died covering the Iraq war—many more—than in any other conflict in history. As of this writing, at least 135 journalists have been killed in Iraq since March 2003. That's more than the total number killed in World War II and Vietnam combined. The "journalist" number in Iraq doesn't even include what the Committee to Protect Journalists calls "media support workers." Interpreters such as Rafraf fall into that category, along with "fixers" . . . locals who know the ins and outs of a particular region. Adding that number swells the journalist death toll in Iraq to close to 200.*

While "combat" deaths accounted for the overwhelming majority of deaths in earlier wars, the leading cause of death for journalists in Iraq is murder. They are specifically targeted for who they are and what they do. There has never been a more dangerous place for journalists to work in history.

Insurgents in Iraq targeted the military and foreign journalists as a matter of tactics. But they targeted Iraqis who worked with them as a matter of vengeance. No mercy was to be given to Iraqis who would so casually turn their back on their country and work for the enemy. Translator, cook, machinist . . . it didn't matter what you did for Americans. Anything was enough to get you killed.

Insurgents began hunting down translators who worked for Americans. They murdered them in their homes, in their cars, wherever they could find them. Often they murdered their families too.

By late summer Rafraf started feeling the pressure. It came from people in her neighborhood as well as from those she met while working on stories. She was warned, usually out of genuine concern, that being seen with Americans was not in her best interests. Sometimes the warnings sounded more like threats.

Rafraf assumed the U.S. military would make security in Iraq their top priority, giving the insurgency no breathing room to gain ground. The first few months after the fall of Baghdad had seen a growing peace. The truck bombings in August, she hoped, were spectacular yet isolated incidents. She was wrong.

---

* Source: Committee to Protect Journalists, "Iraq: Journalists in Danger," October 2008.

By September 2003, the relative calm in Baghdad had completely unraveled. Terrorist attacks on military and civilian targets rose at an alarming pace.

The morning of September 25 began for Rafraf like any other morning. An NBC driver picked her up from her house just before seven o'clock in the morning. She and the driver crawled their way through the congested morning traffic. They were just minutes from the small hotel that housed the NBC bureau when they heard and felt a tremendous explosion.

It was a homemade bomb that had been placed on the sidewalk, hidden from view by the hotel generator. The blast shattered the first floor windows of the Al Aike hotel, and damaged a neighboring restaurant. It was the first attack in Baghdad to directly target foreign journalists and it was effective. A security guard employed by the hotel was killed and an NBC soundman was injured. The hotel employee, Awais Ali, was thirty-six years old, with a pregnant wife and four children. An Iraqi police officer told the *Los Angeles Times*, "NBC should do more to protect itself." [*]

Rafraf arrived for work just a few minutes after the explosion. An American tank blocked the road a hundred yards from the hotel, so Rafraf jumped out of the NBC car and ran to the scene.

She saw John Zito, an NBC producer, standing on the street in front of the hotel.

"What happened?" she asked. "Is everyone okay?"

"A bomb," he answered still obviously in shock. "They bombed us."

She wanted to know more, but John was trying to sort out the details. He quickly hurried away to check on other staff members who had been in the hotel.

Rafraf was left standing on the street. Any optimism she had about the future of her country was fading fast.

---

[*] Source: *Los Angeles Times*, September 25, 2003.

A short time later she learned about the death of the hotel employee.

Rafraf liked Awais. He always made sure to check on her as he was making his rounds. Just the night before he had told her the good news . . . that despite earlier difficulties in his wife's pregnancy, the most recent doctor's visit had gone well. His new baby was expected to be healthy.

The wife's younger sister, Awais's sister in-law, was also an employee at the hotel. She arrived hysterical later that morning.

"You have to talk to her," John told Rafraf, "she should hear the news from you. It will be easier for her."

It was the last thing Rafraf wanted to do. But someone needed to tell Awais's family what had happened. NBC was thought to be the target of the attack. Even though Awais worked for the hotel, not the network, the mere presence of the American journalists had cost him his life.

Rafraf first told the sister, then accompanied her to speak with the rest of the family. She cried with them and tried to offer an explanation for the unexplainable.

OVER THE NEXT FEW MONTHS, the violence seemed to grow exponentially. More bombings, more ambushes, more trouble.

On November 29, Rafraf accompanied correspondent Jim Maceda on a trip to Hilla, a town near the ancient city of Babylon. A British security consultant was assigned to travel with the two-vehicle convoy. Iraqi drivers were at the wheel of both vehicles. The crew also included a female producer, a cameraman, and a soundman.

The purpose of security consultants, at the time, was to simply keep the journalists out of trouble. The network required every staff member working in the war zone to undergo specialized training, including combat first aid, to help insure their survival. Part of the training included navigating hostile checkpoints and even simulated kidnappings. But nothing can replace having armed security on hand.

Most of the security consultants were former British Royal Marines. Many were veterans of the "troubles" in Northern Ireland and had firsthand experience with terrorism. Their job was to look for and anticipate danger, and steer the reporters clear of it.

By November, the security consultants had begun carrying sidearms, typically 9 mm pistols. But that was more suitable to stopping a mugger than a terrorist attack. The consultants' brains were their primary defensive weapons.

The camera shoot in Hilla went off without a hitch, and the NBC entourage piled into their cars for the drive back to Baghdad. Rafraf got in the first vehicle with Sa'ad, an Iraqi cameraman, a soundman named Omar, and the driver. The security consultant, producer, and correspondent were in the second vehicle.

Driving in Iraq was dangerous enough on its own. The second it became clear that Saddam Hussein was no longer in power, speed limits seemed to disappear. With no police officers to issue fines, traffic lights (the few that worked) were merely suggestions. Stop signs barely caused drivers to tap the brakes at all. The roads, from back streets to main highways, became a free-for-all. And no highway was more important at the time than Highway 8.

Highway 8 is the primary thoroughfare stretching from south to north across the country. It extends from the port city of Basra in the far south all the way to Baghdad, about three hundred miles. The highway, similar to an American interstate, is how military convoys, relief aid, and construction supplies moved north from Kuwait to Baghdad and points beyond.

The NBC convoy flew along the four-lane road, heading north back to the city. The drivers pushed the heavily loaded sedans as fast as they could go. At times, speeds topped one hundred miles per hour. For most of the drive, it was business as usual.

Rafraf didn't see the trouble coming, but she felt it. The driver of her car slammed on the brakes and swerved hard. He had just rounded a bend in the road and roared headlong into chaos.

Two vehicles were burning on the highway in front of them. Orange flames poured out of the windows, and black smoke billowed into the sky. People, angry men, were shouting and dancing around the SUVs. The traffic lanes on both sides of the road were partially blocked.

At first Rafraf assumed there had been an accident, but drawing nearer, she knew the awful truth. They had driven upon the scene of an ambush. It had happened just minutes earlier.

The vehicles weren't military—they belonged to civilians. And they were mangled—not from a crash but from an explosion. Bullet holes dotted what was left of the doors and windows.

The worst part was the bodies. Sa'ad saw them too.

"Go around," the cameraman said to the driver. "Don't slow down."

The driver swerved left into the oncoming-traffic lane, then right. The scene rolled past in what seemed like slow motion. Rafraf counted at least two bodies, burned beyond recognition and sprawled out on the asphalt. She watched a man pull yet another smoldering body out of an SUV and drag it mercilessly toward the crowd. He dropped the body just a few feet from Rafraf's window and began stomping on it. Another man ran up to the victim's corpse and stomped on his head.

Rafraf, unable to believe what she was seeing, held her digital camera to the glass and took a picture.

Then all hell broke loose.

Perhaps someone saw her take the picture. Or maybe they noticed the TV camera sitting on Sa'ad's lap in the front seat. Maybe someone in the crowd noticed the blond producer sitting in the second vehicle. Whatever the trigger, the seething crowd suddenly realized that more "Westerners" were in their midst. More targets of their anger.

Thump!

The first rock smashed into the car. Then a second.

Thump!

"Lock the doors," Sa'ad shouted.

The crowd started rushing the vehicles. Guns could be drawn within seconds.

"Go," Rafraf screamed. "Go!"

The driver floored the accelerator.

Thump! Another rock.

Rafraf's vehicle cleared the scene and roared away. She looked over her shoulder at the second car. If the angry mob managed to stop the vehicle, it would mean certain death for everyone inside.

The driver of that vehicle knew it too. He was accelerating as fast as possible. Rocks and fists flew in the air as the second car narrowly cleared the crowd.

The NBC convoy escaped . . . but just barely. The passengers from both cars watched nervously out the back windows, expecting to see men with guns or cars chasing them. Luckily, there were neither.

Not until the group made it back to the hotel and the NBC bureau did they learn the full extent of what they had seen. Insurgents had ambushed a convoy of Spanish intelligence agents with grenades and automatic weapons. Seven men had been killed.

But a heroic act of courage also occurred on Highway 8 that day. It happened minutes, perhaps even seconds, after Rafraf's convoy left the scene.

Eight men were in the Spanish convoy, and one of them had survived the initial barrage of bullets. The angry mob discovered the survivor and was about to burn him alive when a small Iraqi police unit rushed to the scene.

The commander of the unit, putting his own life in great peril, rescued the survivor from the angry mob. The man reportedly told the insurgents he was going to put the Spaniard in jail. Instead, he rushed the survivor to a U.S. military base nearby, thereby saving his life.

If the attack on the hotel hadn't convinced Rafraf, the narrow escape from the ambush sealed it. Working with the Americans was a dangerous job, and it would only get worse.

In the following weeks, the violence in and around Baghdad would reach a fever pitch. The country, once hopeful that the fall of Saddam Hussein would usher in a new era of peace and prosperity, fell further into chaos.

FIVE

HUMILITY

Sometimes you learn things about yourself that cause you to rethink who you are. Things you're not proud of. My first extended tour in the war zone taught me things about myself and my faith that I didn't want to know.

I had, throughout my life, created an illusion in my mind of who I was. I had faced plenty of dangers on the job . . . riots, wildfires, and severe weather from hurricanes and blizzards to tornadoes. I had also held what, in my view, was one of the more dangerous jobs in the military. I flew army helicopters and had survived what I considered a couple of close calls.

In the summer of 1995, the engine of a Huey I was piloting exploded in flight. I was flying low along the coast of Rhode Island with another pilot and a crew chief. The other pilot was a Vietnam veteran, with vastly more experience than me. When the engine blew, the senior pilot took control of the aircraft and we autorotated to safety. Everything went by the book. I did the things I was supposed to do . . . made the Mayday call, monitored the rpm of the rotor system, and helped the pilot gauge his landing. But the ten to fifteen seconds between the engine's blowing up and our skids hitting the beach were the most terrifying of my life.

I didn't fly the next day, but knew I had to get back in the air as soon as possible. By the end of the week, I was flying again. A little jumpy, but in my view a better pilot for having gone through the experience. I thought I was brave.

But I'm not brave. My experiences in Iraq taught me that.

I was often scared. Afraid not just of what might happen to me or the people I was with, but of what I might see or be a part of.

During the first few weeks of the war, an area near the border between southern Iraq and Kuwait became particularly troublesome with frequent ambushes. The ambushes weren't to kill, but to steal. Food, money, camera equipment . . . if it had value, it was worth stealing.

Many of those doing the ambushing didn't have guns. So how do you stop a car without using guns?

You use children.

Just before we crossed the border, the soldier driving a Humvee we were following stopped to warn us, "Watch out for children lying in the road."

"Children?" I asked. "Why children?"

"Because they know you won't run them over. They line up little kids, five or six years old, across the road and force you to stop. When you do, people swarm the vehicle. They smash the windows with rocks, drag people out. You don't want that to happen."

"So what are we supposed to do?" I asked.

"You don't stop. No matter what."

I couldn't imagine a worse situation. It was designed to leave a compassionate person with no choice but to become a victim. The soldier told me he didn't know of any military people who had actually run over children. The Iraqis, he said, figured military vehicles wouldn't bother stopping, so they usually reserved the tactic for civilians. That meant us.

I prayed we would never face such an impossible dilemma. Every time we rounded a corner, I worried there would be children—tiny, barefoot, and dirty—lying head to foot across the road. The thought

of it made driving across the border so stressful that it literally nause-
ated me.

Thankfully, we were never forced into that situation. That prayer
was answered.

While that exact scenario didn't present itself, we were often surrounded by Iraqis including children. They would clamor around the
vehicle asking for food, water, money, or candy. Adults would beg to
use our cell phones, desperate to reach relatives who had fled to other
countries. If our windows were open, they would thrust phone numbers at us and shout the names of people we were to call. It was often
chaotic, and several times I thought we were going to run over someone trying to get to our vehicle.

Against the advice of our security adviser, I lent my phone to a
man in Safwan—a village in southeastern Iraq on the border with
Kuwait. The man was part of a massive, restless crowd waiting for
handouts of relief supplies from the Red Crescent (the Arab world's
version of the Red Cross). I had waded into the crowd looking for
people who spoke English to interview. The man tried to leave with
the phone, but I held him in place.

"Make the call," I said. "Now."

He did, then quickly passed my phone off to someone else, who
tried to run away, but I grabbed him.

"That's my phone," I said, "please give it back." I had to pry it
from his hands.

In that same crowd, I first realized some people in Iraq would
very much like to kill me.

Most of the people, thousands of them, who had gathered in a
vacant dirt lot on the outer edge of the village were extremely poor.
They lived in a mostly rural area with a total population of just a few
thousand. Their homes were made of mud bricks made from the
desert; some seemed on the verge of collapsing under their own
weight. Many of the people who gathered to receive aid were dirty,
from head to toe. Their clothes were tattered, and their teeth were in
terrible shape.

The crowd was just a degree short of a mob. Not so much enraged, but panicked at the prospect that they would starve to death
with no government food-distribution system to sustain them. They
shouted and sang in unison.

"We give our blood and hearts to Saddam!" went the cry in
Arabic.

The people swarmed the two Red Crescent eighteen-wheel trucks
as soon as they arrived. Dozens of young men swarmed to the front
of the crowd as soon as the doors of the truck trailers were opened.
Punches were thrown, and people were pushed to the ground as men,
women, and children fought their way to the open trailers.

There was no sense of shared suffering. The pecking order for receiving supplies was simple: survival of the fittest. I saw old women
pushed to the ground, and an elderly man punched in the face.

A few American and British soldiers were mingling within the
crowd for security. I saw them break up a few fights, but for the most
part they tried to stay out of the fray. I watched as a mother with a
baby in her arms and several children in tow was shuffled empty-
handed away from the trucks. Young, strong men who made it to the
front would leave with four or five boxes of food, complaining that it
wasn't enough.

Red Crescent officials begged for patience. They promised there
was more than enough food for everyone, but the riot only intensi-
fied.

I tried to interview a few people in the crowd. I knew some
spoke a smattering of English, but those who would speak simply
repeated the same mantra: "Saddam is great, America must go." An
American soldier told me the anti-American chants only began
when the TV cameras arrived. He said the people were afraid . . . not
of the foreigners, but of what remained of Saddam's government
structure.

The only thing keeping the situation from turning into a full-
blown riot were the guns. The British army had surrounded the aid
station with armored personnel carriers. Soldiers manned .50-caliber

machine guns on top of the vehicles and kept them pointed toward the crowd.

Then I saw him. He wasn't part of the crowd, he was on the periphery, monitoring it. He stood just at the edge of the action, seemingly taking notes in his head of who spoke to foreign journalists and who didn't. His clothes weren't just clean . . . they were spotless. His hair was perfectly trimmed, and he wore a watch that surely cost more money than most Iraqis would ever see. His arms were folded across his chest.

No one stood within fifteen feet of the man. He was clearly feared, and unapproachable. I figured he also spoke English, so I walked up to him with Mark, my cameraman, in tow.

"Can I ask you some questions?" I began.

He had startling green eyes and seemed insulted that I had dared approach him, much less ask a question. Then he seemed to realize this might be an opportunity.

"What do you wish to ask?" His English was perfect.

"About the war," I said, "about Saddam Hussein. Do you think America did the right thing going to war?"

He looked at me suspiciously. "Are you an American?"

For the record, many journalists I know do not answer that question honestly when traveling in a hostile country. They will typically say they're from Canada. Nobody hates Canadians.

But as a former military officer, I had sworn an oath to "support and defend the Constitution of the United States against all enemies, foreign and domestic; that I will bear true faith and allegiance to the same . . ."

I was no longer in the military, but I had never "unsworn" that oath. I certainly wasn't going to go all squishy on where I was from simply because a guy who didn't like my country had asked.

"Yes," I said, "I'm an American."

I saw him do the math in his head. Could he kill me on the spot and get away before being gunned down by the British soldiers? Would the cameraman try to intervene? I actually saw his eyes fill with hate. I can't explain how I knew . . . but I knew. The man's body seemed to vibrate with anticipation. I realized I was standing much too close to him. He could stab me with a knife or shoot me in the gut with a gun that nobody but he or I would ever see.

Instead of killing me, he smiled. His teeth were white and perfect.

"We hate America," he began. "You have no right to be here."

He continued speaking, but I found that I wasn't really listening. Not because he was saying things I didn't want to hear, but because I realized that even as he spoke, this man was trying to figure out how to kill me. It dawned on me that he was probably a high-level member of the Baath Party. Perhaps he was an enforcer, or one of Saddam's secret police, who ruled communities with an iron fist. Torturing and killing were said to be part of a day's work for them. Killing me would be easy.

I glanced around and noticed the soldiers had all retreated to their armored vehicles. And where were the other reporters?

"Thanks a lot," I said to the Iraqi, giving him the quickest brush-off I could. "Good luck with everything."

I backed away, grabbed Mark, and said, "I think we should get out of here. Let's see if everyone's back at the bus."

The bus belonged to the Red Crescent. They had invited the media to ride with them on the trip, so the bus was our only way of getting back to Kuwait.

"Good plan," he said. "I just want to grab a couple more shots. I'm right behind you."

I headed back to the bus while Mark wandered off in search of video.

As I reached the edge of the crowd, alarm bells started ringing in my head. No longer were any journalists or soldiers on foot visible. What's more, the Red Crescent volunteers were jumping out of the truck trailers and heading to the cabs. They didn't even bother closing the trailer doors.

Thankfully, the Red Crescent bus was still there, but it was about to move.

My Kuwaiti "fixer" Fallah and his wife were on the bus. Fallah's job with NBC included more than translation; he was invaluable in helping us navigate the political and cultural landscape of Kuwait, and keeping us out of trouble. He and his wife had never set foot in Iraq and thought the trip to Safwan would be a grand adventure. But at first sight of the angry crowd, they rethought their decision. They never got off the bus.

Fallah stood in the open door, a panicked look in his eyes.

"Don, get on the bus," he yelled as I approached. "The driver says it's not safe to stay. We are leaving."

I saw Fallah's wife, Laila, looking out the bus window. Her eyes were as big as saucers. She was scared to death. What I didn't know at the time was that a man armed with a large knife had stormed onto the bus moments earlier and demanded money from the passengers. Laila gave him all she had.

I turned and looked for Mark. He was still somewhere in the crowd.

"No, we have to wait for Mark," I yelled back.

Fallah pointed toward the military and the trucks. "Look," he pleaded, "everyone is leaving."

"Just wait!" I yelled. "Don't leave, just give me one minute."

Against all of my instincts, I turned and ran back into the crowd.

I had been so caught up in work, that somehow I hadn't noticed the mood of the crowd growing even angrier. The situation was on the verge of spiraling out of control. By the time I waded back in to look for Mark, there was no missing it. The sense of panic and anger had dramatically escalated. Suddenly, everyone seemed to be looking at me. I started yelling for Mark and jumping up to see over the sea of heads. I was sure "Mr. Green Eyes" was looking for me as well. What a great opportunity he would have to kill me.

I thought it would be easy to find Mark. How hard is it to spot an American with a giant video camera who's several inches taller than everyone around him? But I couldn't find him! In a panic, I ran back to the area where we had separated, and I finally spotted him. He was crouched low to the ground, engrossed in taking whatever "perfect" shot he was looking for. He was oblivious of the growing peril around him.

"Dude, we have got to get out of here," I said when I reached him.

"Almost finished," he said.

"No," I yelled. "Seriously!" I grabbed his shoulder and pulled him up. "The bus is leaving without us."

"Oh, crap."

We both took off at a dead run toward the bus. It was, indeed, leaving without us.

We cleared the crowd and chased the bus, screaming for it to stop. I could see Fallah standing on the step at the open bus door. He motioned frantically for us to catch up.

The driver slowed just enough for us to jump on.

I tried to look nonchalant as I walked down the aisle toward my seat. But who was I fooling? When I looked back toward the crowd, I saw pandemonium.

Two tractor-trailer rigs were accelerating as fast as they could out of the crowd, but the Iraqis were attempting to stop the trucks. Men were hanging on the sides of the trailers, one from a trailer door like Eddie Murphy in *Beverly Hills Cop*. The door swung wildly as the truck turned hard onto a dirt road, but the man didn't let go.

Then the shooting started.

Whump . . . whump . . . whump!

One of the British soldiers opened up with his .50-caliber machine gun.

Whump . . . whump . . . whump!

They were probably warning shots. I didn't see anybody hit by bullets, but the Iraqis flew off the trucks like fleas being shaken from a dog.

Whump . . . whump . . . whump!

The soldier kept firing as our bus and the trucks raced away down the dirt road. A couple of cars peeled out down the road to give chase, but the soldiers intervened and stopped them.

We left Safwan with the sound of gunfire echoing in our ears, and a growing sense that things were going to get a lot worse. Two days later military officials declared Safwan "off-limits" to journalists.

BEFORE THE WAR STARTED, I thought of myself as the daring, intrepid correspondent that my wife and my NBC bio said I was. But as terrorist attacks, missiles, bombs, impossible situations, and close calls began to add up, my self-image changed dramatically.

For the first time in my life I felt real, sustained fear. I knew that being afraid was a logical response to the situations we sometimes found ourselves in, but the people around me didn't seem to fear any-thing. Hundreds of reporters were covering the war, and many faced much more danger than I did. They seemed impervious to the danger.

I could hide the fear. I could function. But I felt a gnawing sense of failure nonetheless.

I had gone to Kuwait some three months earlier filled with hope. Kiki and I had earnestly prayed for protection and strength from God. We were both confident that I would be safe no matter what dangers swirled around me. She reminded me daily that God had a plan for my life, and as long as I listened to His voice, I had nothing to fear. I saved all of her e-mails.

"You are in the safest place . . . right in the middle of God's perfect will," Kiki wrote to me. "You are where you are for a reason. We don't have to know that reason for it to work out. Remember the disciples asked Jesus, 'What is the most important thing we can do?' and he an-swered, 'Just believe.'"

I also had hundreds of people praying for me. Old friends I hadn't heard from in years would see me on the *Nightly News* and send e-mails encouraging me. I even heard from viewers I had never met.

One viewer wrote after seeing me standing on the roof of a hotel wearing my gas mask:

"While watching you, you seemed like the most alone person in the world and that is why I found your email address and sent you a note as someone on MSNBC commented that you guys might like to get an email from the folks back here to let you know how much we appreciate and support you. In any case, I felt a connection with you and I just wanted to share with you that my thoughts and prayers are with you, the folks there with you and your family back at home."

THE E-MAILS HELPED ME, BUT my primary source of strength during that first trip to the war zone was the Bible. For one of the only extended periods of my life, I read God's word almost every day. I needed the affirmation that it was God's will for me to be there. I needed the strength that comes with that knowledge.

I repeatedly turned to the twenty-seventh psalm:

> *The LORD is my light and my salvation—*
> *whom shall I fear?*
> *The LORD is the stronghold of my life—*
> *of whom shall I be afraid?*
> *When evil men advance against me*
> *to devour my flesh,*
> *when my enemies and my foes attack me,*
> *they will stumble and fall.*
> *Though an army besiege me,*
> *my heart will not fear;*
> *though war break out against me,*
> *even then will I be confident.*

I knew I was living in God's will . . . but for how long? The Bible mentions the word *fear* more than three hundred times. Many times it tells us to have no fear. Still, there it was.

Fear lurked in the corners of my mind, waiting for the opportunity to lead me in the wrong direction. I could feel it trying to creep in. I felt guilty for allowing even the smallest hint of fear to take hold. I felt that I was letting down God, my family, and my employer.

I had spent three and a half months covering the buildup to war and the first six weeks of fighting. I ventured into Iraq at least a dozen times in the month following the Safwan incident and each time faced dangerous situations.

By the end of April 2003, I had the distinct feeling that it was time for me to leave. It wasn't fear that told me to go; I'm not sure it was God either. But it was time.

I was the first NBC correspondent sent to Kuwait in advance of the war, and I was among the last of the early wave still in place. NBC would have to send another person to replace me for a couple of weeks, but I had had enough.

I called New York and told them to get me out. I wasn't running away, but I wasn't volunteering to stay either.

I would return home both thankful and humbled. If it was God's will that I go to Iraq, then what had I accomplished? God had been faithful to me; I wasn't at all sure I'd been faithful to him.

SIX

ROTATION

The day I left the war, April 25, 2003, was one of the happiest days of my life. By my count, I had spent more than one hundred days away from my home in Atlanta. I was never more thrilled to be on a plane.

I was rewarded for my long stay with a week off that didn't count against my vacation time. I quickly learned that the stress of the past months had been harder on my family than I'd expected.

Rachael and Madison, both normally straight-A students, were having problems in school. Rachael was two months shy of her eleventh birthday. She was ordinarily outgoing and smart, and always happy. But when I returned home, I found her withdrawn.

Madison, my youngest, turned eight while I was gone. Her grades had dramatically slipped, and for the first time in her young life she even got in trouble at school.

With Kiki, the effects of the stress were visible. She had gained weight, which no woman I know actually wants to do, her face had broken out for the first time since high school, and she looked tired.

I felt guilty for putting them through the last few months, and I felt even more sympathy and respect for the families of U.S. troops. Many of them would worry about their loved ones for more than a year and face multiple deployments. While my family could simply turn on the TV to see how I was doing, military families could only worry and pray that sedans would not come to their houses carrying bad news.

The week off passed too quickly, and I was soon back to the normal grind of covering news in the United States. I hoped I wouldn't be asked to return to Iraq.

AS USUAL, OVER THE NEXT few months I covered a wide range of stories. In May, I was in Jackson, Tennessee, reporting on the aftermath of deadly tornadoes. In June, it was flooding across the Southeast. August brought a fight over the Ten Commandments at the Alabama State court building. In September, I was at a fatal nursing-home fire in Nashville.

I followed the news from Iraq as closely as any American, but I was glad I wasn't there. Yet, as the months passed, I started getting the feeling that my time away from the war was too good to last.

"WE NEED YOU TO DO a month in Baghdad," said the voice on the other end of the line. It was NBC's director of national news. "Are you up for it?"

It was mid-January 2004. I had returned home from the war nine months earlier. I never made it to Baghdad during my first stint covering the war, but I knew the security situation was deteriorating there.

My brain screamed *NO,* but my mouth betrayed me:

"Sure. When do you need me?"

"We're thinking the first of February. Do you think you can do that?"

I love how bosses ask things like that. What could I say, "I'm busy that month"? Technically, I could have said no. Postings to war zones are strictly voluntary. But I felt I would let the network down if I refused.

"Just let me check with Kiki." I knew that Kiki would reluctantly agree, but it still had to be a family decision.

"Great." He knew the answer too.

By early 2004—almost a year after the war started—NBC's method of operation in Baghdad had settled into a routine. Richard Engel, a truly fearless correspondent hired shortly after the fall of Baghdad, was assigned to cover Iraq full-time. Richard speaks fluent Arabic and may very well be bulletproof. He seemed at home in the chaos of postwar Iraq.

But the stress of working in a war zone builds up over time, so the network implemented a rotation plan.

Correspondents, producers, camera crews, even bureau chiefs from NBC operations worldwide, would work in Baghdad for one month at a time, then be rotated back to their normal duty stations. For staffers based in London and other locations outside of the United States, two or three trips a year to Iraq would become the norm.

Richard Engel was rotating out of Baghdad for the month of February, so my job was to fill his place until he returned. I wasn't looking forward to it.

Violence in Iraq had been rising sharply since the bombing of the NBC hotel. Ambushes of civilian convoys, the use of "improvised explosive devices" or IEDs, and suicide bombings were commonplace.

"Don't worry," Karl Bostic told me the night before we drove into Iraq. "We've got it pretty much down to a science. It's sort of a drill."

We were having a drink in the lounge of our hotel in Amman, Jordan. Karl, a producer based in the London bureau, was rotating into Baghdad with me for the month to serve as bureau chief.

"How long is the drive?" I already knew the answer but hoped it would magically change.

"It's about twelve hours, depending on checkpoints," he said. It was not the answer I wanted to hear.

*   *   *

BY 4 A.M. THE FOLLOWING morning we were out of the hotel and on the road. A few hours later, we reached the Iraq border and transferred our gear into two SUVs with Iraqi drivers employed by NBC.

Karl rode shotgun in my Suburban; I rode in the backseat with a security guy named Craig. Craig, like the others, was a former British Royal Marine. He had a 9 mm handgun and an AK-47 assault rifle. We would be the rear vehicle in the convoy. The first Suburban carried another security guy, a cameraman, and a soundman.

"Put your body armor against the door, mate," Craig told me. "The first few hours aren't too bad. We'll stop and put on our kit before Ramadi."

The SUVs had no armor to protect from bullets. The security guys had rigged metal plates behind the backseats to provide some protection, but bullets could easily penetrate the doors. Bulletproof vests shoved against the doors would be our only barrier from bullets fired from the side of the road.

Karl turned and looked at me seriously. "I shouldn't have said it's just a drill."

"What?" I asked.

"Last night. This is actually the most dangerous part. But these guys know what they're doing."

With that, we began our race to Baghdad. The drivers pushed the Suburbans as fast as they would go. The big SUVs were heavily loaded, but still managed nearly 100 mph on the four-lane highway.

Craig rechecked the magazines in his weapons, turned around in his seat, and began scanning the road behind us.

"What are you looking for?" I asked.

"Fast cars, usually big BMWs or Opels. If they come up on us, it's bad news."

Ambushes occurred daily on the highway from Jordan to Baghdad. The bad guys could be insurgents, or simply robbers, but the targets and tactics were the same. Convoys such as ours were prized targets for either group. We were foreigners. We carried expensive gear, and cash.

Word traveled quickly when a convoy of Suburbans was on the road. Bad guys would wait just off the highway until foreigners passed, then chase after the convoys in much faster vehicles. The good news, at least for us, was that they didn't immediately open fire when they reached a convoy.

The tactic was to race up alongside the vehicles, have a quick look at the passengers and equipment, then fall back. Minutes later the sedan would race up again with armed men shooting from the windows and the sunroof.

Convoys would be riddled with bullets, vehicles would crash at high speed, people would die.

But our guys had figured out how this worked. They would watch for any vehicle approaching at high speed. If the vehicle looked suspicious when it came alongside, the security men would display their weapons and motion for the other car to keep moving. With the element of surprise lost, the bad guys would slam on their brakes and turn around. They were looking for an easy target, not a gunfight.

So Craig would ride to Baghdad facing backward, looking for trouble in the form of a shiny BMW.

"Where are the safeties?" I asked Craig. If he got shot or needed me to help, I wanted to be ready.

He showed me the safety-on and safety-off positions for both of his weapons.

"They're locked and loaded?"

"Yeah," he said, "ready to roll."

"Good."

With that, we were off.

IN FEBRUARY 2004, THE IPOD had not yet taken over the music world, so I brought a CD Walkman with me on the trip, and an assortment of music. Shortly after crossing the border, I put Third Day's *Offerings* CD into the Walkman, plugged in my headphones, and pressed play.

I knew the guys from Third Day. I had interviewed them twice for stories on the popularity of Christian music. I spent a few hours with the band while they worked to build a house for Habitat for Humanity in Atlanta and was impressed by their love of God and passion for people. They express that passion beautifully through rock 'n' roll music.

Third Day would be part of my spiritual arsenal for my second extended trip to the war; they would help me keep my focus on God. I hoped listening to their music would fortify my soul and keep fear from taking hold.

For hours, the desert rolled by my window, little more than a brown blur. I would have noticed, but what I now understand as my extreme-stress reaction kicked in. I fell asleep.

Sleeping through periods of high danger is definitely not a reaction that would serve me well in most situations . . . but on a seven-hour "death ride" across western Iraq, it turned out to be quite a blessing.

We raced across the desert, uncertain of what lay ahead of us, and wary of what might be coming from behind us. I slept with the *Offerings* album playing over and over in my head.

The message of the music was simple; God is good and he loves me: "Who is this King of Glory that pursues me with his love?"

A sound track of faith, with music and lyrics by Mac Powell.

"Hey, mate," said Craig, waking me with a nudge, "snap to."

The Suburbans were coming to a stop on the side of the road.

"What's up?" I asked, a bit groggy.

"Time for the kit." He was talking about our Kevlar helmets and body armor. The British have a funny way of calling everything from technical gadgets to power tools "kit."

We climbed out of the SUVs and strapped on our military-style helmets. Then came the heavy vests.

NBC had spared no expense on the body armor for its crews in the war zone. Unlike the bulletproof vests that police officers often wear, or the slim flak jackets worn by soldiers at the time, our body armor was enormous, bulky, and heavy.

"Level-four protection," we were told by the folks who issued our battle gear.

The armor was actually a heavy vest made of a high-tech, bullet-resistant fabric called Kevlar. Attached to the vest was a removable ceramic plate in the chest area capable of stopping bullets from high-powered military rifles. Even the neck was protected with a flip-up Kevlar collar. A fold-down flap of even more Kevlar hung in the front of the vest to cover the groin area.

Wearing the kit was hot and uncomfortable, but vastly superior to being dead. I had worn mine many times during my first stint covering the war. While technically making us safer, the body armor had one serious flaw. It was bright blue—even the helmet.

The initial thinking before the war started was that Iraqis would adhere to the Geneva convention, meaning noncombatants such as journalists would be off-limits. The bright blue coloring was supposed to make us safer by showing the enemy that we weren't part of the fight. Instead, it made us bright blue, shiny targets in a sea of desert camouflage.

Still, to borrow a phrase from former defense secretary Donald Rumsfeld, "You go to war with the armor you have—not the armor you might want or wish to have at a later time."*

In my case, I would go to war looking like a giant blueberry . . . with a Walkman.

"We'll need this for the rest of the way," Craig said as he strapped on his armor. "It's a bit dicey through Ramadi and Fallujah."

As if to emphasize the point, he stepped out a few yards into the desert and test-fired both of his weapons.

We climbed back into the SUVs and continued the high-speed journey. We were considerably less comfortable but much safer with our kits on, rather than simply jammed against the doors.

---

* The actual quote uses the word *army*, not *armor*. Rumsfeld was responding to a question from a soldier about the lack of protective equipment: "You go to war with the army you have—not the army you might want or wish to have at a later time."

We were now just two hours from Baghdad. Small communities began to dot the desert, and with them evidence of fighting and violence. Palm trees rose above sand-covered houses with flat roofs. The villages seemed to grow larger in population as we drew closer to Baghdad. Even from the highway, I could see bullet holes and battle damage on some of the buildings.

"What happened to the power lines?" I asked Karl as we neared the city.

Massive, high-tension power lines had run parallel to the road. The towers, similar to those in the United States, were made of steel. But the towers were all snapped in half. And not just a few, but every tower for miles. They still stood fifty feet or so high, then, were simply snapped like toothpicks. My first thought was that they had been targeted by missiles, or perhaps blown up by insurgents.

"Looters," Karl told me. "They steal the cables, and without the tension, the whole string of them comes crashing down."

"I guess that explains why they don't have electricity," I said. "That and the fact that they kill the contractors who try to fix the lines."

It sounded absurd even as I said it, but that was the reality of Iraq. Death and brokenness.

About seventy miles west of Baghdad sits the city of Ramadi. With more than four hundred thousand residents, most of whom are Sunni Muslims, the city sprawls on both sides of the highway. The Euphrates River forms the city's northern boundary and, at one point, can be seen just a few hundred yards off the highway.

We passed through Ramadi as quickly as possible. I saw Craig tense visibly every time a car entered the highway behind us. His attention was almost always focused out the back window, or to the side, which is why he didn't see the Iraqis with guns blocking the road ahead.

"That doesn't look good," I said.

Karl saw the roadblock too. For the first time since I had met him the night before, he looked nervous.

A white Toyota pickup was parked across the road about a quarter mile in front of us. Markings on its side indicated that it might be an Iraqi police vehicle, but there was no way to tell for sure. Even if it was a police vehicle, the armed men manning the checkpoint might not be friends.

I remembered the warnings during survival training nearly eighteen months earlier. Checkpoints are dangerous, no matter who's running them. Kidnappings, murders, and tragic misunderstandings happen there with alarming frequency.

The men running this checkpoint had chosen their spot well. There was no way off the highway, and with traffic filling in behind us, turning around wasn't an option.

"Do you think those are really cops?" I asked Craig. The checkpoint now had his full attention.

"No telling, mate." The anxiety in his voice was clear. He put his weapons on the floorboard and covered them with gear.

"Just keep your head down, and hopefully we can talk our way through," he said.

I reached over and locked my door. I figured anything that would delay my being dragged out of the vehicle would help.

The lead SUV of our convoy was the first to be stopped by the gunmen. Craig watched intently.

I knew what would happen if things went south. I could see it in Craig's body language. His hands were inches away from the hidden rifle. If shooting started, or if the gunmen began dragging people out of the lead vehicle, Craig was going to open fire.

It would not go well. At least half a dozen men were manning the checkpoint, all armed with Kalashnikov rifles. Still, it's better to die trying than doing nothing at all. I made a mental note to remember to turn off the safety after I grabbed the 9 mm.

Then I closed my eyes and said a silent prayer.

You sent me here, I reminded God, knowing of course he didn't need it. *I'm trusting you not to get me killed before I even make it to Baghdad.* I added, *Please*, for good measure, then opened my eyes.

One of the gunmen approached the driver's door of the lead vehicle. The man said something that I couldn't hear and wouldn't have understood if I had. Other gunmen looked into the rear and side windows of the SUV. Nobody moved inside.

Then the men stepped away from the Suburban.

The moment of truth.

An excruciating half second.

A slight nod of the head.

The lead Suburban pulled away without another look. We followed immediately behind, and the gunmen didn't even bother stopping us.

I tried my best to look bored and detached as we rolled slowly by the white Toyota.

I couldn't tell by looking at them if the gunmen had been police officers working under an agreement with the United States to provide security, or if I had simply overestimated our value as insurgent targets. Maybe they were looking for someone in particular, or maybe our driver had performed an Iraqi version of the Jedi mind trick from *Star Wars* on them.

Either way, I was relieved to be past the checkpoint. I silently said one more prayer:

Thanks for that, and sorry about the whole "you sent me here" thing.

SEVEN

BAGHDAD

Baghdad was a contradiction in almost every way. Even time seemed in conflict with itself; carts drawn by donkeys were mixed into traffic with thousands of cars and trucks.

The relatively light traffic we had experienced during our long drive across the desert quickly gave way to an enormous snarl of cars that I soon learned was the norm—even without donkeys slowing things down.

I arrived in Baghdad on February 1, 2004. It had been just under eleven months since the beginning of the war, and over twelve hours since we left the hotel in Jordan.

The sprawling city of nearly 5 million was in motion, but to my surprise it wasn't in ruin. Bullet holes and scorch marks left by bombs were visible on a few buildings, though most of what I could see was still standing.

While a number of high-rise buildings were scattered throughout the city, Baghdad didn't have what most people would consider a "skyline." The city was modern by many standards, but few would confuse it with an American city of similar size; Atlanta, Dallas, and Miami look nothing like Baghdad.

The most striking features of the city, from my vantage point, were the domes and minarets of dozens, or perhaps hundreds, of mosques. The blue tiles that adorned the domes added vibrant color to otherwise muted tones. The tall towers adjacent to the domes, the minarets, cast long shadows across sand-colored neighborhoods as we crawled past.

There were large apartment buildings, and neighborhoods of one- or two-story concrete-block homes with flat roofs. All of it looked solid, formidable, and decades old.

In some areas, damage from the war was much more visible. Twisted metal, piles of brick and concrete, were all that remained of a few buildings, particularly those where antiaircraft guns had been based, or which had been important strategic targets.

A complex that had once housed communications equipment and antennas still stood . . . but just barely. It had been blown almost entirely apart. Wire and sharp-looking pieces of metal stuck awkwardly out of what little remained of the building's walls.

Our convoy of two Suburbans reached Baghdad just before five o'clock in the afternoon. The city was awash in the warm glow of a sun that would set within the hour. But the scene was anything but serene.

The crush of traffic continued to increase as we neared the center of the city. Within the span of a city block, one could see just about every imaginable type of vehicle.

Tanks and armored personnel carriers shared the roads and sidewalks with cars, trucks, bicycles, motorcycles, and donkey carts. Black smoke billowed from diesel engines; blue smoke poured from the tailpipes of run-down cars. The blare of horns filled the air, which smelled of dirt and diesel.

Armed Iraqi men in civilian clothes stood guard in front of mosques, businesses, and at the entrances to neighborhoods.

The look on my face must have telegraphed concern.

"He's okay," Karl said as our SUV crept past a man holding a Kalashnikov rifle.

"How do you know?" I asked suspiciously.

Karl pointed to the badge hanging around the man's neck. "That badge. That means he's got permission from the Coalition authority to have the gun."

"So he's on our side," I said, more of a statement than a question.

"Not necessarily, mate," said Craig. He had learned long ago not to let his guard down. He watched the man out of the corner of his eye until we had passed, then turned his attention to the next man with a gun. "Not necessarily."

But as alarming as the guns were, they seemed to me a lot less dangerous than the other drivers around us.

The rules of the road were simple. Look out for yourself and get there first—no matter what.

Iraqi citizens were allowed to own cars during Saddam's regime, but most could never afford them. The government imposed a staggering tax on vehicles brought into the country, tripling their price.

When the regime fell, so did the tax. New and used cars flooded into the country, and vehicle prices plummeted. Suddenly, people who had never dreamed of affording a car found they could get their hands on one.

Others chose to steal them. Carjackings, unheard of in Iraq before the war, became commonplace in the power vacuum of wartime Iraq.

No driver's license? No problem. There was no government to issue a license . . . or to register vehicles. Police had much higher priorities than issuing traffic tickets.

Intersections were a particular challenge. Most had been designed to work with traffic lights, but none of the lights were working. Under normal circumstances, a police officer would direct traffic if a signal was out. But nothing about Baghdad was normal.

Then, of course, came the traffic circles.

I've never understood the world's fascination with traffic circles. I'm sure some transportation engineers will put forth solid arguments that they are the most efficient method for merging traffic. Clearly the rest of the world believes this. Traffic circles infest the roadways in Europe, Asia, and the Arabian Peninsula. Even the United States has traffic circles, though I suspect most are purely for entertainment value.

Traffic circles, to put it simply, bring out the worst in people.

This was painfully evident at the Kahramana Square traffic circle in central Baghdad. The circle sits on a peninsula, surrounded on three sides by the Tigris River. It was the last major intersection our convoy had to navigate before reaching our hotel, which also sat on the peninsula just south of the Green Zone. The Kahramana Square traffic circle, which collects traffic on major highways running both north-south and east-west through the city, is one of the busiest and most important intersections in Baghdad.

There was surely nothing else on earth like it.

Tanks and military convoys, as you might imagine, typically had the right of way on Iraqi roads. With attacks on such convoys a daily, if not hourly, occurrence, soldiers tended to get jumpy when drivers of other vehicles got too close. For the most part, that was fine with Iraqi drivers. Most wanted to stay as far as possible from American military vehicles because they attracted bombs and bullets.

But with the exception of the aforementioned tanks, the concept of right of way, especially in the Kahramana Square traffic circle, was nonexistent. Cars careened over the sidewalk and plowed across the grass in the center of the square. Drivers commonly drove the wrong way against the flow of traffic. It was such complete chaos that some police officers were actually diverted from more important jobs to try to maintain control. But the cops were unarmed and thus woefully ineffective.

As our SUVs entered the circle, I suddenly remembered that I was violating what had become rule number one of my professional life. I was letting somebody else drive.

While working in local news, I was involved in three traffic accidents. All happened while I was a passenger in a news vehicle with someone else driving. Each of the wrecks was my driver's fault and could easily have been prevented. Thankfully, no one was hurt in the accidents, but I wasn't happy about any of them.

The last straw came after a live shot for the four-o'clock news in San Diego. I was riding back to the station as the passenger in an unmarked vehicle. We were cruising westbound on Interstate 8, in no particular hurry.

Then for a reason that made sense only to him, the driver unbuckled his seat belt and floored the accelerator.

"What are you doing?" I yelled.

"Driving," he said. "Shut up."

I looked at the speedometer. We were going just shy of 100 mph and weaving in and out of cars in the afternoon traffic.

"Slow down!" I shouted. "What's the hurry?"

"Shut up."

I thought he might have decided to commit suicide and take me with him.

"Why did you take your seat belt off?" I asked incredulously.

His answer was one of the stupidest things I have ever heard: "Because I know I'll die if I crash going this fast. So it makes me safer to take off the seat belt. This way I'm more careful."

My life was in the hands of a moron. We made it back to the station in one piece, but I vowed it would never happen again.

The next day I drove my own car to my story—I literally followed the news van. I've driven myself to every story since.

Except in Iraq.

I suddenly found myself a passenger in a vehicle that was rushing headlong into what may have been the most dangerous intersection in the world. By my count, fifteen lanes of traffic were either entering or exiting the melee.

Our driver joined the fracas without even touching the brakes. I looked to my right and saw a beat-up sedan careen toward our SUV.

I closed my eyes and braced for impact.

Nothing.

I felt the big Suburban lurch left, then right, but the expected crash never came.

A few seconds later we shot out of the traffic circle and down a four-lane boulevard. Within a quarter of a mile we arrived at what would be my home for the next month.

CONTRARY TO WHAT MOST PEOPLE in the United States thought, journalists in Iraq did not live in the Green Zone. That heavily protected area—once home to Saddam's central presidential palace—was now reserved for government workers, military personnel, contractors, and others who had specific needs to be there.

The Green Zone consisted of about thirteen hundred acres near the geographical center of Baghdad. It was completely surrounded by concrete blast walls. Soldiers patrolled the perimeter in vehicles and on foot. The few ways in and out of the zone all featured multiple checkpoints. Everyone trying to enter was searched, then searched again.

Once inside the walls of the compound, the chaos of the city was replaced by relative serenity. Soldiers and diplomats walked from building to building without fear of being ambushed. There was always the chance of a mortar attack, but as far as Iraq went, no place was safer than the Green Zone.

It would have been nice to live in the Green Zone, but journalists lived in houses, apartments, and hotels scattered throughout the city.

The bombing of NBC's hotel four months before my arrival had convinced the network to make drastic changes. The first priority was to find a hotel that could adequately be defended against bomb blasts or a kidnapping raid by insurgents. Network officials decided against moving the bureau to the Palestine hotel, which housed many Western journalists. Instead they found a little-known hotel called Al Hamra, which would allow NBC to implement its own security measures.

Unlike most of the other hotels in Baghdad, Al Hamra did not sit directly next to a major road. While it was near the thoroughfare that connected to the nearby traffic circle, the hotel was down a cul-de-sac in what could best be described as a residential neighborhood.

Immediately surrounding the hotel were homes, an apartment building, and several family-run restaurants. All of this sat within a residential block that was shaped like a triangle. The hotel itself sat more than a hundred yards from the highway.

Two other side streets led into the neighborhood. Both were heavily guarded, and neither led directly to the hotel.

The hotel was no longer simply a collection of buildings, but was a secure compound.

NBC's security measures began at the main highway, where Iraqi guards manned a checkpoint at the entrance to the cul-de-sac.

When our SUVs arrived, the security men stopped the vehicles, despite knowing who we were.

The checkpoint looked like something from a spy movie set in the Cold War. A small booth was next to a heavy metal gate that could be raised and lowered by hand. The gate was similar to the automated gates often found at railroad crossings.

Beyond the gate, concrete barriers and strands of concertina wire blocked sections of the narrow road leading to the hotel. The barriers and wire were designed to keep vehicles from approaching the hotel at high speed. Navigating the cul-de-sac meant zigzagging between the wire and the concrete. Top speed could be little more than the speed of a walk.

One of the Iraqi security guards greeted the driver of the first SUV, then immediately raised the gate. The second security guard seemed barely paying attention.

"I can't bloody believe it," Craig said. He jumped out of our Suburban and headed toward the gate guard. "How many times do I have to go through this?" He demanded, "Stop! Put the gate back down."

I saw the Iraqi guard do as he was told, then begin pleading his case. It was obvious who we all were. Why delay our getting to the hotel any longer than necessary?

But Craig would have none of it. He had helped design the security system for the hotel and was responsible for the training of the Iraqi guards.

"How many times do I have to tell you to search every vehicle?" He pointed to the other man. "And what are you doing? Where's the mirror?"

Adequately chastised, the guard picked up a pole with a mirror attached and began walking around the vehicle. The mirror allowed him to see if explosives or anything suspicious was attached to the underside. Of course there was nothing, but laziness or familiarity was a good way to get people killed.

After the underside of both vehicles had been searched, the gate was again raised, and we were allowed inside.

AL HAMRA DOMINATED ITS COZY surroundings. The main building stood fourteen stories tall, with a smaller building attached on the north side, plus a swimming pool, restaurant, and shops in the lobby. Concrete steps led to the hotel entrance, which had sliding glass doors and plate-glass windows.

The entire complex was the color of desert sand. It looked sturdy and somewhat imposing. The upper windows, partially obscured by overhanging balconies, seemed too small to be in balance. Each of the ninety-six rooms, it seemed to me, had squinty eyes overlooking the city.

It was by no means the best hotel in the city, but by Iraqi standards, Al Hamra was luxurious. I suspect business travelers accustomed to Western hotels would give Al Hamra a two- or three-star rating at best. But luxury was subjective. The hotel boasted a five-star rating.

During better times, it was often filled with newlywed couples on honeymoons. The first-floor restaurant included a large dance floor and party area. It hosted weddings, and sometimes entire families stayed in the hotel rooms during the festivities.

The first thing I noticed as our Suburbans pulled to the front of the hotel was the wall. NBC had gone to considerable expense to erect a massive blast wall that completely surrounded the hotel. The twelve-foot-tall barrier was built of concrete sand bags and reinforced with steel bars. It was designed to keep car or truck bombs from getting close enough to the hotel to destroy it. If the bombs detonated outside the barrier, its shape would direct the force of the blast up and away from the hotel.

We parked in an area reserved for NBC vehicles, featuring yet another gate and a guard. We unloaded our gear and headed for the entrance.

I was happy to be off the road.

EIGHT

THE BUREAU

The NBC News bureau was on the ninth floor of Al Hamra. "The workspace," as most employees called it, consisted of several suites cobbled together with adjoining doors. The main work area was once a living room, but it no longer resembled anything comfortable. Two long, plastic-topped tables were pushed together to provide a single gathering point.

The table seated at least eight people, with two computer workstations, phones, and Internet connections for laptops. Broadcast engineers from the network had installed an intricate satellite system, which included dishes on the roof and an entire room full of sophisticated electronics. Part of the system included the communications package, which most people simply called comms. To the user, *comms* is nothing more than a phone sitting on a table, or a DSL line providing an Internet connection. But somewhere in another room, sophisticated electronics were required to make it all work.

When comms worked properly, phone lines on the worktables acted as if they were in 30 Rockefeller Center in New York. Picking up the phone in the Baghdad bureau was like picking up a phone in New York City. No country codes needed to be dialed. Calls within the NBC system could simply be made by dialing a four-digit extension.

Two small offices directly adjoined the main workroom. The smaller was reserved for the bureau chief. Bureau chiefs, even those appointed for a month at a time, made personnel, financial, and other business decisions that demanded privacy.

Like the workspace itself, the bureau chief's office was simply a cramped room with a desk, phone, computer, and a small sofa. The Baghdad bureau had nothing fancy.

A balcony that jutted off the main room afforded an unobstructed view of the southern part of Baghdad. From the balcony, the four-lane highway leading to the Kahramana Square traffic circle was visible between the apartment buildings and businesses. Beyond that highway, Baghdad sprawled toward the south. Minarets, palm trees, apartment buildings, and concrete-block homes seemed to stretch as far as the eye could see.

Almost daily, staff members would run out onto the balcony after hearing an explosion trying to pinpoint where it happened.

The opposite end of the room contained a small but complete galley-style kitchen.

The other office connected to the main room was for translators. The five translators, three men and two women, included Rafraf.

The satellite system allowed the bureau to do more than just broadcast a signal back to New York. It could also receive television feeds from around the world. Part of the job for translators was to monitor Arabic-language news networks such as Al Jazeera and Al Arabiya to see what was being reported about the region.

Monitors in the translators' office remained on Arabic media stations twenty-four hours a day. The main room also had three desks and several relatively comfortable chairs.

Rafraf tried her best not to sit in any of them.

It wasn't technically a rule, but the Iraqi translators were assumed to stay in their room during the day. Generally, half a dozen producers, correspondents, cameramen, and other crew members would be using the seats at the main table. But Rafraf had no interest in being shuffled off to a side room.

The action, after all, happened in the main room: stories were discussed, plans and decisions were made, scripts were typed.

Shortly after beginning the job, Rafraf began sitting at the far corner of the table. The seat had a computer workstation, which Rafraf quickly claimed as her own.

Prior to going to work for NBC, Rafraf had never seen the Internet—not even once. Internet access wasn't available at the university, and Internet cafés didn't exist. Rafraf had heard about the Internet but never dreamed she would have access to the world of information it provided.

Her computer skills, in fact, were nonexistent. Shortly before the war started, her little brother Rami had convinced their father that a computer would be a useful tool at the family's stationery shop.

Rami had just finished taking a computer course and was officially the family's expert in all things technical. A computer, he told his father, could be loaded with an Arabic version of Microsoft Word. The system would not, of course, be connected to the Internet. Such a connection was not even possible for Iraqis. But it would allow the stationery shop to offer the valuable service of editing and printing résumés and other job-related materials. Kamal reluctantly agreed. He diverted a few hundred dinars from the shop's small operating budget and bought the family's first computer.

"What good is that?" Rafraf asked suspiciously. Her brother was busy hooking the vintage, 1980s model IBM PC to a black-and-white monitor. The machine had a floppy disk and no hard drive at all.

"You can do so many things with it," Rami said, somewhat in awe of the technology.

"Like what?" she asked, unconvinced.

Rami told her about Excel, about Microsoft Paint, about programs that would make life easier in so many ways. Programs that, Rami knew, the vintage eighties PC wouldn't actually run, and which the family didn't own. But the first important step had been taken.

Rafraf saw through the optimism. She didn't bother with the computer at all. It functioned as a word processor in the shop until the war started. Then, like everything else in Iraq, it broke.

NBC's computers, on the other hand, were magic. From the first moment Carol Grisanti logged Rafraf on as "guest" and opened Internet Explorer, Rafraf was hooked.

One of Rafraf's daily assignments was to read Arabic-language newspapers online and peruse Web sites for clues about the insurgency and other potential dangers. She quickly learned that the world she thought she knew bore little resemblance to reality.

To begin with, Iraq was not, it seemed, the center of the universe. Residents of all countries, the most obvious example being Americans, tend to feel the world revolves around them. It is a natural part of the human condition.

But throughout her entire life, Rafraf believed Iraq was a dominant player on the world stage. Saddam, after all, was one of the world's greatest leaders. His army was so powerful that, to defeat Iraq during the first Gulf War, America had to assemble a vast coalition of thirty-three other nations, simply to match Iraq's military might.

Saddam's image was on the cover of every textbook Rafraf had read since childhood. Math, history, science, even English. Surely he was the smartest man in the world.

Saddam Hussein was second only to Allah. He was the most powerful man in the world. The cowardly American president George Bush was no match for him in any way.

So strong was her belief that Saddam Hussein could not be beaten, even months after the fall of Baghdad, Rafraf was certain he was still in control of the country. Her work for Americans, she reasoned, would be forgiven as a necessity of the times. She needed the American money, but longed for the day the Iraqi government—Saddam's government—returned to power.

Saddam wasn't really in hiding. Had he not vowed to fight to the end?

Saddam was simply allowing the American army to think it had established a victory. It was all part of a brilliant plan. Somewhere Saddam was massing the greatest army in history. He would soon sweep back into Baghdad, retaking the city and the country in days. It was inevitable.

Everyone Rafraf knew believed the same thing. Rafraf believed it until the day she discovered Google.

THE FIRST THING RAFRAF GOOGLED on the Internet was the Iraq War. She wanted to see the war through the world's eyes. She wanted to feel the pride she had felt during the first weeks of combat. Pride that Iraq's army, led by Saddam, had fought so fiercely. She wanted to read for herself that the world had seen Iraq's greatness.

Rafraf could barely hold back the tears as she read the world's view of Iraq's defeat. The outcome was determined the moment the American president gave the order to strike.

Her country was not, she determined, the center of the universe.

It was merely a dot in a book of a million words.

She spent the following weeks devouring information. The feeling began to overwhelm her that she had never actually used her eyes or ears before. She had lived her life simply being fed information. What others may have known to be propaganda, she had believed as truth. She felt naïve and angry at the same time and vowed that in this new world . . . the Google world . . . she would find the truth for herself.

NBC was the key that would allow her to find truth.

But that was only one reason Rafraf claimed the seat with the computer at the far corner of the table. The other was causing her daily grief.

Rafraf believed the other translators didn't like her. She was the youngest of the Iraqi employees. She clearly had the least amount of seniority. Yet from the first week on the job, she seemed to be getting the best assignments.

"She's just a child," one of the men had complained to Carol shortly after Rafraf was hired. "She's immature and thinks she knows things. This is not a job for an immature child.

"She considers herself equal to me. She won't even call me mister, she just calls me by name. It's not proper."

Was there a grain of truth in what he had to say? Perhaps, thought Rafraf. But this was America! The rules she had rebelled against her entire life don't apply in America. Whether it was sovereign territory or not, Rafraf considered everything within the walls of the workspace "America."

None of the other translators had complained about Rafraf. She suspected, however, that the only other Iraqi woman working for NBC wanted Rafraf to go away.

Rabia was somewhat older than Rafraf. She was quiet, perhaps even shy around the Americans.

"Do you want to advance in this career?" Rabia asked Rafraf shortly after their first meeting.

"Of course," Rafraf replied.

"You're so pretty, don't you think you should be in front of the camera?"

Rafraf had already learned that when a woman began a conversation with "you're so pretty," what followed would not be good.

"I just want to do my job," Rafraf replied. "That's all."

"Well," continued Rabia, "I have a friend who works at Egyptian television. She tells me they are looking for a woman to be a correspondent in Iraq. I think you should apply for that job."

"I don't want to be a correspondent." Rafraf thought about adding she was not even sure what a correspondent did, but decided not to.

"Well, then you could be a producer," Rabia pressed on. "The Egyptian channel pays well too."

"I want to work here," Rafraf answered firmly.

It was only the partial truth. Rafraf wanted the job, of course, but what she really wanted could be summed up in two words: a future.

Only the Americans, in her view, offered a future.

Rafraf gathered up her belongings and, without asking permission from anyone, took the spot at the corner of the big table. If the Americans told her to go back with the others, she would. But they never did.

BY FEBRUARY 2004, RAFRAF'S POSITION within the bureau was well established. Assignments for each day were written on a dry-erase board that hung in the main workspace. Rafraf made sure to look at the board each day before she left for home. Her name was always near the top.

When they were not working on a breaking news story, the schedule for Iraqis at the bureau was somewhat predictable. The workweek consisted of six days, Saturday through Thursday. Friday is a holy day in Islam. It's the day most Iraqis take off.

Rafraf usually arrived for work at Al Hamra before 8 a.m. Like the other Iraqi employees, she had no car of her own. Buses and taxis were considered unsafe and unpredictable, so NBC drivers shuttled workers to and from the Iraqis' homes.

Rafraf was already irritated on the evening of February 1, 2004. It had been a slow day at the bureau, and on such days she usually left by 5 p.m. She logged off the computer and packed her things, but by five forty-five the driver assigned to take her home still hadn't arrived.

She was sitting on the edge of the table watching the clock when the newly arrived members of the convoy from Jordan began piling into the room.

After more than seven months on the job, the "new" of Americans and British citizens had worn off for Rafraf. No longer did she eagerly anticipate new arrivals to the bureau.

Westerners, she had discovered, weren't all that exotic or different after all. Plus, she probably already knew most of the producers and camera crews rotating in for their month of war duty. By February, the path to Baghdad for most NBC crews based outside the United

States was well worn indeed. All that changed, from Rafraf's viewpoint, were the faces.

She had heard, however, that a correspondent whom she hadn't met was coming to the bureau. That could be trouble.

Correspondents, in Rafraf's view, did the least amount of work and, based on what she saw, made the most money of any of the Americans. They tended to tell people what to do and had the power to get away with it. What's more, they had ideas for stories that made no sense and usually raised the prospect of getting someone killed.

She liked them personally and got along well with all of the reporters she worked with. She was particularly fond of Richard Engel and Kevin Sites. They spent more time than anyone else in Baghdad and always treated Rafraf as a friend and colleague.

She trusted Richard and Kevin but viewed the "temporary" correspondents with caution.

She still wasn't absolutely convinced she could trust these Americans and other foreigners in the first place. They were, after all, the people who had invaded her country and turned the world upside down. Maybe not them specifically, but their countries.

Rafraf's views toward the war, Americans, the people she worked with, and her future were in conflict. Her inner struggle with who she was and where she was heading raged as viciously as the war itself.

Unlike everyone around her, who seemed so sure of who they were and in which direction their lives were going, Rafraf was confused.

Wouldn't it be easier to pick a side? She could simply hate these invaders. Plenty of Iraqis did.

But to what end?

Killing them didn't seem to discourage them. Even as the Iraqi resistance gained strength, so did the resolve of the U.S. troops they were battling. The Americans were digging in for the long haul.

What purpose did killing innocent people serve? In recent weeks insurgents had increased their attacks on shopping centers, mosques, funerals—anywhere people gathered in large numbers.

Siding with the Americans, while profitable, felt like a betrayal. But siding with the insurgency felt like murder. For Rafraf and many fellow Iraqis it was an almost impossible dilemma.

So Rafraf took the practical route. She did her job the best she could. She collected her salary. She prayed to Allah that someday things would change. She watched the clock and waited for her ride.

THE PEOPLE FROM THE CONVOY filed into the office looking ragged and disheveled. Rafraf had never been on the drive, but she had heard it was a difficult trip. The arriving crews always looked the same.

As she suspected, she did know most of the members of the convoy.

Craig, the British security man, immediately began briefing anyone who'd listen on the important details of the trip.

The cameraman from London, Steve O'Neil, Rafraf thought of as great fun. O'Neil was considered by all who had worked with him to be completely, perhaps even certifiably, nuts. He relished working in war zones and only seemed to smile more as the danger increased. He was about fifty years old, and almost impossible to keep up with.

Karl Bostic, the incoming bureau chief, had pulled a half dozen similar tours in the last months. He had a great sense of humor, was easygoing, but left no mistake about who was in charge.

The gruff, gregarious Iranian-American producer named Babak Benham was also a bureau veteran.

The only person she didn't know, in fact had never even heard of, was the correspondent. He was almost a foot taller than Rafraf, with blond hair and blue eyes. He came into the room dragging a huge duffel bag of gear and wearing a look of stunned relief. He wore jeans, a khaki shirt, and a gray microfiber vest that didn't match.

He began introducing himself to the rest of the bureau just as Rafraf received word that her ride was waiting downstairs.

He shook hands with both men and women and would occasionally hug people he must have known from previous assignments.

Rafraf wanted to leave, but didn't want to appear rude. She waited until he made it to her side of the table.

"I'm Don Teague," he said in what Rafraf later learned was a California accent, "it's nice to meet you." She noticed he didn't offer a handshake.

"I'm Rafraf." She mustered up a pleasant smile. She waited for what always happened next.

"Wait. What's your name?" he asked, puzzled.

"Raf-raf," she replied, emphasizing each syllable so he could understand.

"Oh. What an interesting name." That's what they always said. It was not an insult, but certainly not a compliment.

"My ride is waiting for me," Rafraf said matter-of-factly. She gathered her things and slipped out of the room as the introductions continued.

I'll bet he takes my seat, she thought to herself as she walked down the hallway toward the elevator. *They always take my seat.*

NINE

GET TO WORK

I was tired after the long road trip from Jordan. With the introductions and reunions behind me, I wanted to check e-mails and make a call home to Kiki and the girls. I spotted an empty seat with a computer monitor at the far corner of the table and took it.

But as exhausted as I was after a long day on the road, Karl suddenly seemed energized.

"Are you ready to see the Green Zone?" he asked excitedly. It had been barely half an hour since we arrived at the hotel.

"Now," I asked, "seriously?" The last thing I wanted to do was go back outside the protective area of the hotel compound. My nerves were still bristling from the ride in.

"Yes," he said eagerly. "I have to go over to the convention center and check on some things. It will be a good time to show you around. Security lines are shorter at night too."

The convention center was one of the largest Iraqi government buildings within the fortified Green Zone. Major news organizations were allowed to keep small offices there. When the Coalition authority or the emerging Iraqi government had an announcement to make or held a press conference, it was in the convention center.

Paul Nassar noticed the concern on my face. Paul was a London-based producer for the network. Of Lebanese descent, Paul spoke fluent Arabic and English with the accent of a well-educated Londoner.

I worked with Paul for weeks in Kuwait during the buildup to the war. He was an intelligent, compassionate man with a good sense of humor. He was also ridiculously good-looking, an observation Kiki made every time she saw him.

Paul had been David Bloom's producer during the war. He rode to war with David and was at his side when he died. He stayed with David's remains through what turned out to be a perilous, four-day journey from the battlefield back to Kuwait.

Ten months after the ordeal, Paul was still cloaked in a mist of sadness.

"Karl, why don't you wait until tomorrow?" Paul offered. "We have to go there for the briefing in the morning anyway."

"I just thought he'd like to get his bearings right away," Karl said. It struck me as an honest answer. Karl seemed to thrive on adrenaline.

"Yeah, I'd just as soon get settled in tonight and go in the morning," I said, "unless there's something that can't wait."

"No, not at all," Karl said, already heading for the door. "See you in the morning."

I used the bureau phone to call home, then headed down one floor to my room to unpack.

ALL OF THE ROOMS AT Al Hamra were technically considered suites. My room was the smallest they offered. It was basically a longer-than-average hotel room with a kitchenette and dining area on one end. A sofa, chair, and bed were at the other end of the room, nearest the window. The furniture was serviceable, but hardly five-star.

The room had a worn, brownish colored carpet, white walls, and a large window on the south end.

Our British security folks explained to me that NBC had gone to considerable expense to coat the windows of the rooms with "blast gel." It would not, of course, stop bullets or missiles. But the gel would keep the window from shattering into a million deadly projectiles if a bomb went off outside.

I looked out the window and discovered I could easily see the highway we had driven in on from my room. That meant an attacker on the main highway could launch a rocket-propelled grenade into the room or spray it with bullets.

"Not good," I said to myself, noting the bed's proximity to the window.

So before my first night's sleep, I did some rearranging. I moved the dining table to the opposite end of the room and dragged my bed as far away from the window as possible. I moved a chair close to the bed, between where my body would lie and the window. I pulled out my body armor and draped it over the chair.

I surveyed the room and took a mental picture, mapping out an escape route. Finally, I pulled an LED flashlight out of my bag and placed it on the chair next to the bed. I'd have to remember to grab the flashlight and the body armor if a bomb blast shook the hotel.

RAFRAF SPENT THE NEXT DAY with Sa'ad, the Iraqi cameraman, shooting video in a nearby market. Despite the mounting violence, Iraq's economy was showing signs of bouncing back.

The video would be used in upcoming reports. Rafraf had learned that video used in a taped story was called b-roll, but she wasn't sure why the Americans called it that.

She returned to the bureau late in the afternoon and saw the new correspondent at the table. He looked much better than when she'd first met him. He seemed energetic and rested.

And he was sitting in her seat.

The Americans, she thought, were so predictable. She knew they all brought their own laptop computers but they were too lazy to use them. Instead, they just took her computer.

She sat in an empty seat, without a computer monitor, and tried to look nonchalant about it.

The producers, Paul and Babak, were sitting at the table too. They were engrossed in their computers.

"What's everyone doing?" Rafraf finally prodded.

"Playing marbles," replied Babak. "It's a computer game Don showed us."

Rafraf peeked at what was ordinarily her computer screen. Hundreds of brightly colored balls were on the screen. Don was busy trying to rearrange them.

It figures, she thought to herself, *the whole world is going crazy and the Americans are playing computer games.*

Don must have read her mind. He finished his game, clicked off, and turned his attention toward Rafraf. "So you're from here? From Baghdad?"

"Yes."

"And you speak English?"

"Yes."

It was the same drill every few weeks. Rafraf had grown tired of answering the same questions over and over. Of course she was from Baghdad. Where else would she be from? She learned English in school. She had nine brothers and sisters. Same questions, different American.

Most of the others stopped asking after the first few questions. But not this one.

"Are you a Shiite or a Sunni?"

Rafraf wondered if he knew the difference. She certainly wasn't in the habit of telling people which branch of Islam her family followed, and most people didn't ask.

"We are not really either." It was her default brush-off, which usually ended this line of questioning.

"You've got to be one or the other," he insisted. "You can't be both, which means you can't be either."

That, thought Rafraf, made no sense.

"And since you went to college," he continued, "I'm guessing more Sunni than Shiite."

"Well, you're wrong," Rafraf answered with the briefest hint of annoyance. "If you get good grades, you go to college, and that's that. It doesn't matter about those other things."

"Interesting," he said with what seemed like real interest.

Rafraf prepared herself for the next question. But she wasn't prepared for what he said next.

"I'm sorry about your country," Don said genuinely. "I know things are bad right now, but it won't always be this way."

To Rafraf, it seemed an unreasonable thing to say. Just the day before, eleven Iraqis had been killed in a coordinated truck-bomb attack in Kirkuk. There was no end to the violence in sight.

"Yes, it will," Rafraf said. "It will get worse."

"I don't expect you to believe it now, but you'll see. You'll get your country back."

AND I MEANT IT. I didn't consider the war about taking over another country. In my view, America fought wars for just purposes: to free others from tyranny, to spread democracy, to defend allies from oppressors. I would never have joined the army if I had thought its purpose was to take over other countries. I would not have agreed to cover the war if I believed that to be the case. I would have stayed as far away as possible.

Still, I couldn't blame this young Iraqi woman for believing otherwise. It was true that Saddam Hussein had lived in palaces with gold-plated toilets while his country suffered. But the Americans, in the view of many Iraqis, were beginning to repeat the same mistakes.

Saddam's palaces were not immediately turned over to the people of Iraq. They were, instead, filled with new occupants. The Americans—like Saddam's government before them—carried guns, gave orders, and killed people.

I knew there was good reason for the Americans to take over Saddam's palaces. First of all, they were vacant. It certainly wouldn't do to start kicking people out of homes or taking over schools to house U.S. soldiers. The palaces were large and sat on several acres of land. They also had fortified walls and were built with security in mind.

The presidential palaces seemed obvious places for the Americans to set up camp, but many Iraqis didn't see it that way. For them, there was little difference between the former occupants of the palaces and the latter.

I WAS IMMEDIATELY INTRIGUED BY Rafraf. She looked impossibly young to be working for NBC and could easily have passed for a teenager. The effect was amplified by a fairly serious case of acne.

I took my first trip into the Green Zone on the morning of my first full day in Baghdad. While there, I noticed many of the Iraqi women employed by the United States had skin problems similar to Rafraf's. I wondered if it was related to a particular kind of makeup, or perhaps it was something in the diet. No doubt the stress of the situation didn't help.

Simply getting into the Green Zone was more stress than most people would ever voluntarily put themselves through. The ordeal could take hours.

The Green Zone had only a handful of entrances, and they were frequent targets of insurgent attacks. What better way to kill large numbers of Americans or Iraqi sympathizers than to simply drive a car bomb into the line of people waiting to get in. Suicide bombers would also wait in line to enter the zone wearing bomb-laden vests. When they reached the first checkpoint to be searched, they would simply blow themselves up, along with everyone around them.

Most of the entrances broke the line into two segments. One was for Iraqi contractors and citizens who had legitimate business inside the secure compound. The other was for Americans and other Western contractors. Fortunately, journalists were also allowed to use the second line, which was much shorter.

The military had taken steps to make the line area as secure as possible. I noted armed soldiers at high vantage points with weapons trained in our direction. I assumed there were snipers using high-powered scopes to have a good look at all our faces. Military vehicles were also parked at the nearest intersection, evaluating each car heading toward the checkpoint. But there was no way to provide complete security.

I determined that standing in line to enter the Green Zone was a high-risk activity and made a mental note to only go during off-peak hours when possible. I could see why Karl had been so keen on going in the off-hours the night before.

Perhaps the stress, or years of living what I could only imagine was a hard life, was responsible for the acne. I couldn't know for sure.

Still, Rafraf was obviously a beautiful woman. She had large black eyes that were penetrating. They were highlighted by pink eye shadow. Her face was oval, and her eyes showed what looked to me to be a hint of Asian ancestry.

Her face was all that was visible. A traditional head scarf covered every strand of her hair and was tightly wrapped around her head, ears, and the sides of her face. It was so tight that it looked uncomfortable.

While the scarf was traditional in design, I wondered about the color. It was bright pink and perfectly matched the color of her eye shadow.

Her clothing was fashionable and modern. She wore bell-bottom jeans that were at least three inches too long for her legs and a white turtleneck sweater. It covered the skin on her neck and its sleeves covered her arms and hands almost to the tips of her fingers. She was, it seemed, covered up as much as possible without wearing a veil over her face.

Most of the Iraqi women I had seen so far had worn the effects of their hard lives. They seemed prematurely old, worn down, and ragged.

Rafraf was radiant, even with the pink eye shadow and the too-long clothing. I assumed because of her clothing and education that she was from a family of importance. I had no idea how wrong I was.

"Can I show you a game?" she asked.

I was surprised by the question. I had expected Rafraf to be timid. the Arab women I had met in the past seemed much more guarded.

"Sure," I said. "What is it?"

"I'll have to get on the computer." Perhaps the others in the room knew this was Rafraf reclaiming her territory. I was clueless.

"Okay," I said, moving to the next seat.

Rafraf wasted no time getting in the chair and working the keyboard. She navigated to an Internet gaming site and pulled up a page.

"It's called TextTwist," she said excitedly. "I'm very good at it."

She spoke with an accent that I couldn't quite place. Her speech carried the occasional mispronunciations of a native Arabic speaker. After my first tour in Kuwait and Iraq, I had heard the linguistic quirks many times. *Electricity* would come out as "elk-tricity." Sometimes *b*'s and *p*'s would be reversed, leading to the comical description of a "parking dog."

As Rafraf continued speaking, I finally pinpointed the accent. It was British. I wondered how far back the original English man or woman had been in the sequence that eventually ended with Rafraf speaking with a British accent. Perhaps her elementary-school teacher had learned English in the United Kingdom?

Rafraf explained the game. The screen showed a six-letter word with its letters scrambled, a timer, and a row of boxes.

The letters *V, T, E, R, S, and I* appeared on the screen.

"You have to make as many words as you can from the letters," she said. She quickly moved the mouse and clicked *T-I-E*. The computer made a happy sound, and the word *tie* filled one of the empty boxes.

"You get points for every word. If you don't guess the longest word, you don't get to move to the next word."

"And then the game ends?" I asked.

"Yes." She moved the mouse again. "For example, the longest word this will spell is *strive*."

She clicked each of the letters. The computer made an even happier sound than the first, then displayed a message: *You got the longest word! You qualify for the next round.*

"That seems easy enough," I said.

"But it gets harder as you go, and you only have two minutes to find the longest word."

The next screen came up. The letters *F, A, T, U, R, and L* appeared on the screen.

"*Turf!*" I practically yelled. She clicked the letters and spelled the word. The computer made a happy sound.

"*Fault!*" I said. Another happy sound.

But I had nothing else. The screen still had several empty boxes . . . including one that would use all of the letters. I stared, but nothing came to me.

"It's your language," Rafraf teased. "I just barely speak English and I can do better than you."

"*Future!*" I yelled.

Rafraf looked at me as if I were an idiot. "No."

Suddenly, the computer started making a sound that was not at all happy. It was the ticking of a clock. I had just ten seconds to find the answer, and the pressure was on.

But before the timer expired, Rafraf went to work with the mouse. She clicked on each of the letters in sequence . . . *A-R-T-F-U-L.* She beat the ticking clock with just two seconds to spare.

"*Artful,*" she said cheerfully. The computer made a happy sound and displayed the congratulations screen.

"I knew that," I said. "I was just testing you."

"You shouldn't do that, mate," Paul chimed in from across the table.

"Oh, really?" I asked somewhat skeptically. "You guys play this game too?"

They all nodded.

"Who has the high score?" I already knew the answer. It was written across Rafraf's face.

The rest of the table answered in unison: "She does."

But how can she? I thought to myself. Rafraf was clearly not a native English speaker. She spoke the language well, but even during a few short conversations I had noticed flaws in her grammar.

"How do you know so many words?" I asked her.

Rafraf shrugged but didn't answer. Her attention was focused on the next string of letters.

P-W-A-R-D-U was displayed on the screen.

"*Ward!*" I said.

"Of course." She didn't bother clicking on the letters.

I looked at the boxes and noticed she had already entered *ward* in one of them.

The ten-second timer started counting down. Rafraf looked at me, and I had the feeling I was being tested. Not by the game this time, but by her.

I shrugged my shoulders, and she began clicking on the letters.

"*Upward,*" she said after spelling out the word. She beat the timer with a second to spare. The computer made a happy sound.

"How do you do that?" I repeated.

"I just do. I don't always know what the words mean. But if I see a word once in my life, I will always remember it."

She was trying to play it off, but Rafraf was clearly a very intelligent woman.

I resolved then and there that I wouldn't leave Baghdad until I beat Rafraf at TextTwist.

BOOM!

An explosion in the distance. It was close enough to hear, close enough to feel, but far enough away that it probably wasn't a threat to the hotel.

The sound got my attention, but the rest of the table paid scant attention.

"What was that?" I asked, though the answer seemed obvious.

Paul looked at the clock on the wall. "Either a truck bomb or the military blowing up a weapons cache. But it's late in the day for a controlled blast, so my guess is truck bomb."

I could feel the adrenaline start to pump in my body.

"So are we going to check it out?" I asked. I wondered why nobody was heading for the door.

"We'll know what it was soon enough," answered Babak. "The agencies will get there first anyway. We only go to the really bad ones. If it was bad, it'll show up on the wires in a bit."

The agencies were news-gathering organizations such as the Associated Press, Reuters, and Iraqi Television. They had Arabic-speaking camera crews on a hair trigger to respond to bombings and other breaking news throughout the region. Their camera crews were often at the scene of explosions and ambushes before the first ambulances.

Although NBC News is a huge organization, its operation in Baghdad was tiny in comparison to the combined staff of the agencies. It made more sense to simply buy the video shot by others than to risk valuable personnel by sending them to the scene of every bomb blast. Insurgents had begun setting off secondary explosions minutes after attacks to kill journalists and others who responded to an attack. Most reporters were happy to let things settle down a bit before racing to the scene.

All of the networks relied heavily on agency video, which is why the same pictures often appeared on every major newscast. Networks such as NBC pay a hefty annual fee to have access to the pictures and to limit the exposure of their staff members.

"I think that's the first one of the day," Paul said.

"You can always hear them like that?" I asked.

"All the time. Sometimes the whole building shakes."

I noticed as we spoke that Rafraf was transfixed on the computer game. The happy sound of the next level being reached would occasionally chime in as we casually discussed the ongoing destruction of Baghdad. I couldn't tell if she was paying attention to the conversation or not.

I tried to see the situation from her point of view. This was her country . . . her city. Every time a bomb exploded in the distance, people were dying. More often than not, some or all of those people were Iraqis. Her neighbors, maybe even her friends or members of her family, were being blown to pieces. She too would have to wait to read the wires to know for sure.

In the meantime, she unscrambled words with a vengeance. Her country and her life were in complete turmoil. The Americans and British were responsible.

But in TextTwist, she could beat them at their own game . . . in their own language. It wasn't a major victory. But even a small victory is better than losing.

The wires never did reveal the source of the explosion. It was surprising how often that happened in Baghdad. Something would blow up; there was no missing that an explosion had occurred. But if by chance nobody died, then nobody cared.

MY FIRST FULL DAY HAD been relatively tranquil. First came the uneventful trip into the Green Zone that morning to meet and greet some military and political contacts. Then a quiet afternoon of "reading in" with the rest of the Baghdad rotation.

Reading in is news speak for cruising the Internet for information about the news of the day. It's an odd term, used in odd ways.

If the phone rings, for example, at seven thirty in the morning and the executive producer from the *Nightly News* is on the other end of the line, it's a good bet that producer has already "read in." If I hadn't, the conversation would go in either of precisely two ways.

"Teague," the producer would say, "we're going to make a run at the du jour story today. It was on page four of the *Times.*" *Du jour* is a French term that means "of the day."

"Soup du jour" is on a menu; the "story du jour" is usually in the *New York Times.* The producers in New York never called it the du jour story, but the phrase ran through my head every time the phone rang.

For some reason, most of the producers also called correspondents only by their last names. Teague, Tibbles, Faw, Sanders, Thompson. It never bothered me, but I always thought it kind of odd.

Since producers always read the *New York Times* and the *Washington Post* before the ink had dried (or seconds after they were posted online), chances were good that whatever the du jour story was, I knew nothing about it. Particularly since I would often be in the field, or on the road, or simply busy doing something else. But saying so in that way was a bad idea.

So there were two possible responses to the "What do you know about the du jour story from the *Times*?" question.

"What's the du jour story?" was the worst possible answer. It implied that despite my currently standing in the middle of an ice storm, a hurricane, or a war zone, I didn't know more about everything than everybody else. But that's what correspondents are expected to know.

"I haven't had a chance to read in yet. Give me five minutes and I'll call you back" was a much better answer. It got the point across that I wasn't ready to discuss details of du jour but was probably aware of it. And it implied that learning everything there was to know about it was already next up on my agenda.

So "reading in," which to an outsider looks like a person sitting around wasting time on the Drudge Report, is critical to remaining employed as a network correspondent.

During my first full day in Baghdad, I spent most of my time on the computer. I read the scripts for stories that Richard Engel and other correspondents had produced from the bureau. I searched the wires looking for signs of improvement.

"Isn't it news that no Americans have been killed in the last week?" I asked. It had been six days since a roadside bomb had killed three soldiers south of Baghdad. I hoped it was the beginning of a trend.

"It won't last," Paul said bleakly. "It never lasts."

And he was right. The following day, an American soldier was killed by an improvised explosive device, an IED in military jargon. The brief pause in American deaths had come to an end.

Rafraf was the first person in the office the following morning. No shoots were scheduled for the day, but that was about to change.

Rafraf had learned that the arrival of new people in Baghdad followed a predictable pattern. If events didn't dictate the schedule (major attacks or press conferences that had to be covered), then the new staffers would spend a day or two at most getting oriented. This was the time when they came up with the strangest ideas for stories.

Don had been in Baghdad for two days. It was about time, thought Rafraf, for him to begin suggesting stories about things that didn't really matter.

She took her favorite seat and waited.

"Good morning, Rafraf," Don said as he entered the office. He was dragging the same duffel bag that he'd carried when she first saw him two nights before. He didn't sit, but went straight to the kitchen. "Can I get you some coffee?"

Rafraf had tasted coffee exactly once in her life. It was the strong, almost peppery blend favored in many Arab countries. She hated the stuff.

But apparently, Americans, particularly journalists, were addicted to coffee. Rafraf watched with amusement as he started unpacking the duffel bag in the kitchen. It contained dozens of shining bags.

"What's all that?" she asked.

"Starbucks," he said excitedly. "There should be at least a month's supply."

"No thank you," she said simply. She watched him stuff one of the cabinets full of the bags. "I don't like coffee."

"How can you not like coffee? I'm pretty sure it's a rule that you can't work for NBC unless you drink coffee, so you'd better get used to it."

He continued loading the coffee into the cabinet. Then he popped his head into the office. "I found some tea. How do you like it?"

Was he serious? Surely this guy wasn't actually going to make her a cup of tea? Rafraf pretended she hadn't heard him.

"What? You don't drink tea either?" he persisted.

"With lots of sugar?" she offered, thinking perhaps she was about to be the butt of a joke.

"Got it." He ducked his head back into the kitchen.

The next few minutes were impossibly loud. Cabinets were slammed, pots and pans were clanged, drawers were pulled open, then abruptly closed. Finally, she heard the familiar whistle of a tea-kettle coming to a boil. A moment later, Don came to the table carrying two cups of tea.

"I wasn't sure how much sugar you wanted," he said, offering her one of them.

"Thank you." She took the cup. She noticed the tea bag in his cup. "Why aren't you having coffee?"

Don looked embarrassed. "I couldn't figure out how to make it," he said sheepishly. "There's no coffeepot in there."

He took a sip of his tea and made a face.

"BROTHER DON!" KARL BOSTIC SAID cheerfully as he entered the room.

"Good morning," I said. "I have a special delivery for you from Frieda."

Frieda was my bureau chief in Atlanta. She had once been the London bureau chief and knew Karl well.

Karl looked excited. "Is it what I think it is?"

"It is if you think it's a whole boatload of grits." I grabbed the duffel bag from the kitchen and pulled out ten boxes of Quaker instant grits. "She says you've got a thing for grits."

"Yes!" Karl was like a kid on Christmas morning.

"So, what's the plan?" he continued. "We've got to pitch some stuff to *Nightly*. Any ideas yet?"

I followed Karl into his office and sat down.

I told him about some stories that I'd seen on the wires. One was a brief mention that the number of weddings in Iraq had risen sharply in recent months. With Valentine's Day just around the corner, I thought that might make the point that even in the midst of a war, love prevails.

"I could see that," Karl said. Bureau chiefs didn't have any actual say about which stories made it into a show. But it was always a good idea to run story ideas past them first. They generally had a good nose for news, and a better understanding of the types of stories the executives in New York were looking for.

"Also, they're trying to get the Baghdad Zoo open again," I continued. "Apparently it's a joint effort with a zoo in North Carolina."

"Okay. Anything with a harder edge?"

"Cell phones. As you know, Iraqis weren't allowed to have cell phones under Saddam. With him gone, they're about to get cell service for the first time ever. I saw a White House press release that says half a million Iraqis have already signed up."

"They're throwing the switch next week, right?" Karl asked.

"Right. Since landline phone service is so bad here, a lot of homes and businesses have never even had a phone. Cell phones could change everything."

"Good. That's plenty to keep us busy in between bombings and ambushes."

Sadly, it turned out that Paul had been right about the relative quiet not lasting. Later that day, February 3, an American soldier was killed by a bomb near the town of Haswah. It was the first U.S. casualty in what would become one of the bloodiest months yet in Iraq.

But one American death, no matter how tragic, was not considered major news in the States. Newspapers and television networks mentioned the attack, updated the growing death toll, and moved on.

I knew my time would soon be taken covering bigger acts of violence, so I quickly turned my attention to the stories Karl and I had discussed. After leaving his office, I told those gathered around the table my story ideas and asked who wanted to do what.

Babak and another producer named Rachel Levin would shoulder most of the producing load for the stories. I had often

worked with Rachel during my first trip to the war zone a year earlier. Like just about everyone else assigned to Baghdad, she seemed
fearless.

Paul was due to leave Iraq for London midmonth, and his plate
was already full working on other stories for Richard Engel and Kevin
Sites.

Richard may have been out of the country, but stories pitched by
correspondents continue with or without them.

Field producers were extremely capable. They could pull together
all the elements of a story, conduct interviews, supervise the camera
crews, even write the scripts without help from a correspondent if
necessary. It was through the hard work of producers that just over
three dozen NBC correspondents seemed to be everywhere at once.
Perhaps a story took three or four days to shoot and to conduct all of
the interviews. Frequently the correspondent would only work on the
story for one or two of those days, then write the script when all of
the fieldwork had been completed.

I typically tried to be a part of all of the shooting days except that
spent standing around while camera crews shot b-roll. Baghdad
would be no exception.

After speaking with the producers, I turned my attention to
Rafraf. I had met all the translators who worked in the bureau, and
Rafraf had impressed me immediately. I could tell she was smart, and
her English was easy for me to understand.

"What do you think about the wedding story?" I asked. "Does that
sound like a real story to you?"

"What do you mean?" she replied.

"I mean, do you think it's true? Are more people getting married
now that Saddam is gone?"

"I think so, yes." She didn't look convinced.

"Well, I don't want to pitch it if it's not true. How can we check
the numbers for ourselves?"

"I can go down to the office that issues wedding licenses. They
can tell me what the real numbers are. How soon do you want
them?"

"As soon as possible," I said. "It's eleven days until Valentine's Day, that's probably when the story will air."

"Okay. I'll go today."

To my surprise, she got up and left.

Now that's initiative, I thought.

WHO CARES ABOUT WEDDINGS? was the thought running through her head as Rafraf left the office. *There are people dying, and this guy wants to go to a wedding?*

Not that she planned to argue the point. Money was money, and after the last few months, Rafraf looked forward to a story that didn't involve body parts.

She hadn't planned to go right then and there to the wedding-license office. She was actually just going to the bakery downstairs to get her daily pastry. But Don seemed so pleased when she got up, maybe she'd just go to the office after all.

But first, the bakery.

It was by far the best part of Al Hamra. A bakery and sweets shop was tucked into a side building on the first floor. Rafraf had developed a serious weakness for chocolate. She rode the elevator downstairs and headed straight for the bakery.

Sarah worked at the bakery. She was twenty-one years old and was one of the few Christians Rafraf knew. The young women had become friends.

"Where are you off to today?" Sarah asked, noting Rafraf was carrying her purse.

"A stupid story about weddings." Rafraf didn't have to order. Sarah had already pulled her favorite piece of cake out of the counter.

"Weddings? Why weddings?"

"I have no idea." Rafraf paid for her cake with a 250-dinar note . . . the equivalent of about twenty-five cents in U.S. currency.

It had been nearly a year since the destruction of Saddam's government, but Rafraf still did a double take every time she looked at the new Iraqi currency. Saddam Hussein's image had appeared on the dinar for Rafraf's entire life. Money simply wasn't money without his thick mustache and fatherly appearance.

This was the new Iraq. Saddam's face no longer appeared on the currency; it had been replaced by the Iraqi flag. Rafraf wondered how long it would be before the dinar was redesigned once again. It was just a matter of time, she thought, before George Bush's face was on the bill. She was certain of that.

"And when will your wedding be?" Sarah asked mischievously. She was one of the few people who knew that, despite enormous risk, Rafraf had dated some boys in secret.

"Never," Rafraf answered seriously, "I will never get married."

"Oh, sure you will," Sarah said happily, "and I want to dance at your wedding."

Rafraf smiled at that. "Deal," she said, taking her bag with the cake in it. "I'll see you later."

Rafraf had meant it when she said she would never get married. Despite some loosening of the cultural rules that had forced Rafraf's parents to marry against their will, arranged marriage was still the norm for many Iraqi families. Rafraf would never stand for that.

Her father had already begun hinting around at the possibility of marrying his willful daughter off, and in Rafraf's view the prospects were not good. Kamal would try to make a match that would increase his standing in the community or within the family.

Kamal had, in fact, already suggested to one of his brothers that Rafraf's younger sister Sama marry his son.

Sama was barely sixteen years old at the time. Rafraf considered her a bit of an airhead—another term she had learned from American movies—but she was quite fond of her little sister. Sama was cute, with a bubbly personality, and she was always funny, though rarely on purpose. But if their father had his way, Sama would be forced to marry her first cousin. Rafraf knew that was considered taboo in many countries, but it was simply a matter of routine in Iraq.

"Never," she repeated to herself as she walked out of Al Hamra toward the main highway. Five minutes later she flagged a taxi and was on her way to the office that issued the licenses. The NBC security detail would have preferred she wait for a company driver and car, but Rafraf was in a hurry. She never worried about riding in a taxi.

THE LICENSE BUILDING WAS PACKED. There was hardly enough room to breathe, much less navigate from one office to the next looking for the right person to talk to. Rafraf felt claustrophobic, but wasn't sure if it was from the crush of people or the unnatural happiness.

Young women were everywhere, some accompanied by their future husbands, but all accompanied by their mothers. Everybody seemed to be talking at the same time. Wedding dresses, living arrangements, guest lists—all the things new brides obsess about were under relentless, excited discussion. Rafraf wanted out of the license office as soon as possible.

Thankfully she found the right office, and after being handed up the chain of bureaucracy several times, she was face-to-face with the person who had the information she needed.

"Is it really true that more people are getting married now?" she asked.

"Did you not just see for yourself?" the woman replied. "It's craziness. We've had more applications in the last month than in all of the last year before the war."

"Do you know why?"

The woman shrugged. "Some say because you can marry whoever you want now." She lowered her voice and continued in a conspiratorial tone, "You know, without intervention."

Rafraf knew what the woman meant. Saddam's government and Baath Party officials had always managed to find reasons not to issue certain people marriage licenses. Sometimes a bribe was necessary to complete the application, in other cases there was simply no getting past official opposition to a marriage.

It seemed far more trouble than it was worth to Rafraf. She thanked the woman and waded out through the mass of brides to her taxi. She couldn't help thinking of them as hypnotized zombies like the ones she had seen in American movies.

They all looked so happy, but she knew it was a lie. Once they were married, these women would simply become the property of their husbands. They could be beaten, abused, or violated at will and have no recourse. Rafraf knew dozens of young women who were married. None of them were happy. Some of them wanted desperately to die.

"Never, never, never," she repeated over and over as she finally cleared the crowd of zombie brides and returned to the waiting taxi.

It wasn't that she hadn't been asked. Her latest boyfriend had even proposed to Rafraf just a few months before, and she had initially accepted.

But marrying Firas was out of the question.

It wasn't that there was anything specifically wrong with Firas. He was tall and good-looking, with brownish hair and expressive hazel eyes. His family was wealthy, and he always wore fashionable clothing. He was somewhat shy, but quickly opened up when he got to know somebody.

No, Rafraf thought, there was nothing wrong with Firas that wasn't wrong with many Iraqi men. He was stuck where he was, unable to imagine anything else but his current life. And he was extremely jealous.

"I don't want you working for the Americans," he had told her in November. They were eating at the student cafeteria at Baghdad University. Rafraf was no longer a student, but the cafeteria was the only place she and Firas could actually eat a meal together without creating a scandal. Going together to a proper restaurant was out of the question.

"Oh, so now you're one of them?" she said bitterly. "The insurgents have you now?"

"Of course not," he said, "they're a bunch of idiots. But I don't trust the Americans either. And I don't think you should be with them."

"It's my job. I'm making good money. And I do trust them. Nobody has done anything wrong to me except Iraqis."

"What does that mean?"

"Nothing," she answered, not wanting to go into details.

"It's not right. You shouldn't be making money. It's an insult to me and to your father. When we are married, you're quitting. You should be at home raising children and cooking for me. That's the Iraqi way. What you're doing is wrong."

"I'm not quitting."

"People are talking about you," he cautioned. "They see you come and go every day with a different man driving you. Different cars and different men every day! They say you are not acting right."

"Are you serious? Those are drivers who work for NBC. They change cars because it's too dangerous to be seen all the time in the same car going to the same place."

"And still you do that when you could marry me? My mother has already spoken with your mother. She says your father will be agreeable."

"What if I'm not agreeable?" Rafraf shot back.

"It's not up to you. And NBC will soon leave, so it just won't matter."

"There will be other jobs," Rafraf said simply. "I don't have to be what you want me to be. I want to be somebody I choose."

"We'll see," Firas answered in a tone that struck Rafraf with finality.

"No, you'll see. I would never marry you!"

With that, Rafraf stood and left Firas with a plate of half-eaten lamb.

"Rafraf!" he called after her.

She turned and saw him holding the knife they had used to cut the lamb. He held it by the blade with the handle pointing toward her.

"Here, you might as well cut out my heart. If you're leaving me, I won't need it."

"I'm sorry." She turned and walked away.

He tried to talk to her the next day, but she avoided him. It had been almost three months since that day in the cafeteria, and the two hadn't spoken a single word.

I HAD SPENT PLENTY OF time driving around Baghdad since my arrival earlier in the week, but for security reasons we didn't spend much time simply out among the people.

The management at NBC had determined that the city was far too dangerous for its employees to eat in public restaurants or to shop in markets. So my first few days consisted mostly of trips in and out of the Green Zone, and brief opportunities to do "man on the street" interviews with Iraqis.

I was anxious to get out of the hotel and begin the day-to-day work of gathering news. The wedding story was the perfect chance to meet some ordinary Iraqis and start getting a feel for what they really thought about the future of their country.

So, security contingent in tow, we set out to begin blowing the lid off Iraqi weddings. First stop, a wedding-dress shop, where the little old woman who ran things said business was indeed booming.

Second stop, the wedding-license office, where we spoke with brides-to-be and their mothers.

Rafraf proved to be much more than just a capable translator. In many ways, she functioned as a producer on the wedding story. She found all of the characters, researched information, coordinated the shooting, and conducted some of the interviews on her own.

Eventually we found ourselves at an outdoor wedding celebration. The bride and groom, and hundreds of their family members and friends, met in a parking lot near Baghdad's Al Jadriyah bridge. The bridge spans the Tigris River just south of the Green Zone. The actual wedding ceremony had taken place an hour earlier, but the real celebration began with what Iraqis called the *zeffa*.

The *zeffa*, I learned, was a tradition similar to a parade. In days past, the groom and his entire family would walk together to the bride's house to collect his prize . . . the bride. There, the two families would join together for the *zeffa* leading back to the groom's house. The joyous procession, with much dancing in the streets and singing, had another purpose.

Parading the bride and groom through the streets advertised for all to see that the couple were, from that point forward, allowed to be seen together in public. In a culture that imposed severe penalties upon contact between unmarried men and women, the *zeffa* could prevent a potentially serious misunderstanding.

It was still done in the same way in smaller communities through-out the country. But Baghdad was a huge city. With brides and grooms often living several miles apart, the modern *zeffa* was a variation on the theme. For all but the poorest of families, walking had been replaced by rented buses and every car or minivan the families could commandeer. Hundreds of passengers would pile into the vehicles, then honk and weave through traffic on the way to the Al Jadriyah bridge.

"Why this bridge?" I asked Rafraf. "What's so special about stand-ing in the parking lot there, as opposed to anywhere else?"

The parking lot wasn't much to look at. Weeds grew through the crumbling asphalt. The painted lines that marked parking stalls were cracked and faded. The lamps that should have lit the parking lot at night were broken and dangling from poles.

"Because of the wedding island," Rafraf said matter-of-factly. "Look down there."

Just past the edge of the bridge, right on the bank of the Tigris River, there was indeed an island, lush and green. Its trees and foliage were nourished by the river. The river, at least a quarter mile wide, was gently flowing. It looked serene enough, but I knew the river was highly polluted; it contained a toxic mix of raw sewage, industrial waste, pesticides, and oil by-products.

Technically, it wasn't really an island. Every inch of the wedding island—which was about the size of a city park—sat on the northern bank of the river. But for Iraqis, it was an island nonetheless, an escape from everyday reality.

A closer look revealed a number of buildings that looked like apartments nestled among the trees. There was a restaurant, a banquet hall, a park complete with swings, and a swimming pool.

"Why do they call that the wedding island?" I asked.

"Because that's where people go after they are married," Rafraf said.

"Like for honeymoons?"

"Yes. It's so they don't have to just go right back home. So they can be alone together. You have to show identification before you can enter the gate to prove you are married."

It struck me as sad; a weekend in a cramped apartment on the banks of a polluted river was all the honeymoon most Iraqis would ever have.

I gestured toward the bride and groom standing in the parking lot next to the bridge. "Will they go to the wedding island after this?"

Rafraf's face turned serious. "No," she said simply, "nobody can go there now."

"Really? Why not?"

"Because the Americans took it. See?" She pointed to the northernmost part of the park. Dozens of military supply trucks were parked near a checkpoint. Armed soldiers roamed what should have been a strolling path for newlyweds. "They've taken everything. Even the honeymoons."

"So why do they come here?"

"Because where else can they go? At least they can see the wedding island from here. It's as close as they can get."

I WADED BACK THROUGH THE crowd and found my producer, Madeleine, standing near the bride and groom.

"Does she look happy to you?" Madeleine asked. She had to yell to be heard above the crowd.

"He does," I said. The groom, who appeared to be nearly forty years old, had allowed a smile to crack what seemed a stoic face. He had the look of a cat that had swallowed a canary without anybody noticing.

"But I don't think she wants to be here." Madeleine nodded toward the bride, who seemed to nod back with her eyes.

The bride was barely twenty years old. She wore thick makeup. Her cheeks were far too rosy. Her lips, too red. Her eyes looked as if they were pleading for a way out.

The dancing grew to a fever pitch. Iraqi women were making the traditional *la,la,la,la* noise with one hand covering their mouths.

I was about to ask the bride some questions about her wedding day when the shooting started.

Bang! Bang! Bang!

The shots came in rapid succession.

My first instinct was to dive for cover, but nobody else seemed at all concerned.

Bang! Bang! Bang!

"La, la, la, la!"

Weddings, I knew, were prime targets for insurgent attacks. The past few months had seen several massacres at wedding celebrations just like this one. But the shooting wasn't coming from outside the wedding party, but within.

Bang, bang, bang.

I spotted the guns. Two men held AK-47 rifles. The barrels were pointed toward the air. As the men danced in celebration, they would occasionally pull the trigger, spitting 7.62-millimeter bullets into the sky at nearly twenty-five hundred feet per second.

Rafraf saw the concern on my face.

"That's what we do at weddings," she said. "On Thursday nights, you can hear guns all across Baghdad. There's no need to worry."

"Those bullets have to come down somewhere," I said. "Don't people get killed by falling rounds?"

"Sometimes." She shrugged. "That's the way it is. If it's the will of Allah, so be it."

The sun was beginning to set. Our security guys had told us we should be back to the hotel before dark.

"Congratulations," I offered to the bride and groom before retreating back to our cars.

As we pulled out of the parking lot, another wedding party drove past us on the bridge. This one was even more boisterous than the *zeffa* we were leaving.

People were literally hanging on to the sides of buses and mini-vans. Two men sat on the hood of one of the cars; the driver had to stick his head out the window to see around them. Both of the men were shooting AK-47s into the evening sky. The bullets sailed happily off to points unknown.

I made a mental note to avoid standing outside on Thursday evenings.

Don Teague, U.S. Army pilot

Rafraf on a Baghdad rooftop

Don reporting outside
a communications building

Rafraf before a statue
of Saddam Hussein

Don in an oil field in southern Iraq

A bomb crater at the entrance to the Green Zone. *Photo by Rich Galen.*

The aftermath of an IED b *Photo by Air Force Staff Sergeant Reynaldo Ramon.*

Rafraf's neighborhood in Baghdad, where a bomb has exploded nearby

The river of sewage in
Rafraf's neighborhood

Rafraf mugs for the camera

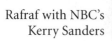

Rafraf working with
NBC's Rachel Levin

Rafraf with NBC's
Kerry Sanders

Rafraf before lion cages at the Baghdad Zoo

Rafraf enjoying the sprinklers at the Baghdad Zoo

A U.S. soldier with Iraqi children. *Photo by Staff Sergeant Brian Ferguson.*

Al Rasheed Street in Baghdad

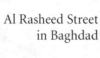

Don interviewing an American soldier at the school immediately before the bombing

Debris from the school bomb

Bombed communications building in Baghdad

Don interviewing the
wedding dress merchant

Don with the painting
Two Faces of Iraq in
Baghdad

The rush for goods that
sparked the Safwan riot

The riot at Safwan

Rafraf ready to board
for her first plane ride

Rafraf uses a cell phone

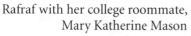

Rafraf's first American Christmas at
Kerry Sanders's home in Florida

Rafraf with her college roommate,
Mary Katherine Mason

Don, Madison, Kiki, Rachae[
and Rafraf at home in Texa[
*Photo by Tobin Smith,
www.photobinphotography.co[*

Rafraf settles into her dorm
room at the University of
Southern Florida

Rafraf anticipating a
new future

TEN

BAD THINGS

The word should have been obvious. The letters were right there in front of her, but Rafraf couldn't see them.

E-R-E-R-A-D.

She had already picked out the short words. *Red* was obvious. So was *dare*. But for some reason these letters had Rafraf stumped.

"I'm stupid," she said. "I can't do anything."

"You're not stupid," Don said. "It's supposed to be hard. It wouldn't be a game if it was always obvious."

"But look. There are four spaces for six-letter words, and I don't know any of them." The game's ten-second countdown began. Rafraf pushed the computer mouse away in frustration. "I'm stupid."

To a casual observer, it may have looked as if Rafraf were being overly dramatic as a way to attract attention. But her self-loathing was real.

Rafraf had always been prone to mood swings. She could go from a joyous high to a crashing low in minutes. She and, more important, those around her had lived with the ups and downs for her entire life. But over the last few months, the condition had gotten much worse.

Rafraf tried to appear cheerful, but she had seen so much in the last year: bombs, bodies, and the threat of more violence at every turn. She tried to push the images out of her head, but she couldn't. They sat just at the edge of her consciousness and would jump out at her in moments of weakness.

Sometimes something as simple as a word, even one not directed at her, could trigger an image and send Rafraf reeling into despair.

She felt stupid, alone, and trapped.

That obnoxious countdown clock only made it worse.

"*Reader,*" Don offered. "Like a person who reads."

Rafraf typed in the letters and hit enter as the counter hit zero.

The computer made a happy sound.

Rafraf and Don celebrated for a split second, then looked back to the screen. With TextTwist, you never really had time to relish your genius. The next set of letters immediately demanded attention.

R-O-D-M-E-F.

Rafraf saw *deform* immediately. She could have entered it and been ready to move on, but she didn't.

She wondered if Don would offer to help right away or let her struggle with the word before jumping in at the last second. Was he playing some kind of game? If he knew the answer, why didn't he just say so?

Rafraf thought she was good at reading people, but she was having a hard time figuring Don out.

Why did he ask so many questions? He said it was because that's what reporters do, but nobody else asked her so much about her life.

He also seemed obsessed with getting her to drink coffee. He had finally figured out how to make coffee with the French press in the kitchen and drank Starbucks constantly.

First he would bring a pot of water to a boil on the stove, then add the hot water and coffee grounds to the press. The next step was the most delicate. The filter of the press had to be pushed down from top to bottom, collecting the grounds at the bottom of the press. It all seemed like way too much work.

"It's not against your religion," he pointed out. "It's not like I'm trying to make you eat bacon or drink beer. Why don't you just have a cup?"

"No. I just don't like it."

"Okay," he said with a touch of defeat in his voice, "what do you like?"

"I'll show you," she said excitedly. "Let's go." She grabbed her purse and headed for the door.

With what seemed like considerable reluctance on his part, Don got up from the table and followed.

"Where exactly are we going?" he asked with a touch of suspicion.

"You'll just have to wait and see." She smiled. The two walked the rest of the length of the hallway toward the elevators in silence.

The elevators of Al Hamra were tiny by American standards. Six adults could cram inside and close the doors, but it was an uncomfortably tight fit.

Rafraf pushed the down button, and the nearest elevator doors opened immediately. They boarded the empty elevator, and the doors closed.

"One," she said, motioning toward the buttons.

"Oh, right." Don pressed the button. He seemed uncomfortable.

"You're not afraid of elevators, are you?"

"No," he said simply. "But where are we going again? If we're leaving the area, we really need to let somebody know."

"I told you, you'll have to wait."

The remaining moments passed in silence as the lift journeyed toward the first floor.

Don seemed to be standing as far away from her as possible. He didn't look at her, but stood staring at the doors as if willing them to open.

Rafraf could tell he was uncomfortable with being alone on the elevator with her. He was obviously not an expert on Muslim culture or religious traditions, but he probably knew that many would frown upon the two riding alone together in an elevator.

Rafraf didn't worry about such things while at Al Hamra. The hotel was her island of independence.

Ding.

The doors opened on the first floor. Rafraf noticed Don let out a sigh of relief as the two stepped off.

"Follow me," Rafraf said excitedly. She headed not for the front entrance of the lobby, but for the back door that led to the pool.

"Is the pool heated?" Don asked as they walked across the empty deck. February in Baghdad wasn't really swimming-pool weather. Still, the water looked clean and inviting.

"I don't know." Rafraf shrugged. "I can't swim."

Don stopped in his tracks. "How can you not swim? Everybody swims."

"Not in Baghdad. I've never even been in a pool. Where could I learn to swim?" She pushed open the doors to the adjoining building and continued down yet another hallway.

"How about the river? You could swim in the Tigris."

"Would you swim in that river?" she asked. "You've seen it."

"I guess not. I'm going to have to get a list of things you haven't done. Ever been on an airplane?"

"No."

"Driven a car?"

"Never."

"Can you ride a bike?"

"Yeah, right."

"Have you ridden an escalator?"

"A what?"

"You know, like stairs that move."

"Of course not. We don't have those here."

"Do you have drive-throughs? You know, restaurants that give you your food in your car?"

"That's stupid. Are all Americans that lazy?"

"We're not lazy," Don said defensively. "We're just usually in too much of a hurry to stop and eat."

"Well, we don't have those here." Her face broadened into a smile as they finally reached the right door.

"But we do have this," she said proudly.

The smell of sweets poured through the open door. The bakery shop was warmly lit. It was, in Rafraf's view, one of the most magical places in all Iraq.

Chocolate cakes, brightly colored cookies, and tarts were arranged in rows and placed under a long glass countertop. Goodies were stacked on trays along the wall behind the cash register and sat on plates lining the main counter.

Her friend Sarah was standing behind the counter. The two exchanged a quick greeting in Arabic.

"Do they make all of this here?" Don asked, his eyes wide with delight.

"They do," Rafraf said, smiling. "See, everything isn't bad here. What do you want?"

"I'll try whatever you think is best. It all looks good."

"Okay." Rafraf quickly ordered an assortment of treats, which Sarah put into a paper bag.

Don tried to pay for the goods but Rafraf wouldn't let him. She purposefully pulled out a wad of dinar notes that was much bigger than required and peeled off the necessary payment.

"Try the rolled one with the red stuff in it first," she suggested as they headed back toward the bureau.

Don was too busy eating to answer.

WHEN THE BRASS AT NBC asked me to do a month in Baghdad, I insisted on one condition before agreeing.

"You have to let me tell positive stories," I said to one of the senior international producers at the *Nightly News*. "I know plenty of bad things are going on, and I'll report that too, but I know there's good happening there that we're not seeing."

"Do you really think so?" was the reply.

"Of course."

A research group had recently released an extensive survey of Iraqis. They said it was the first such poll ever taken. It showed a majority of Iraqis considered themselves better off after the U.S. invasion than before. The group, Oxford Research International, conducted another national survey of Iraqis while I was there, in February 2004. It revealed that a strong majority of Iraqis, 71 percent, had a positive view of the direction their country was going. Almost 80 percent of Iraqis said their lives were as good or better than they had been before the war began. And overwhelming percentages of those surveyed opposed attacks against U.S. forces, foreign-aid workers, and Iraqis who worked with foreigners.*

That's not to say they were thrilled with the continued American presence. Only 49 percent of Iraqis polled said it was right for the United States to invade their country, and many Iraqis were dismayed that the American military had not managed to establish security. Iraqis were also split on the overall result of the U.S.-led invasion: 41 percent said it liberated the country, while 41 percent said it humiliated Iraq. Residents were frustrated by the continued need for so many American troops, but a majority didn't want the foreign forces to leave until security improved and a strong Iraqi government was in place.

I relayed the poll results to the senior producer in New York.

"We're not seeing that story," I said. "If Iraqis really feel they're better off, the American people need to know that."

"I agree completely" came the answer from New York. "If you find something positive to report, by all means do it. We'll put it on the air."

But bad news has a nasty way of getting in the way of good news. And in Iraq, there was plenty of bad news to go around.

---

* Oxford Research International, "National Survey of Iraq," February 2004.

* * *

FEBRUARY 10 SHOULD HAVE BEEN a beautiful day. The sun was out, the wind was calm, and temperatures were pleasant. All in all, if you had to stand in a long line, February 10 had all the makings of a nice day to do so.

But at nine thirty in the morning on February 10, a suicide bomber blew up a pickup truck full of explosives outside a police station in a town just south of Baghdad called Iskandariya. Hundreds of Iraqis were waiting in line to fill out applications to join the police force. More than 50 people were killed, and at least 150 were wounded.

Less than twenty-four hours later, yet another devastating attack took place.

Hundreds of young men had lined up in front an Iraqi army recruiting station in Baghdad less than a mile from the fortified Green Zone. Some were just kids. Others were older, with wives and children of their own. What all of the men had in common was a desire to help their country get back on its feet.

They were the perfect target for terrorists. Shortly after seven thirty on the morning of February 11, a car carrying several hundred pounds of explosives drove slowly past the hopeful new recruits. When the man behind the wheel determined he could kill the maximum amount of people, he detonated the car bomb. The blast killed forty-seven men and wounded scores more.

I arrived at the scene of the explosion a short time later. MSNBC wanted live reports from the location, and with a heavy military presence our security guys determined it would be safe to broadcast with our remote satellite truck. U.S. military vehicles had established a cordon around the blast site, so we couldn't get closer than about a hundred yards. That was close enough for me.

The smell of blood lingered in the air. Perhaps I imagined it, but I couldn't seem to get the coppery taste off my tongue.

This had been the deadliest twenty-four-hour period in Iraq

since the beginning of the war . . . and the killing was far from over.

My plan to tell positive stories was quickly coming unraveled.

AS IF TO PUNCTUATE THE point, senior political and military officials summoned journalists to the Green Zone the following day.

Military intelligence officials had intercepted a letter from Abu Musab al Zarqawi, the Jordanian terrorist who had formed a new and deadly group called Al Qaeda in Iraq.

The letter laid out AQI's battle plan for defeating the United States in Iraq.*

"This is a blueprint for terror in Iraq," said Dan Senor, the Bush administration's senior adviser in Iraq. "It outlines very clearly that the blueprint calls for unleashing civil war, provoking one ethnic group in Iraq against another ethnic group with the hope of tearing the country apart. It talks about continued attacks against any individual working with the Coalition."**

Along with both harassing and spectacular attacks against Coalition forces, the plan called for a stepped-up campaign of terror against Iraqis. Police officers, Iraqi soldiers, contractors who supported the United States, they would all be specifically targeted. So would innocent civilians. The idea was to create so much chaos that the weak-willed Americans would pull out of Iraq on their own or be forced out by Iraqis.

Ample evidence suggested that fighters from countries outside of Iraq were already pouring into the country to take on the American army. The military had captured or killed many foreign insurgents who had recently entered Iraq. I wondered if re-

---

* February 2004, Coalition Provisional Authority English translation of Musab al Zarqawi letter obtained by U.S. government in Iraq.

** February 11, 2004, transcript of Coalition Provisional Authority briefing, Baghdad, Iraq.

leasing the Zarqawi letter would only increase the influx of terrorists.

"Despite the fact the author says this isn't a call to arms," I said to Brigadier General Mark Kimmitt, "I'm curious if you're concerned that releasing this to the world will have the opposite effect of bringing more people from outside the country in, exposing them to this message?"

"No," replied the general, "we believe that by handing this document out to everybody in Iraq and everybody in the world, the plans of the terrorists are laid out for everyone to see. What they need to understand is that when everybody in Iraq, both Coalition and Iraqi citizens, read this document, they'll fully understand what the terrorists are up to."

I COULDN'T TELL IF RAFRAF fully realized what the terrorists were up to. I knew, perhaps more than she did, that working for NBC made her a prime target for insurgents, but she seemed unconcerned.

I wondered what she thought of the U.S. invasion of her country. Did she think Iraqis were better off?

"You humiliated us," she offered during yet another game of TextTwist. As usual, all her clothing matched. A blue sweater, baby blue head scarf, and blue eye shadow. She sat low in her chair as if trying to disappear from the room and focused her eyes intently on the computer. "Thousands of people are dead because of President Bush."

"You don't like Bush?" I asked, already knowing the answer but hoping to prompt a deeper conversation.

"No, I hate him."

"But you don't hate Americans?" I said with a note of suspicion.

"Of course not."

"But we elected Bush, and we'll probably reelect him in November. He represents America. But you don't hate Americans . . . just the president?"

"You can't control what he does."

"Rafraf," I said sincerely, "Americans supported this war. There's opposition to it now, but something like ninety percent of us thought getting rid of Saddam was the right thing to do at the time."

"Including you?"

"Yes," I said plainly. "His government agents raped women and tortured families. He went to war with his neighbors, and he made billions of dollars while allowing his country to starve. He used chemical weapons against his own people. How could you possibly not think it was good to get rid of him?"

"You don't understand Arab countries. We had respect because he was strong. He fought for us, and he stood up to the rest of the world. In Arab countries, your leader is everything. He said he would fight the Americans to the death."

"But he didn't," I shot back. "He crawled into a hole and hid like a rat."

Saddam had been captured hiding underground about two months earlier—in December 2003. A general with the army's Fourth Infantry Division had used the "like a rat" phrase, and I repeated it without thinking about how it would affect Rafraf.

I wasn't prepared for her response. Tears streamed down her face. She started to say something but couldn't.

"I'm sorry," I said. "I didn't know he meant that much to you."

After a moment, she composed herself and continued, "He was no different than any other president in the world. They all do the same things."

"He killed tens of thousands of his own people," I said. "The reason Iraqis say they're better off now is because they don't have to fear him. I know innocent civilians have died in this war, but even more were dying because of Saddam."

"But with Saddam," she said, "they brought it on themselves. If he killed people, it's because they broke the rules."

She couldn't be serious, I thought. Rafraf's own father had been imprisoned by Saddam's government simply for being a possible witness to a crime. How could she possibly believe that it was okay for Saddam to kill citizens.

"You can't mean that!" I insisted. "Saddam murdered people by the thousands."

"Everybody in Iraq knew the rules: Don't speak about the government, don't say anything bad about Saddam or the Baath Party. Keep your mouth shut and you'll be okay. Sure, he killed people, but that's because they broke the rules."

"That's not the way the world works, Rafraf. At least not most of the world."

"Sure it is. Are you telling me that if George Bush heard people saying bad things about him that he wouldn't have them killed?"

"Are you serious? That's exactly what I'm saying."

I knew Rafraf had a college degree. The war had interrupted her senior year, but she did finally manage to graduate. Didn't courses in Iraqi universities at least touch on the subjects of democracy and free speech?

"Of course I'm serious," she said. "If people in the U.S. say bad things about George Bush, he'll kill them or put them in prison."

"No, he won't. There are millions of Americans who can't stand him. They have protests in the streets. They write editorials in newspapers about how much they hate him. They make movies about what an idiot they think he is."

"And he does nothing about this? He just lets people say anything they want?"

"Yes. Don't you get it? That's what this is all about. He doesn't have to like what people say about him, but we have the right to say it. And we have the right to replace him with somebody else if we don't like the job he's doing. That's what democracy is."

Rafraf seemed to have a hard time believing me. "He wouldn't even put them in prison for saying those things? You're telling the truth?"

"Of course I am. America isn't here to take over your country. We're here to give it back to you. If you guys would just stop bombing each other, we'd leave."

"Maybe you think so, but I don't think you'll ever leave. And Iraq is embarrassed in front of the rest of the world."

"You'll see. Maybe not right now, but someday you'll know the truth."

"Hopefully, but I still hate him."

And she had every right in the world to do so.

ON VALENTINE'S DAY, A PARTY was held at Al Hamra. I wasn't sure exactly who was throwing the party, or what the specific purpose was. But if anything, journalists stationed in Baghdad desperately needed a party.

By nine o'clock at night, the hotel's restaurant and its adjoining ballroom were filled with reporters representing television networks and newspapers from every corner of the planet.

A British reporter from the *Times* of London was there. He wore jeans and a cashmere sports coat, and told stories of daring while embedded with U.S. troops. Just a day earlier he had been involved in a terrible accident while riding in an American Humvee.

I was particularly happy to see another Brit at the party. Rupert had just arrived for a tour in Baghdad the previous day.

Rupert was the chief of security for NBC during my months in Kuwait. He was with me for most of my trips into Iraq, and I liked him tremendously. Rupert didn't look much like a soldier. He was in his late forties or early fifties, with a friendly face and a quick wit.

He was also one of the most experienced military men in Great Britain. Prior to his work with NBC, he had risen to the rank of sergeant major of the British Royal Marines. A veteran of the conflict in Northern Ireland, Rupert was an expert on terrorism and terrorists.

"I was hoping you wouldn't be here," I said to him after we exchanged a quick greeting.

"What do you mean?" he asked.

"Well, nobody else here really knows me. But you know what a chicken I really am. I could fool the rest of them, but it's too late to fool you."

"Bloody hell, you're one of the few reporters I've ever known with any common sense."

"Really? I was scared to death the whole time we were in Iraq last time. I figured you had me pegged for a coward."

"You were a military man," he said, "you know how dangerous this is. The rest of these people think this is a game. Self-preservation is a good trait to have."

"I'll toast to that." I lifted my glass.

While we were toasting, Paul Nassar was dancing and working up a sweat. His month in Baghdad was over on February 15, and his birthday had been just a few days earlier, so he treated the Valentine's party as if it were meant for him.

Paul had no shortage of dance partners that night. I noticed him dancing with a young woman. She had blond hair and braces and looked to be in her mid to late twenties. Something about her, even from a distance, spoke of sadness.

"Who's that?" I asked when Paul came over to toast his good fortune at going home in one piece.

"She's an American, Marla Ruzicka. We did a story on her a couple of months ago."

"She's not a journalist?"

"No," Paul said, "she's an activist from California. She represents Iraqi families who have had relatives killed in the war. She goes to the U.S. and demands they pay reparations."

"Do they?"

"Oh, yes. She gets them thousands of dollars." Paul took a sip of his beer and looked over toward Marla. "She's here all by herself. No security or even a support staff. Just her and a translator traipsing around Iraq . . . foolish if you ask me. She shows up after there's been a battle or a bombing and just starts talking to the survivors. She's got guts, I'll give her that."

Everyone in Baghdad knew Marla. You didn't have to agree with her politics to see she was a bright and giving young woman. She was an antiwar activist, in the middle of the battle, putting her beliefs into action. I learned she was friends with practically every reporter in Baghdad.

She was a thorn in the side of U.S. military officials for sure, but even they respected her dedication and fearlessness.

But the Marla I met on Valentine's night in Baghdad seemed a far cry from a daring activist. I spotted her sitting alone in front of what looked like a giant birthday cake. She looked exhausted, as if she hadn't slept in weeks. I wondered how she had managed the energy to dance earlier in the evening.

"Hi, Marla," I said as I sat down across the cake from her. "I'm with NBC News, I'm Don."

"Hi," she said, her eyes focused somewhere in the distance. She could have been anywhere in the world, but one thing I knew for sure . . . she wasn't really in the room. I wondered what horrible image she was reliving in her mind.

"Are you okay?"

"I'm fine. I'm just fine."

She didn't seem fine.

"So you're here by yourself?" I asked. "Where do you live?"

"In a house."

"Do you have security, or do you just drive around by yourself?"

"I don't need security. These people know I'm on their side, they would never . . ."

She didn't finish the sentence. Her mind drifted off to some other place.

I stayed for a moment to make sure she really was okay. She just swayed back and forth to the music, her eyes focused somewhere far away.

Marla died the next year. She and an Iraqi translator were driving the treacherous road to the Baghdad airport when their car was hit by a roadside bomb. Marla was twenty-nine years old.

* * *

I LEFT THE PARTY AT around midnight to make my way up to the workspace. A live feed of the *Nightly News* was available from one of the satellite dishes there.

Because of the time difference, *Nightly* came on while most of Baghdad slept. We typically watched a tape of the show the following morning, but I wanted to make sure the wedding story had actually made it into the show and looked okay.

It was often nerve-racking seeing my stories air for the first time. Because of the limited staff in Baghdad, the editing of stories—combining video, sound bites, narration, etc.—happened back in the States. I recorded my voice to tape in Baghdad, then all of the raw video was sent with my voice to Atlanta, where an editor and a producer would do the edit.

As a result, I saw my work for the first time along with about 10 million other people. If something went awry—a forgotten sound bite or a wrong video used to cover a segment of the story—it would be too late to fix it.

I was pleased with the wedding spot, which was the first positive story I had managed to get on the air in my two weeks in Baghdad.

Satisfied, I went back to my room, double-checked that my body armor was in position on the chair next to my bed, and went to sleep.

THE FIRST THING RAFRAF DID upon arrival at the bureau the following morning was find the tape of the *Nightly News* and watch the wedding story.

She was unimpressed. "I thought there would be more," she told Madeleine, who had produced the story with us.

Madeleine had a funny habit of twirling her sandy blond hair with her fingers. During times of intense concentration or stress, she actually twirled with both hands.

"I think we crammed a lot into two minutes." Madeleine was only twirling with one hand. "You didn't like the story?"

"It was okay," Rafraf said.

She didn't know why the story disappointed her. Perhaps it was just her aversion to getting married? Still, she was pleased to see a story that she was so deeply involved with get on the air.

If this kept up, she thought, maybe NBC would make her a producer too.

Don had already requested her for another story the next day, and she was eager to show her skills again.

ELEVEN

THE SCHOOL

I t had once been one of the better schools in Baghdad. The middle school stood proudly—a two-story, gleaming structure of white brick and concrete.

Dirt streets led in all directions away from the school. Just across the road, single-level houses built of concrete sat dwarfed by the immense school.

When the wind blew, which was always, the dirt from the roads and the yards would swirl into dust devils. A thin layer of dirt covered everything.

Everything, that is, except the school. It was brand-new. Not a streak on any window or a crack in any wall. It featured an arched entryway into a central courtyard, and arched windows repeating the theme.

The school, Rafraf knew, had been considered a showcase by Saddam Hussein. The neighborhood—in an agricultural area about twelve miles southwest of central Baghdad—was home to those who'd worked at one of Saddam's presidential palaces nearby. The workers were largely unskilled: housecleaners, lawn mowers, and handymen. They weren't highly paid but their children had been rewarded with one of the finest schools in Iraq.

From this school, Iraqi troops launched surface-to-air missiles and other antiaircraft fire at U.S. warplanes during the opening days of the war. The Iraqi military had used schools and even hospitals as antiaircraft and ammunition storage sites. In some instances, munitions were also discovered near mosques.

As a result, American warplanes trying to destroy the antiaircraft guns would also destroy the schools they were located in. Bombs, after all, were only so precise.

But this school had been given a new life.

A Civil Affairs unit from the U.S. Army Reserve had spent much of the past year, and several hundred thousand dollars, rebuilding the school. It was part of the effort to "win the hearts and minds" of Iraqis. The school was, by all accounts, better than new.

"This is the kind of story I came here to tell," Don said to Rafraf as the convoy of two NBC Suburbans wove through the morning traffic.

It was considered a risk to drive anywhere in or around Baghdad at the time, but the school was located in what was considered a relatively docile area.

Rafraf was somewhat amused by Don's enthusiasm. It was, after all, just a school. And it wouldn't have needed rebuilding if the Americans hadn't blown it up in the first place.

They passed Rafraf's neighborhood along the way. She could just see her house down the road, but decided not to say anything.

It was February 16, 2004. The violence in Baghdad had grown more intense by the day, but this day was supposed to be fun. Rafraf was pleased to be working on a story that didn't involve bodies in the street.

A short time later, after turning off the main highway and taking a long dirt road south, they arrived at the school. A low concrete wall surrounded the school; a large concrete gathering area between the wall and main building also served as a parking lot. A double set of iron gates were opened to allow the news vehicles in.

The journalists were escorted to the school by three U.S. army

Humvees. Soldiers manned M60 machine guns atop each of the vehicles, which remained parked on the road near the gate.

Also outside the gate were dozens, perhaps hundreds, of young men. Many stood with their arms folded across their chests, or hands on their hips. Some of the men smiled and waved as our Suburbans entered the school. None of them seemed to have a better place to be that day.

The soldiers had invited NBC News to the school to see for themselves how much Iraqis appreciated the effort the United States was undertaking to rebuild the shattered country. A brief ceremony was planned in which the commander of the Civil Affairs Battalion would hand over the keys to the school to the principal.

The soldiers laughed and even kicked soccer balls with children who would soon attend the school. Schoolteachers, soldiers, journalists, and children enjoyed chocolate cake, Coca-Cola, and ice cream, and smiles were plentiful.

It was a pleasant, warm day.

Rafraf translated as Don interviewed some of the students. She liked children and was happy to be surrounded by so many of them. They were happy to have their school back, but, like any kids, were not thrilled about actually going back to class. They said the American soldiers who had helped rebuild the school were nice and would give them candy sometimes.

Rupert discussed the security situation with the soldiers. The army had promised the visit to the school would be under the tightest of security. They said there was nothing to fear in this neighborhood because the people here knew the United States was trying to make things better for them.

Rupert was so sure of the safety of the situation that he told everyone they could leave their body armor and helmets in the vehicles.

Babak, who was producing the story, rounded up other people for Don to interview. He also helped out another news crew that would only be in Baghdad for three days.

The crew and correspondent, Rafraf learned, were from NBC's Spanish-language network, Telemundo. Rafraf helped them too, impressing them not just with her English skills, but with a workable knowledge of Spanish. She had learned Spanish in college, but rarely had an opportunity to use it.

The cake eating and interviews lasted almost two hours.

"It's about time to get out of here," Rafraf heard the army commander tell the journalists.

"Okay," Babak replied. "We've just got one quick interview left and we're ready to go."

The iron gates opened, and the soldiers began piling into their Humvees.

Nobody noticed that the crowd of Iraqi men was no longer gathered around the gates to the school. The dirt road, which was packed with people just moments earlier, was empty.

THE FINAL INTERVIEW WAS WITH the leader of the neighborhood where the school was located. I had Rafraf ask if it was okay to call him a mayor so viewers in the United States would understand his title. He said yes.

We stood with the mayor in front of the school so it could be seen in the background of the interview. Rafraf, a soundman, two cameramen, and I were all facing him, with our backs to the iron gates about one hundred feet away.

Suddenly my ears were on fire. Instant, tremendous pain enveloped my head, followed by a high-pitched ringing. I saw the mayor's eyes go wide with fear. A millisecond later my brain registered the explosion.

Boom!

It was so close—right in front of the gate!

I felt the concussion push my body toward the school.

I turned instinctively toward the noise and saw the fireball, with smoke billowing into the air. The smoke rose high above the nearby palm trees, perhaps a hundred feet or more.

I saw bodies on the ground, but couldn't tell if they were hurt or diving for cover.

Then came the sound of broken glass. The windows of the school shattered and crashed down around us. Bits of metal and dirt fell from the sky.

A three-foot brick wall was next to the school a few yards away. A split second after the blast, I ran for the wall and dove behind it. Others around me were doing the same thing. We all expected a barrage of gunfire or perhaps another bomb.

Everyone, except Rafraf. She hadn't moved a muscle. I saw her standing exactly where she had been when the bomb went off. She seemed frozen with shock. Her face registered the fear and confusion, but somehow the signal to run hadn't made it from her brain to her feet.

"Rafraf," I yelled, "come here!" She turned and looked at me, tears streaming down her face.

I remembered countless nightmares I had endured over the years when something chased me but I couldn't run. I imagined she was living through such a nightmare. Everything around her was chaos, but she stood statue still in the middle of it looking frail and paralyzed.

I stood and motioned frantically for her to come behind the wall.

"What happened?" she cried.

"Just get over here, there could be an ambush or another bomb."

I felt guilty for not grabbing her and pulling her with me when I dove for cover. Everything just happened so fast, we were all acting on instinct. Her instinct was to freeze in place.

Thankfully, Rafraf finally rushed over and crawled next to me behind the wall.

Out on the road, the soldiers got out of their vehicles to check on the wounded. I could see at least one soldier lying on the ground, but I couldn't tell if he was seriously injured or just dazed from the blast.

What happened next both terrified and infuriated me.

The crowd of Iraqi men that had so quickly vanished before the blast suddenly reappeared. Many were shouting and raising their fists in the air in anger.

I expected the soldiers who had escorted us into the school to at least look our way to make sure we were okay. They had, after all, promised to provide security.

Instead, they jumped into their vehicles, pointed their machine guns toward the angry mob, and roared away down the dirt road. They were gone within sixty seconds of the bombing. I guessed it was their standard operating procedure to immediately leave a potential ambush, but what about us?

We were on our own. Stunned, surrounded, and in deep trouble. We had several serious problems.

First, we had to get back to our vehicles. The two Suburbans were parked right next to the gate, about seventy-five feet from our hiding position. One of the SUVs had a broken windshield, but both were otherwise intact despite being just a few yards from the bomb when it went off.

Second, once we got to the vehicles, we would have to get through the gates, past the crowd, and out of the area before whoever set off the bomb decided to finish the job.

Finally, we would have to survive the ambush that we all knew awaited us just down the road.

I saw Rupert crawling toward our Suburbans. He had his 9 mm in one hand, and a radio in the other.

"We have to go," I said to Rafraf. "We've got to get out of here now."

This time, she didn't need any encouragement. It was too far to crawl to the SUVs, so we both took off at a dead run. I grabbed the cameraman's tripod along the way. I figured if we survived, he'd appreciate having his $3,000 piece of equipment with him. I didn't think much of it at the time, but later it dawned on me that weighing myself down with a heavy tripod shouldn't have been a high priority while fleeing for my life.

In the army, we were taught that people fight the way they train.

If you do something often enough in peacetime training, you'll do it automatically in battle—even when bullets are flying. After fifteen years as a TV reporter, I was well trained at carrying tripods.

We made it safely to our Suburbans and dove to the ground next to Rupert and his gun.

"I can't bloody believe it," Rupert said. I could tell he felt it was somehow his fault that we were attacked. Of course it wasn't, but that's the kind of guy Rupert is.

"Do you think there's another bomb out there?" I asked.

"It's likely. I'm surprised they're not shooting at us yet. I'll bet they open up when we hit the road."

That was all the convincing I needed. I opened the back door of the SUV and started grabbing body armor and helmets. I threw everything I could find out of the vehicle. Rupert and our camera crew quickly donned their gear. The crew members from the other SUV did the same thing.

Less than two minutes had passed since the blast. It seemed much longer, but time slows down during times of high stress. I knew driving through the gates, through the growing crowd of Iraqis, would be the most dangerous event in my life.

Then I noticed Rafraf; she was crouched next to me, silently awaiting the order to jump into the vehicle.

"Where's your body armor?" I asked, noticing for the first time that she wasn't wearing any.

"I don't have a vest," she said. "It's at the hotel."

I unleashed a string of profanity. "How could you not have body armor?" I demanded. "Everybody is supposed to have it!"

"Well, I don't have it with me. It's okay, let's go."

It clearly wasn't okay. I let loose another string of profanity. Rafraf needed to be protected.

"Time to go," Rupert interjected. Everyone began loading into the SUVs.

"You're wearing mine," I finally said. I took off my gear and began to put it over Rafraf's head.

"No!" she said. "You have a family. It's yours."

"Look, you're here because of me. I'm not going to let you get killed just because I wanted to do a story. Now put on the freakin' body armor."

"It's not right."

I tightened the Velcro straps around her. It was way too big for her, but the Kevlar and ceramic plates would do the job. She tried to protest again.

"Look," I said, "don't get me wrong, I'm not planning to get killed either. I'll sit in the middle seat. If they start shooting, I'll hide behind you."

I was trying to lighten the mood. That is, if threatening to use a 110-pound woman as a human shield is lightening the mood.

It worked.

"Okay. You can hide behind me." She offered the least convincing smile I had ever seen.

We climbed into the SUVs.

Someone opened the gates and we roared out onto the dirt road.

RAFRAF COULDN'T BELIEVE INSURGENTS HAD set a bomb off at a school opening! She tried not to cry, but couldn't help herself.

Who were the targets? The military, the reporters, the children? None of it made any sense.

She dared a peak out of her window as the SUV turned onto the dirt road. She didn't see any dead bodies on the ground, but the blast had been so big . . . and close.

She didn't see children anywhere. Where had they all gone? Did someone warn them of the blast ahead of time?

The exact location where the bomb had been buried was obvious. It was directly across from the front gate of the school, just on the other side of the road. Metal construction debris surrounded a small crater in the dirt road.

Rafraf had noticed the pile of debris when she first entered the school. She thought it was piled up to await pickup by a cleanup crew.

Now she knew the truth; the metal debris was intended to kill people.

The bomber had buried a ten-pound block of a military explosive called C-4 beneath the surface of the road, then used the metal to cover up his handiwork. The apparent goal was to turn the bits of steel, iron, glass, and aluminum into shrapnel. The construction debris would increase the lethality of the blast, and if it worked as planned, the shrapnel would kill dozens of people.

Rafraf wondered how many of the angry young men gathering around the blast site had known it would happen. Word must have spread ahead of time; there was no other explanation for the lack of bodies on the ground.

Then she remembered her digital camera. She had been taking snapshots throughout the day and realized it was still in her hand. She knew from experience that the camera attracted the wrong kind of attention in situations like the one she was currently in. But she couldn't help herself.

As the SUV passed the blast site, she raised the camera and snapped a picture. If she survived this day, she would want to remember it.

Then she scooched down as low as possible in the seat and leaned against Don. She wanted to be as far away from the door, and the angry mob outside it, as possible.

Don pulled her away from the door. She tried to wipe her tears with her other hand but suddenly realized he was holding it as he shielded her.

Is he trying to protect me? she thought to herself. *Or hide behind me?*

A moment later, he abruptly let go of her. As she sat up, she caught Ibrahim's eye in the rearview mirror.

He didn't look happy.

*   *   *

WE WERE SUPPOSED TO DIE that day. That was the insurgents' plan.

We learned from the military a few days later that the reason we hadn't been killed was because the bomber planted his explosive too deep in the ground.

Because of the depth of the hole, the force of the blast sent the shrapnel flying upward, instead of horizontally through all of our bodies.

What's more, there had indeed been a second bomb. It was identical to the first and was designed to kill us as we tended to the victims of the first blast, or tried to escape.

An army ordnance team found the second bomb buried about fifty feet from the first. It was the same size, ten pounds of military-grade plastic explosive (C-4), with a detonator that could be triggered remotely.

The second explosive was wrapped in Styrofoam . . . Styrofoam that had hundreds of nails and bits of sharp metal embedded in it.

The bomb was not buried as deep as the first. If it had gone off, it would have killed or seriously injured all of us.

"You got lucky," one of the soldiers said over the phone. "The detonator must have malfunctioned."

I SUPPOSE IT COULD HAVE been luck, but to me the incident at the school had God's fingerprints all over it. I believe he can and does intervene in human events. I don't pretend to understand his timing or his ways, but I believe God allows some things for a purpose.

But what purpose? I thought to myself.

That night, I prayed and thanked God for protecting me. I thanked him for giving me the strength to believe in him in the first place, and I thanked him for sparing my family the anguish of losing me on a dirt road in southern Baghdad.

"I guess you brought me here for a reason," I said.

I promised to get out of God's way and let him reveal that reason to me. I promised to continue trusting him.

I thanked God for faulty detonators.

TWELVE

FAMILY

The job was beginning to take its toll on Rafraf. It wasn't just the growing dangers she faced; the biggest stress came from her family.

Her father was having second thoughts about her work for the Americans. At first he was so thrilled to have money pouring into the family that it didn't matter. But by late February his attitude had changed.

On February 20, four days after the bombing at the school, the phone in the bureau rang. Rafraf was shocked to learn it was Kamal calling for her.

How did he even get this number? she thought to herself.

"Come home now," her father commanded. "You are finished working for the Americans."

"I can't, they need me here." The truth, Rafraf thought, was that she needed them.

"You are making me look bad," he insisted. "It's not right for a daughter to work like you are. You make more money than me, but you live in my house. I would rather not have the money than suffer this humiliation anymore."

Rafraf understood what her father was going through, but she wasn't ready to give up her newfound independence. Perhaps that's why she spoke to him in a way she would never have before surrounding herself with Americans. She respected her father, but not enough to do as he wished. Maybe the Americans were changing her.

"Then I won't live in your house," she said plainly. "I'll live with my sister, or here at the hotel. They say it would be safer for me here anyway."

Rafraf had spent a few nights at the hotel in previous months. Usually nights when work on a story went late, or she had to leave early on a long drive the next morning. NBC had plenty of spare rooms and thought nothing of putting her up in one.

For Rafraf, staying at the hotel was the lap of luxury. She had never before slept in a proper bed. Even while working for NBC and making more money than anyone else in her family, Rafraf still slept on a thin mat on the tile living-room floor with her sister.

She still had just as many chores at home as ever, even while supporting the family financially. Before she could leave for work every day, she had to wake up early and iron her brother's police uniform.

Ayser considered it beneath his dignity to iron his own uniform. That was women's work, and Ayser always seemed to think Rafraf's job was to do whatever he wanted. She did her best to avoid him, but couldn't avoid the stupid uniform. Every day, it was hers to iron.

He also told Rafraf things that she didn't want to hear.

Just a few weeks earlier, Ayser confided in Rafraf that he was dating a woman from across the city, and he planned to marry her.

"Have you told Mom and Dad?" Rafraf asked.

"No, they would never accept it."

"Then why tell me?" she asked suspiciously. Rafraf knew the answer. Ayser hoped she would accidentally reveal the wedding plans to one of their parents. Their rage would be directed at her for trying to keep the secret, rather than at him.

"Because I have to tell someone," he said, "and I know you will not tell them."

* * *

THERE WERE MANY SECRETS IN Rafraf's house. Secrets about money, about relationships, about politics. For as long as she remembered, Rafraf had considered trying to keep secrets an overarching theme of her life.

During childhood, it was an us-against-them game between the children and their parents. But as they grew older, the gamed turned serious.

When she was in high school, Rafraf had involved her favorite younger brother, Rami, in a dangerous secret.

She and Rami were supposed to be going to a neighborhood Baath Party meeting. But Rafraf used the opportunity to sneak away and see her boyfriend, leaving the thirteen-year-old Rami to cover for her absence.

His cover story worked for the meeting, but Jamila was suspicious. She had a feeling Rafraf was sneaking around and went to Rami for the truth.

"Where was your sister this afternoon?" she interrogated.

"She was at the meeting with me," Rami lied.

He watched in horror as his mother got up from the kitchen table where the two were sitting.

"I don't think she was." Jamila took a large knife from a kitchen drawer and walked with it to the stove. "You know what happens if you lie to me."

Rami's eyes grew wide with fear. He watched his mother light one of the burners on the stove, then hold the blade of the knife in the fire.

"I'm not lying," he insisted. "She was with me at the meeting."

"Put your arms on the table," Jamila ordered.

The knife was glowing hot. She returned to the table and sat down, placing the knife down next to Rami's arm. It was so close he could feel the heat.

"Where was your sister?" she asked again.

"She was with me," he pleaded as tears streamed down his cheeks. "I swear."

Rafraf could hear the conversation from the next room. She knew exactly what was happening. She had undergone the same questioning plenty of times.

Don't tell her, she said to herself, *it will only make it worse for both of us.*

She felt guilty for putting her little brother in this situation, but she was also proud of him for trying so hard to protect her.

A moment later she saw a crying Rami run to the bathroom. His mother had not burned Rami with the knife but had sufficiently terrified him.

"You should thank your brother," Jamila said to Rafraf matter-of-factly. "He really does love you."

Rafraf knew it had been wrong to have Rami lie for her. Yes, she had been selfish, but she wasn't trying to get him in trouble. She thanked him later that night and promised she would never put him in such a situation again.

BUT WHILE RAMI LOVED HIS sister, Rafraf suspected her oldest brother, Ayser, loved only himself. He seemed to purposefully put Rafraf in situations that would get her in trouble.

That, she assumed, was why he told her of his secret wedding plans. Even so, that he planned to get married was the best news she'd heard in years.

Maybe he'll finally move out, she thought to herself, *and someone else can iron his uniforms.*

She had other chores at home. She cleaned, looked after her younger siblings, and helped her mother make bread in a clay oven in the backyard every evening.

But at the hotel, Rafraf's time was her own. She could relax, even watch TV in her own room, and, more important, sleep on a real bed.

Someday, Rafraf thought, *I'll have a bed of my very own.* Her dreams for her future were no bigger than that.

There was no way she was quitting. She told her father he was just going to have to get over it and hung up the phone.

She didn't go home again until the next day, when she knew Kamal was at work. She rummaged through her belongings, grabbed enough clothing to last a week, and left.

TWO DAYS LATER, RAFRAF'S MOTHER had a heart attack and had to be rushed to the hospital. Jamila had been shopping at the market when she ran into a neighbor.

"So your son is getting married," the woman had said. "Congratulations are in order, though I wonder if it was necessary for him to look so far from our neighborhood for a bride."

The news sent Jamila reeling. She had battled high blood pressure for several years and had even had episodes with her heart before. But nothing like this.

The shock and humiliation were too much for her to bear. She passed out right there at the market and didn't regain consciousness until she had reached the hospital.

Rafraf had kept her brother's secret. And it almost cost her mother her life.

THE PHONE AT THE BUREAU rang off the hook the day after the bombing at the school. The president of NBC News called to make sure everyone was okay.

Executives at all levels called to say "hang in there."

They asked if I wanted to cut my tour in Baghdad short and go home early.

"No one would blame you if you did," they said.

Ann Curry from the *Today* show called to show her support. My report on the school bombing, she said, had frightened her and just about everyone else who had seen it.

Two of our cameras had been rolling when the bomb exploded at the school. The whole incident had made for interesting television. There was even a shot of me running toward the SUV carrying the $3,000 tripod.

One of the cameras that was rolling was pointing at Rafraf when the bomb went off. It caught, in close-up, the exact moment when a young woman thought she was going to die. The lens only pointed at her for a second before the cameraman dove for cover, but that second captured the fear, regret, panic, and sadness that had frozen Rafraf in place. It was a haunting image.

There was no way I would leave Iraq early. I knew Kiki and the girls wanted me home—I wanted to be home—but I also wanted to leave feeling I had accomplished something. I still had nearly two weeks left before my scheduled departure in March, and I had a lot of stories in the works.

But all that talk of leaving started me thinking. I would soon get to go back to my normal life; people would stop trying to kill me. Rafraf would still be in Baghdad. The bombing at the school would be just one of many attempts on her life. She had already survived more close calls than most people experience in a lifetime.

The bombing at the school had sealed a bond between Rafraf and me. I began thinking of her as a friend, and I was worried for her safety. Somewhere in the recesses of my brain, I wondered if God had something in mind for Rafraf, and if I was supposed to play a part.

I NEEDED TO BURN OFF some anxious energy. A couple of days had passed since the bombing at the school, but my body seemed to still be pumping adrenaline. Fortunately, the Baghdad bureau had just the thing.

On the fifth floor of the hotel was a room with a huge outdoor balcony. Much more than a balcony, the outdoor area was really the roof of an angled part of the building below. It was at least seven hundred square feet and surrounded by a low concrete wall.

Fitness being an important part of survival in Baghdad, the security guys had turned the outdoor area into a well-equipped gym. There was a punching bag, a large mat for stretching and calisthenics, a weight bench, free weights, and dumbbells.

I headed for the gym shortly after sunset.

The balcony had lights but I turned them all off. The last thing I wanted was to be shot by a sniper while doing arm curls or stomach crunches.

Al Hamra was widely known as the hotel housing NBC, and a growing number of Western journalists. A rumor had also been floating around Baghdad that a contingent of Jewish journalists from Israeli television were in the hotel. It wasn't true, but our security team said the rumor alone could be enough to bring on an insurgent attack. Israelis were not welcome in Baghdad.

The sounds of the city filled my ears as soon as I opened the sliding glass doors to the outdoor gym. Honking horns, the belch of diesel truck engines . . . it sounded like any big city in the world.

Except for the gunfire.

Pop. Pop. Pop.

It was off in the distance.

"Nothing to worry about," I said to myself. "Sound travels farther at night, and someone's always shooting at something in Baghdad."

I did some push-ups to warm up my arms and chest, then went to work on the bench.

Using free weights is noisy. There's a lot of clanging as the bar is lifted up and down and the weights bang against one another. Add to that my heavy breathing, and it made sense that I didn't hear the gunfire getting closer.

BANG. BANG.

There was no missing that! The guns were much louder now, and I could hear shouting.

"Not good," I said to myself.

I rolled off the bench and crawled toward the low wall overlooking the street. The chances were good that whoever was shooting wouldn't be looking up toward the fifth floor. I figured it was safe enough for a quick peek.

Two men were running on the street below. They wore dark, civilian clothing and carried AK-47s. I saw one of them duck behind a tree, the other crouched down behind a parked car.

I wasn't sure why, but they didn't look as if they knew what they were doing. They had the look of criminals on the run. But from whom?

I looked farther up the street and saw the answer. A squad-size infantry unit of about ten men was working its way toward the hotel. I couldn't tell from my vantage point if the troops were American or Australian, but I recognized the "bounding overwatch" technique they were using to close in on the gunmen.

I decided the soldiers were mostly likely Australian because an Aussie infantry battalion was stationed in a building under construction near our hotel. I had seen them patrolling, and even training on the surrounding streets. But what I saw this night definitely wasn't training.

The soldiers had split up into two fire teams. One team of five would bound forward ten or twenty yards while the other team stayed in place to provide cover fire if necessary. The squad never made a sound, silently leapfrogging from one cover position to the next, methodically closing the distance to the gunmen.

"I know who's gonna win this," I said to myself.

The gunmen came to the same realization. One of them yelled something, then both of them sprinted from their hiding positions toward a large lawn dotted with trees across from the hotel.

BANG!

A shot was fired but the gunmen kept moving.

It seemed obvious to me how this was going to end, and I had no desire to see it. I crawled back toward the weight bench and tried not to think about what was happening on the darkened street below.

A few minutes later, I heard a half dozen or more gunshots in rapid succession. I never crawled back to the low wall to see what happened.

It made me think once again of Rafraf. Would she die on a street, or in some vacant lot in Baghdad? My mind flashed back to the videotaped image of her face when the bomb exploded. I remembered her standing frozen, with smoke rising behind her, and glass falling from windows.

Suddenly, I realized why I was in Baghdad. My purpose was to get Rafraf out!

God had something in mind for Rafraf, and it wasn't for her to die at the hands of Iraqi insurgents.

THIRTEEN

THE GRAY CAT

Sometimes I feel like a minor character in the story of my own life. Not that I'm not important; I mean, I do pay the bills and stuff like that, but the real stars of my life story are my girls, Rachael and Madison, and my wife. If you think that makes me the best supporting actor, you're still wrong. That role belongs in various degrees to animals.

Kiki loves animals. Not just a little. During our twenty years together, I've lost track of the number of animals she's adopted, rescued, or fostered.

Here's a partial list: six horses, five dogs, two cats, numerous hamsters, a cockatoo, three ducks, a rooster, and a miniature donkey named Brewster. All have been nursed to health, fed, housed, trimmed, trained, vet checked, and loved before being sent to new homes with responsible owners.

Okay, all except the donkey. Brewster still lives with us because he's a really good donkey and he makes us laugh.

I, on the other hand, tend to adopt people. Sometimes just for a day or two, sometimes much longer.

When I was a young reporter in Wichita Falls, Texas, I interviewed a man who was riding his horse from Natchez, Mississippi, to California. He looked like a cowboy from the old West—handlebar mustache, crumpled cowboy hat, and all.

"You'd be surprised what you see along the side of a road from horseback," he told me.

"Like what?" I asked.

"Just stuff. You also meet some darn nice people."

"What do you do with your horse at night?"

"Sometimes we just camp off the road. I'll tie him up to a tree. Usually people let me put him up for the night in their barn. Lots of people have barns."

"How about tonight?"

"Don't rightly know." He talked like a cowboy too.

"Well, my wife and I have horses," I said. "We keep them at a barn not far from here. I'll bet you can keep your horse there tonight."

Then I went too far, speaking as men sometimes do before first checking with their wives.

"And you can stay at our house," I offered. "We've got a spare bedroom."

"Don't you need to check with your wife first?" he prodded, clearly trying to save me from myself.

"No, of course not. She'll think it's a great idea."

But she didn't.

"You're kidding, right?" she asked when I told her the good news on the phone.

"No, I'm bringing him home after work. You'll like him."

Kiki was less than thrilled, but she went along. "Sure, bring him home."

What Kiki remembered, and I had forgotten, was that I had military duty with the Army Reserve the next day. That meant I would be up and out of the house by four o'clock in the morning, leaving my wife and one-year-old daughter alone in the house with a complete stranger.

I was in the running for the worst-husband-ever award, but Kiki handled it.

She fixed the cowboy pancakes, bacon, and eggs the next morning and sent him on his way well fed and rested.

"I've been on the road for a long time," he told Kiki as she drove him back to the barn. "Nobody's ever let me sleep in their house. I don't know how to thank you."

"You just did."

We had only been married for a couple of years, but the traveling cowboy taught us something about ourselves. Kiki and I actually liked opening our home to people in need.

When her younger sister Jessica became pregnant, we didn't hesitate. Jessica was unmarried and didn't earn enough money to raise a baby on her own.

"Of course she can live with us," I told Kiki. "As long as I don't have to change diapers."

Jessica stayed with us through her pregnancy and until her son was six months old.

We all changed diapers.

But even with our "open-house" policy, I knew the call to Kiki from Baghdad would be a surprise.

"So remember that girl I was telling you about?" I began.

"Rifraf something or other."

"*Raf*raf. Anyway, she's really nice and smart, and the thing is, she's not going to survive if she keeps working for NBC."

"And?"

"And, well, I haven't asked her about this," I said cautiously, "but if we could find a way to get her to the U.S., do you think she could stay with us awhile?"

The silence on the other end of the phone was deafening. It occurred to me that most men don't just call up their wives and ask if it's okay to have a twenty-three-year-old woman move into their guest room.

Instead of answering directly, Kiki reminded me of a dream I had had during my first trip to Iraq. She wrote down her dreams every day in a journal; she wrote down mine too when I mentioned them to her.

"You dreamed you were swimming down a muddy river," she began, "and you knew the river was in Iraq. When you reached the mouth of the river, where it emptied into the sea, you came across two cats. Do you remember?"

"Vaguely." I had never given more than a passing thought to dreams or their possible significance. I only told Kiki about my dreams when they were so powerful I had to tell someone.

"Well," she continued, "in your dream you had to choose between the two cats. One was black and the other was gray. You wanted to bring the gray cat home, but the black cat wanted to sharpen its claws on the gray. That's the phrase the black cat used."

"Are you saying Rafraf is the gray cat?"

"I don't know. It was your dream. But I wrote the dream down for a reason. You told me that morning that the dream meant you would have to make a choice in Iraq. That it might be a choice of life or death."

"I should pay more attention to my dreams."

"That's why I write them down."

"So what are you saying?" I finally asked.

"I'm just saying be careful," she said sincerely. "We don't really know anything about her. If you think God is telling you to do this, then the answer is yes. If we can really help her, then I'm all for it. But we just need to be careful."

"All right. She may not even want to leave, or her parents might not let her go. But I wanted to make sure and talk to you about it before I even bring up the idea."

Was Rafraf the gray cat looking for a home, or was she the black cat—a destructive force bent on causing trouble? Kiki's mention of the dream bothered me, but I couldn't pinpoint why. I reminded myself that dreams sometimes don't mean anything at all, but even I wasn't convinced.

If God wants it to happen, I reasoned, doors will open.

*   *   *

IT HAD NEVER OCCURRED TO Rafraf that she might be able to leave Iraq. She was unhappy with the life she knew and sometimes even allowed herself to dream of a new life. But in reality, she never actually believed she would ever be allowed anything else.

She dreamed. She didn't believe.

But when Don spoke about her future, it suddenly seemed anything was possible.

"If we could find a way to get you out of Iraq and into the U.S.," he began tentatively, "would you be interested in going?"

"How would that happen?" Rafraf replied suspiciously.

"To be honest, I have no idea. But you have something to offer. I'll bet we could convince a university to give you a scholarship or something. Surely they'd see that having you in their school would help other students. It's how cultures get to know each other."

Rafraf was bursting on the inside, for the first time in her life contemplating an actual future. One that didn't involve marriage, ironing, and doing as she was told.

"Do you think your parents would let you go?" Don asked.

Rafraf knew her father wouldn't stand for it, but her mother might just accept the idea of her making something better of herself. Jamila could be a hard woman at times, but Rafraf knew her mother loved her. Jamila was always the one pushing Rafraf to get an education. She would see the benefit of her daughter's going to an American college.

"I'll talk to my mother," Rafraf answered finally.

"AND WHAT DO YOU KNOW about this Don?" Jamila asked cautiously. She and Rafraf were preparing dinner in the kitchen.

"He seems very nice," Rafraf said. "He has a wife and two daughters. He says his house is big, and I would have my own room and bathroom."

"In exchange for what?" her mother asked suspiciously. "How do you know anything about his intentions? He's an American. Look outside! You see them running around the streets with guns, and now you want to go there?"

"I think he's honest."

"And this family. They're Christians? You've seen the same American movies I have. There are no morals there. God is either a joke to them or an obsession. What about your culture, your religion?"

"We talked about that. He says I can worship as I please. He looked on the Internet. There are mosques in Atlanta, and something called an Islamic Community Center. He says he'll take me whenever I want."

"Right," her mother snipped, "like you ever go to the mosque here."

"But I pray, Mother, and I wear my scarf and follow the rules."

"And what do you expect me to tell your father? You know he won't stand for such a thing."

"He will if you say it's okay," Rafraf pleaded, "and it's not like I'm leaving forever. It would probably be just a year at the most. Don says that would be long enough for things to get better here."

"So, he really is a fool?"

A moment of silence passed as the women considered the future. Jamila looked at the young woman sitting across from her—her middle child. Rafraf tried to look mature and thoughtful but knew her mother would always see her as a child.

"I'll think of something to tell your father," Jamila finally said.

Rafraf wanted to jump for joy, but thought that would make her look even more like a child. She tried her best to control her emotions.

"Thanks," she said simply.

I WONDERED WHAT KIND OF can of worms I had actually opened.

Shortly after discussing Rafraf's situation with Kiki, I started working on a plan to get Rafraf out of Iraq. My wife had told me to trust what God was telling me and to move forward if I truly believed it was his will. I suspected Kiki had deep reservations about the journey we were about to undertake, but she kept most of them to herself.

Kiki is not a weak-willed woman. She is, in fact, the strongest person I know, male or female. She will, without hesitation, tell me exactly what I'm doing wrong if she thinks I'm really messing up. It's one of the reasons I love her. She made a conscious decision to support the Rafraf plan despite her real concerns about how it might affect the family.

Kiki also had a better sense of how difficult the process would be than I did. I figured that since NBC News was such a prominent and powerful network, pushing the proper paperwork through the system would be easy. The problem was, there *was* no system.

International travel basically requires two important pieces of documentation.

First, you need a passport, which proves you're a citizen of a certain country and have permission to leave it.

Second, you need permission to enter the country you're trying to go to. That usually comes in the form of a visa.

Rafraf faced huge obstacles getting both of those documents.

In February 2004, a functioning Iraqi government didn't actually exist. No agency existed to issue a passport, and Iraq had no international airline service. Without a valid passport Rafraf couldn't travel to another country, even neighboring Jordan or Syria, to catch a plane to the United States.

And the United States was certainly not giving entry visas to Iraqi citizens. The country was literally at war with Iraq. How could it possibly determine which Iraqis had a legitimate reason to enter the United States, and which wanted to bring the fight to American soil?

I should have considered the obstacles before I mentioned the idea to Rafraf, but I thought surely there would be a way to work things out.

I began with Karl Bostic. He had been the Baghdad bureau chief on and off for the better part of a year. He had deep connections within the U.S. government, with nongovernmental agencies, and among Iraqis.

"I think that would be a great idea," Karl told me. "Rafraf is a bright woman. At the very least we could probably find a training program for journalists. NBC might even pay for it."

Rachel Levin also offered to help. I had learned from working with her in Kuwait that Rachel is tenacious and not afraid of anything.

"I can make some calls," she said.

It was a start, but I knew months of work might be ahead.

IN THE MEANTIME, THE BAGHDAD Zoo beckoned.

By American standards, the zoo was little more than a large park with cages. But both Iraqis and Americans had big plans to make the zoo an attraction the city could be proud of.

The young woman in charge of rebuilding the zoo was Farah Marrani. Just a year earlier, Marrani was an unemployed veterinarian living in Baghdad. Iraq's secret police had shut down her practice for reasons she never quite understood, leaving her with no way to do the job she loved. Then the war came.

The Baghdad Zoo was already in bad shape after years of neglect, and the war almost destroyed it. When Baghdad fell, most of the animals in the zoo were either let out of their cages or were eaten by looters. The half dozen animals that remained—the ones too dangerous to steal—were starving.

Fortunately for the animals, Marrani saw a report about the zoo on television and decided she would save it.

I met Marrani just days after cellular phone service became active in Baghdad, and already she had two cell phones. She wore one of them with a cotton cord, wrapped around her neck like a necklace. It rang constantly—usually with offers of financial help from animal lovers around the world.

Marrani, it seemed to me, was a product of the "secular" side of Iraqi culture. She wore jeans, a fashionable top, and most notably, no head scarf. Her hair was relatively short and styled so as not to interfere with her work with animals. I wondered about her background, since she seemed so different from Rafraf. Perhaps she lived in a religiously mixed neighborhood where the stricter norms didn't apply? I didn't ask.

Marrani spoke English well, so I didn't need Rafraf to translate. As Marrani took me and my camera crew around the zoo, Rafraf simply wandered off. Marrani had hired security to protect the zoo; it was among the few relatively safe places in the city.

We caught up with Rafraf later in the day, after the interviews were finished and the camera crew was shooting b-roll.

"Where where you?" I asked. "And why are you all wet?"

Rafraf was soaked with water from head to toe.

"I was walking through the sprinklers," she said as if doing so were something normal people did.

"Should I ask why?"

"Because it's like rain. We never get rain."

"Oh. It rains a lot in Atlanta, so when you get there, you won't have to walk through any more sprinklers."

"I love it here. I used to come here when I was younger."

"Like with your family?"

"Never," she said mischievously. "I came with my boyfriend."

She went on to explain that before the war, the Baghdad Zoo was basically "lovers' lane" for young couples who couldn't be together anywhere else.

"Here nobody cared," she told me. "We could come here and actually hold hands or sometimes even kiss. It was like a safe place."

"But what if somebody you knew was here? Or somebody from your family?"

"Nobody came here but couples. Everybody knew that only couples go to the zoo. That's why we came here."

"And did you come here often?"

Rafraf smiled. "The monkeys know me well."

I couldn't help laughing.

FOURTEEN

TWO FACES OF IRAQ

B y the end of February, my plan to find positive stories was back on track. I had been awfully busy chasing the aftermath of bombings and ambushes over the previous weeks, but I had also covered the wedding story, cell phone service, the rebuilding of the school (even with the bomb), and the zoo story. With less than a week remaining in my tour, I had several other stories in the works. I was feeling pretty good that I had accomplished some of what I wanted to in Iraq.

Except for one thing . . . and it was purely personal.

When I began working for NBC News, I vowed that I would buy art whenever I traveled to some exotic or even interesting place. Shopping for art gave me something to do during my off time on the road, and more important, it would eventually fill my home with art that had stories behind it.

I brought colorful camel blankets back from Kuwait and hung them on the walls. I purchased decorative silver pieces in London, and etchings from a traditional African-American artist in South Carolina.

"Anybody want to go shopping for some paintings?" I asked nobody in particular. "I know we'll have to check with the security guys, but it would be a nice break from the grind."

"Where is there art here?" Rachel Levin asked.

"Rafraf says there's a district where all of the artists have their galleries and studios. She says nobody has thought to bomb it yet, so the artists are still there working."

"I'm in," said Babak.

"Me too," Rachel said eagerly.

To my surprise, so were the security guys. One of them had actually commissioned a painting from one of the artists a few weeks before, but had been too busy providing security for our stories to pick it up.

So the next morning, with Rafraf as our guide, we all loaded up in two cars and headed for the art district.

The district didn't look any different to me from any other commercial area in the city. We saw little more than a few blocks of tiny, nondescript storefronts on narrow streets. Prior to the war, several upscale art galleries had been in the district, but most were now closed. The remaining shops and studios looked as if they could just as easily have sold cigarettes or electronics.

As shopping trips go, it was comical. The security guys didn't want us to stay in one shop, or on one street, for more than a few minutes at a time.

When word spread that Americans were on the street, they figured an attack could be prepared against us within minutes.

So with our cars parked on the road, we all jumped out and practically ran from gallery to gallery looking for something interesting to buy. The security guys took turns either shopping or standing watch outside the galleries with their 9mm pistols. The whole scene reminded me of one of those old Keystone Kops movies—everything about the day seemed sped up and unnatural.

I found the first few galleries disappointing. The art consisted mostly of paintings of sailboats and landscapes that had nothing to do with Iraq. Many of the paintings were on black velvet—the type of kitschy art sold to tourists at theme parks.

Rafraf informed me that the artists were like factory workers on an assembly line. They painted the same painting over and over to be sold as cheap decoration for businesses or hotel rooms.

"Where are the real artists?" I asked.

I was, of course, looking for a tortured soul. A person whose passion for whatever it was that drove him or her could only be expressed through painting. I was looking for Iraq's Picasso or van Gogh. I was getting discouraged.

I was about to leave empty-handed when Rafraf spotted a name on a tiny studio sitting off to the side.

"I know that man," she said excitedly, "he's the most famous painter in Baghdad."

The sign on the door said BAHIR.

Before we entered, Rafraf explained to me that when she was a child, Bahir had a television show on which he taught painting. Every afternoon she would come home from school and watch him paint landscapes and sailboats on television.

Great, I thought to myself, *more sailboats.*

I expected more corporate copies, but when I walked into the dimly lit studio, I was stunned.

The smell of oil paint was thick in the air. Abstract paintings of women hung on the walls. The colors were dark and brooding, like the room itself. Some paintings looked like ancient story lines carved on the walls of Egyptian tombs. The paintings expressed historical, cultural, and religious themes.

This was no gallery; it was a studio of no more than two or three hundred square feet. The artist worked here and, by the looks of things, might have been where he lived too. Dozens of paintings hung on the walls; tubs and cans of paint sat on the floor next to wooden easels. A bare bulb hung from the ceiling, its light barely reaching the darkened corners.

A dark curtain hung across the back of the room hiding what I guessed was a sleeping area.

Bahir barely acknowledged us when we walked in. He was hard at work painting yet another woman's face. He worked without a model;

the face of the woman was clear in his mind, though in the abstract work she was anything but clear on canvas.

"Have a look around," he said in Arabic.

Scores of paintings were on three walls of the tiny studio. I was immediately drawn to one of the oils.

It was, as were most of the others, an abstract work. A mirror image of a woman's face, one face on the right of the canvas looking left, and on the left side of the canvas, what appeared to be the same woman, looking right.

The woman on the right was crying. Thick tears streamed down her face.

The woman on the left of the canvas had no tears. Her face, which at first looked identical to the face on the right, was in fact slightly different. The eyes and corners of her lips hinted at a smile, though no smile was actually visible.

The dominant colors of the painting were dark green and yellow. The woman had green hair, with pale yellow skin. Her cheeks were red, as if flushed with emotion. Her lips were a deeper red, the color of blood. Her eyes were pure black.

Bahir noticed us lingering over the painting and finally approached us. He was warm and friendly, with wild gray hair and an easy smile.

"I am Bahir." He offered a hand.

"I love your work," I said honestly.

He spoke enough English to understand. "Thank you. You are American?"

"Yes," I said simply. "What is this? Is there a story here?"

"Of course. It's called *Two Faces of Iraq*. You see the woman represents Iraq. See her crying?"

"Yes, thick tears."

"That was the past, under Saddam. Iraq was a country in tears for so many years."

"The one on the right is the past?" I repeated, somewhat confused.

Rafraf reminded me that unlike English, Arabic is written from right to left across a page. Likewise, if a story is told on canvas, it would also read from right to left.

"And today?" I asked, turning my attention back to the painting.

"Today, the tears are gone. She has freedom and opportunity."

"And you, are you smiling now like the woman?"

"Of course," he said, once again flashing his friendly smile.

"But it's so dangerous. So many bombings every day. Aren't you afraid?"

"No more than before. Nobody bothers a simple artist. Why would they?"

Why would they blow up children at a school? I thought to myself, but didn't say.

As I examined the painting I noticed a heart separating the two women, the only part of the painting that was symmetrical. A perfectly formed heart, the kind a little girl might use to dot an *i* in a love letter to a boyfriend.

But, like the rest of the painting, the colors of the heart had a mind of their own, changing from deep red on the right to a paler shade on the left.

"And the heart?"

"It's healing."

And there it was, I thought. The reason I had come to Iraq in the first place. I wanted to see firsthand if any good was coming from the war. I wanted to meet somebody who believed, as I did, that freedom was something worth fighting for.

But for me, the painting had even deeper meaning. Was Rafraf the woman on the canvas? Kiki and I hoped we could give her a new life, a better life than the one she knew before the war.

Two Faces of Iraq was a simple painting of a woman, yet it represented so much more. I remembered feeling Rafraf's tears on my arm as we escaped the chaos of the school.

"How much is this?" I feared the price would be more than the limited amount of cash I had available. Credit cards were meaningless in Iraq.

"Ninety dollars?" Bahir said as if unconvinced himself that a painting could command such a price.

"I'll take it."

His smile broadened even more than before.

I bought two other paintings from Bahir as well. One was another abstract painting of women's faces. The untitled work featured seven women, all in red.

The other was one of the ancient-Egyptian-looking works. It had what looked like pharaohs, chariots, religious symbols, and bizarre animals painted in a pattern around a central figure. Its title was *Babylon,* and Bahir told me it represented the religious history of Iraq.

The grand total for my three paintings was less than $200. I was pleased with myself as I watched Bahir remove each of the canvases from its wooden frame so they could be rolled and hidden in my suitcase.

I knew from talking to other journalists that the odds of actually getting home with the paintings were long. Although I had purchased them directly from the artist, had receipts, and even photos of the artist with his works, government officials in neighboring Jordan would likely consider the art "looted treasure." If airport workers in Jordan discovered the paintings, they would confiscate them. Whether they would return them to Iraq or simply sell them for a profit was another matter.

As we left the store and loaded into our cars for the ride back to the hotel, I asked Rafraf what she thought of my purchases.

"Honestly?"

"Yes." I secretly hoped she would see the significance of the work. Or at least appreciate Bahir's bold use of colors and abstract style.

"Remember the first store we went into?"

I did. It was the corporate assembly line. I had half expected to see *Elvis on Velvet* or *Dogs Playing Poker.*

"I liked the painting of the sailboat," she said simply. "You should have bought that."

*   *   *

RAFRAF COULDN'T IMAGINE WHY DON would buy such an ugly painting. She also wondered if Bahir was being entirely truthful about its meaning.

She heard him, of course, when he said the title was *Two Faces of Iraq.* She had believed Bahir when he said it.

But Rafraf knew something about the painting that Don didn't. As Bahir was removing it from the frame, she noticed writing on the back of the canvas, in Arabic. Obviously Don wouldn't know what it said, but Rafraf had no trouble reading it: *When Love Dies.*

That explained the broken heart and the crying woman. To Rafraf, the death of love made much more sense than some made-up story about the painting representing Iraq. The artist had clearly intended it, and Rafraf could feel that connection.

Rafraf wanted to be loved. But she wanted to be loved for who she really was. Why did she have to hide that from people? She hid under her scarf, hid behind her culture. *When Love Dies* was a perfect name for the painting.

Or maybe Bahir changed his mind after titling the painting. That was possible, though not likely in Rafraf's opinion.

Either way, Don seemed happy to have bought the painting that supposedly represented a healing country, but really represented the death of love. Rafraf decided she wouldn't tell him what was written on back of the painting.

Sometimes ignorance was bliss.

FIFTEEN

INSURGENTS

Kevin Sites appears to thrive on adrenaline. He's one of a handful of reporters in the world who, despite having no actual military training, fit seamlessly into the world of fighting men and women. Kevin seems unafraid of war.

Rafraf liked Kevin. He was one of the first NBC correspondents she worked with, and he treated her with respect. Not, she thought, the kind of respect that won't look you in the eye, but the kind of respect that acknowledges hard work and ability.

Kevin was a one-man show. He would spend weeks at a time embedded with American or even Iraqi military units, shooting footage himself with a small camcorder.

Kevin had been in Iraq for almost the entire month of February, though he stepped foot in the bureau only once. He lived and worked with the troops, who were trying to secure the growingly restless city of Fallujah, forty miles west of Baghdad.

He came into the bureau a few days before I was set to leave and introduced himself. He too would soon leave the country before returning in early spring, but he had one story that he needed Rafraf's help with first.

"I want to interview some insurgents," I heard him say to Rafraf.

The thought of doing so had never occurred to me. I considered it a bad idea.

"Do you think you can find some for me to talk to?" Kevin asked her.

Though the insurgency only represented a tiny fraction of the Iraqi population, most Iraqis knew, at least indirectly, of people who were involved. Rafraf assured Kevin that she could probably find someone.

"Why do you want to interview insurgents?" I asked Kevin. "That could be really dangerous."

There was no need to remind Kevin about the murder of *Wall Street Journal* reporter Daniel Pearl. All journalists knew of his terrible fate—kidnapped while investigating alleged terrorists in Pakistan and beheaded by his captors.

I barely knew Kevin, but I certainly didn't want him to meet a similar end. I was also concerned about Rafraf's involvement. Would she understand the potential danger?

"I think the American people need to know why the insurgents are fighting," Kevin said earnestly. "Americans need to know what they're up against."

"But doesn't that also give the insurgents a platform to spread their propaganda?" I asked.

"I guess it's a double-edged sword. But I get to choose what goes on the air. I have to interview them first."

By the next day, Rafraf had set up an interview with a young man who was part of the insurgency. I watched with concern as Kevin and Rafraf left the bureau to conduct the interview.

ONE OF THE CONDITIONS SET by the insurgents was that only Kevin and his interpreter be present for the interview. There would be no additional producers or even a camera crew, and more important, no security.

It would be too dangerous to get in a car with the man, so Rafraf, Kevin, and an Iraqi driver followed in a separate vehicle. The insurgent wove his vehicle through heavy Baghdad traffic heading toward what he promised would be a public area.

But something was wrong. With the NBC vehicle close behind, the insurgent left Baghdad and headed toward a remote farm outside the city. A gate led into the farm and a building sitting by itself several hundred yards from the road.

The insurgent's vehicle headed through the gate without slowing.

A wave of fear gripped Rafraf. She didn't like the look of that building at all. This was no public place.

Kevin was obviously thinking the same thing. "Stop!" he shouted at the NBC driver. "Don't go in the gate."

The driver needed no convincing about the danger of the situation. He slammed on the brakes, and the vehicle skidded to a stop outside the entrance to the farm.

"What's he doing?" Kevin asked Rafraf. "Didn't he say we were going to a public area? I don't like this at all."

The insurgent got out of his vehicle and looked back toward the gate. He waved for the journalists to follow.

"No," Kevin insisted.

"I'll call him," Rafraf said, already dialing her cell phone.

"Tell him to follow us," Kevin said.

The driver turned the vehicle around.

"Where should we go?" Kevin looked to Rafraf for the answer.

"The zoo," she said without hesitation. "Go to the Baghdad Zoo."

Less than an hour later, Rafraf translated as Kevin asked the insurgent questions in a very public area of the Baghdad Zoo. It was so public, in fact, that a police officer stopped to ask why the journalist was interviewing a man wearing a kaffiyeh covering his face. A kaffiyeh is a type of head scarf worn by some Muslim men. They often feature red-and-white, or black-and-white, checkered patterns.

"He was in the army before the war," Rafraf told the police officer. "Now he wants to join the police like you, but he's afraid of retaliation if people see his face."

"Understandable," the police officer said. If he had further suspicions, he didn't show them. He walked slowly away and the interview continued.

The young man, with his face covered to protect his identity, explained how insurgents were organized into cells all across Iraq.

"Nobody knows anybody from other cells," he explained. "We only know our controller. That way if we are caught and tortured, we can't expose the other cells."

The man went on to explain how the battle against the Americans was the holiest of causes, sanctified by Allah himself. It was, in every sense, a religious war.

"But what of killing innocent people?" Kevin asked. "Your fighters have killed hundreds of women and children. Isn't that against the Koran?"

"Anything is justified," responded the man, "if the cause is correct. Allah will approve of what we are doing! The innocent will have their reward in heaven."

Rafraf was struck by the man's anger. How could he think it was okay for innocent children to be targeted? She wished for the interview to be over, but had a terrible feeling that the end of the interview wouldn't really be the end.

RAFRAF WAS RIGHT. TWO DAYS later, the man showed up at her house.

"What do you want?" a shaken Rafraf asked the man. She couldn't believe he was standing at her front door. How did he even know where she lived?

"I've decided that I no longer consent to be interviewed," he said. "You will give me the tapes, and you will not put anything I said on American television."

"I don't have the tapes. They belong to the network. I'm just a translator."

"I don't care. You have until tomorrow morning to get me the tapes."

"I'll see what I can do."

A smug look came across the man's face. "We know where you live. Your whole family in one house? How convenient."

It was a threat and Rafraf knew it.

"I will come to the American hotel tomorrow," he continued, "and you'll give me the tapes."

"Okay. I'll get them."

The truth, she knew, was that she would never be able to get the tapes to the man. Kevin Sites had left Baghdad the day after conducting the interview, and he took the tapes with him.

The good news, if there was any, was that there would be no story. When Rafraf told Kevin of the threat, he decided not to air the interview at all. He didn't want Rafraf or her family in more danger than they were already in. He also revealed a bit of information Rafraf hadn't known.

"I got a picture of his face," Kevin told her over the phone.

"How?" Rafraf asked. "When?"

"Before he covered it up. I pretended I was messing with the settings on the video camera, but I was really getting a close-up of his face. Just in case."

It wasn't much, but Rafraf hoped it was enough to save her life.

As promised, the insurgent showed up at Al Hamra the next morning. He was unarmed, so the security guards allowed him past the checkpoints to the hotel.

Rafraf met him in the lobby.

"You're not getting the tapes," she said boldly. "And you're never going to contact me again, or anybody in my family."

"You don't know who you're dealing with," he smirked.

"As a matter of fact, I do. And not just me. We took pictures of your face. They are very close up."

A look of confusion crossed the man's face. It faded slowly into a realization of what Rafraf was saying.

"If I ever hear another word from you," she continued, "or if anything happens to my family, your picture will be on television that very night. It will also be sent to the U.S. military, and the Iraqi police. You will be dead or in prison before the sun sets."

"You're lying."

"Think what you want." Rafraf hoped the man couldn't see the fear in her eyes. She was playing a role, but was terrified inside. She could feel her hands tremble; she put them in her pockets as if they were cold.

"If you ever bother me again," Rafraf said, "you'll pay."

The man's lips parted as if he had something to say, but nothing came out.

"Go away," Rafraf said.

The terrorist walked away without another word.

Rafraf silently prayed she would never see the man again.

AT ABOUT THE SAME TIME, I was upstairs and violently ill in my hotel room.

Saying I was sick doesn't really do justice to what was happening with my body. My stomach hurt so bad I feared the monster from the *Alien* films was going to burst out of it at any moment.

I had two primary suspects for my gastrointestinal discomfort.

The first suspect had presented itself in my shower about a week prior. The hotel, or at least my bathroom, was having some type of problem with its sewage system. I noticed this, with some concern, about midway through my morning shower.

"What's that awful smell?" I practically gagged.

The answer was literally at my feet. I looked down and saw that I was standing in at least an inch of raw sewage. The vile brown mixture was actually bubbling up through the drain and filling the basin of the shower.

I jumped out of the shower with shampoo still in my hair and called the front desk.

"There's crap seeping into my shower," I said to the hotel manager. "A lot of it."

"Oh," he said with some despair, "that happens sometimes. I'll send a repairman."

The repairman came to the room, spent about an hour repairing the seal between the toilet bowl and the floor, and declared my shower problem cured.

It was cured . . . until the next morning, when I once again experienced an excrement shower.

I sincerely hoped that suspect number one wasn't responsible for my sickness a week later.

Suspect number two, food poisoning, was a much more pleasant thing to think about. The day before my stomach tried to leave my body, we had ordered chicken *schwarma* sandwiches from a new restaurant. Actually, everybody else in the bureau ordered lamb. I was the only one foolish enough to order the chicken.

"Please," I begged God while curled up in the fetal position on my bathroom floor, "let it be the chicken."

Because of my sickness, I had been only vaguely aware of the issue with the insurgent who had been interviewed. I had no idea Rafraf was meeting with the man downstairs, and she apparently didn't think I needed to know about it. She didn't say a word about the meeting.

SIXTEEN

GETTING OUT

Only one road in Iraq was more dangerous than the highway between Amman, Jordan, and Baghdad. It was the stretch of road leading from downtown Baghdad to the airport—in particular the last few miles before reaching the airport.

Baghdad International Airport sits relatively close to the city center; it's about eight miles west of the Green Zone. Because of the airport's importance, the Iraqi government had built a dedicated road—a sort of expressway—to the airport from within the congested part of the city.

In the minds of insurgents, anybody who wasn't an enemy of Iraq would not be on that road. Bombings and ambushes occurred daily, if not hourly. Dozens of people had died on the airport road.

I did my best to avoid the road as much as possible, but as my trip drew to an end, the airport beckoned.

Flying into Iraq had been impossible a month earlier. But by the beginning of March, Royal Jordanian Airlines had begun offering daily round-trip flights from Baghdad to Amman.

If there was any alternative to the twelve-hour drive out of Iraq, I wanted it. Even if the alternative meant tempting fate on the airport highway.

"You're crazy," Craig the security man said when I suggested flying out of Baghdad. "We can't protect you on a plane. The insurgents are just waiting for a chance to shoot down an airliner."

"I'd rather go through five minutes of danger getting up to altitude than twelve hours waiting for an ambush," I said. I didn't mention that with my topsy-turvy stomach, the drive to Jordan would be an unpleasant experience for everyone involved.

"Not me, mate," Craig said honestly. "I'd rather die fighting than falling out of the sky."

"Well, I'm a pilot. I'll take a blaze of glory followed by a smoking hole in the ground over being beheaded on the Internet."

Babak was sitting at his computer listening to our conversation. He was also scheduled to leave and had originally planned to drive out.

"Can I still buy a ticket?" Babak asked.

"Yeah," I said, "there are a bunch of seats."

"Count me in."

"What time is the flight?" Craig asked.

"In the afternoon." I had already bought a one-way ticket out of Baghdad. The flight was to leave the following day.

"Well, that's a positive," Craig said. "Most of the bombs and ambushes happen first thing in the morning. By noon everything has either blown up or been disarmed."

"Great," I said.

I still marveled that the most sophisticated military in the world couldn't protect a five-mile stretch of highway. I knew they were trying, but seriously, it was just five miles!

"Can we take one of the armored cars?" I asked.

"It'll be cramped with all your kit," Craig said, "but that's probably a good call."

NBC had two armored vehicles in Baghdad, but for practical reasons they were rarely used.

The problem with the largest armored vehicle was that it looked like an armored vehicle. Anonymity was a much safer alternative in most cases than armor. An obvious armored car driving through Baghdad was sure to draw fire from insurgents. It was better to not get shot at in the first place.

The second armored vehicle was a Jeep Cherokee. The relatively small SUV was made even more cramped on the inside by the bulk of the steel plates. Its biggest drawback, however, had nothing to do with functionality and everything to do with where it had been.

The Jeep spent most of its time at the NBC bureau in Tel Aviv. Armored by an Israeli company, it had all sorts of Hebrew markings on internal parts. On more than one occasion, searches of the vehicle at checkpoints had turned into tense situations after Iraqi soldiers or police spotted Hebrew words.

It would take a great deal of effort to convince the Iraqis that the journalists weren't actually Israeli spies. Eventually, it was thought, the armored Jeep from Israel would get somebody killed.

But in the winter of 2004, every way out of Baghdad carried a risk of death, so it really was a matter of picking your poison.

We decided on the Jeep, choosing to be as anonymous as possible.

LEAVING SERVED AS A REMINDER, as if I needed one, of how dangerous Baghdad was. It bolstered my determination to get Rafraf out of the country as soon as possible.

We had lunch together the day before my departure from Baghdad. We met at a restaurant just across the street from Al Hamra. The restaurant was within the security cordon set up by NBC, though it wasn't protected by a blast wall.

The other patrons in the tiny establishment were either Australian soldiers or armed security contractors, so at least there wasn't much worry of being kidnapped. Nobody Rafraf knew would ever set foot in such a restaurant, so she felt it was safe for her to be seen there with a man who was not a relative.

I told Rafraf that a number of people had already begun writing letters and making phone calls on her behalf, and that we would intensify our efforts once back in the United States. I assured her that we were all serious about doing our best to get her to the United States, even if for only a short time.

"I'm afraid," Rafraf said as we sampled the hummus.

"Of what?" I asked.

"If I go to America, people will hate me there. And I'll be ugly. At least here I'm pretty."

"You'll be pretty in America, and nobody's going to hate you."

I was trying to sound positive and encouraging, but in reality I wasn't at all convinced Rafraf would make it to the United States.

I could tell Rafraf had something else on her mind. "What's the real problem?"

She broke off a piece of flat bread and kneaded it between her fingers. "I don't know why you're doing this," she finally said. "And why would your wife let me live in your home?"

The truth was that if Rafraf didn't leave Iraq, she was going to die. I felt certain of that, and I knew Kiki felt it too. It was the primary reason Kiki had agreed to open her home to Rafraf. But it seemed too fatalistic to say so out loud, especially to Rafraf.

"Because you've got something to offer the world," I finally said. "Maybe you can teach Americans to understand Muslims, or maybe you'll come back to Iraq someday and become president. I honestly don't know what it is, but God has put you on my heart, and I figured out a long time ago I have to listen to him."

"God speaks to you?" Rafraf asked, clearly skeptical.

"Not with words. But, yes, he speaks to me."

"How, then?"

"I'm not really sure, to be honest. But if you turn to him for guidance, then stay still and listen, you'll know when he's got something to say."

"Allah never speaks to me," Rafraf said flatly.

We had talked about God before, and though we were of different faiths, we had reached a sort of detente on using *God* and *Allah* to describe the same Creator.

"Sure he has," I said, "and he's protected you."

"No. You don't know the things that have happened to me. If you did, you'd know that God doesn't care."

She was angry, but at me or at Allah? I realized that I would never know many things about Rafraf. I was afraid to imagine what she could have gone through that so convinced her Allah didn't love her.

But Rafraf loved Allah. She had told me during one of our many TextTwist sessions, and she went into great detail about the infallibility of the Koran.

"We know Jesus," she had told me. "He was a great prophet of God."

Rafraf was not an expert on Islam. She was a follower, just as I was a follower of Christianity. Her views on religion, as were mine, were personal and probably debatable among those much more knowledgeable than either of us. But I also knew she had read the Koran many times, and I wanted to know her interpretation.

"What does Mohammed say about prophets?" I probed.

"That everything they say is true."

"But didn't Jesus say that he is the only way to God? 'I am the way, and the truth and the life. No one comes to the Father except through me.'* So if you believe Jesus existed and was a prophet of God, and what he said was true, then why do you not believe that he is the way to God? Why does one need the Koran?"

"Mohammed explains that. He says Jesus' words were mistranslated. He was a prophet, but he wasn't the Messiah. His purpose was to prepare the way for Mohammed."

"So you're saying we all worship the same God?" I asked. "The God of Abraham—the God of the Bible? That's Allah? And Christians are stuck one prophet behind? We stopped listening after Jesus, so we missed out on the whole new set of rules set forth in the Koran?"

---

* John 14:6, NIV.

"Yes," Rafraf said.

"Does the Koran say God doesn't care about you?"

"No."

"Then why don't you think God loves you?" I asked sincerely.

"Because he doesn't," she said with sadness.

Now, sitting there in the restaurant, I found it odd that our conversation about life in the United States had veered back into Rafraf's sincere belief that she didn't deserve God's love.

I decided to leave it at that. I rarely discussed faith with others unless they asked, and even then I kept the subject to a minimum.

"Kiki and I both feel very strongly that we should help you. You don't have to do anything in return. That's just the way it is. You can pay us back by leading a long life. Got it?"

"Got it," Rafraf said, finally smiling.

THE DAY DON LEFT BAGHDAD was just another day at the office for Rafraf. The next correspondent, Tom Aspell, arrived in the country the night before, and he was already making plans for the stories he wanted to cover. Rafraf had work to do.

Don spent the morning packing his bags, then came to the bureau to say his final good-byes before heading to the airport.

As he had done on his arrival, he alternated between shaking hands and hugging people. He saved Rafraf until the last.

"Thanks for all the help and the conversation," he said. "Hopefully I'll see you soon, somewhere else."

"Tell your wife thank you for the CD player," Rafraf said.

Don had discovered Rafraf loved music but had no way of playing CDs. His wife bought Rafraf a CD player and somehow got it to one of the producers who'd arrived in Baghdad the day before. Kiki had also sent along a note, telling Rafraf she was praying for her.

"Of course," Don said. It was time for him to go. The others who were leaving were already heading toward the elevators. "I don't know how this works, but am I allowed to give you a hug?"

"Of course." Rafraf smiled.

The two exchanged the briefest of hugs.

"Good," Don said, seeming somewhat embarrassed. "Time to go now."

With that, he was out the door and soon to be out of Iraq.

Would he really try to get her out of the country? Rafraf couldn't know for sure, but she had the feeling things were changing for her.

She resolved to do everything possible from her end to make it happen.

WITH BAGHDAD TRAFFIC SO UNPREDICTABLE, we left the bureau several hours before the plane was scheduled to depart. The treacherous drive to the airport was all that remained of my time in Iraq.

The four-lane highway was mostly free of traffic. I was thankful that the waits were short at both military checkpoints that filtered traffic heading for the airport. With car bombings so frequent on the highway, I tensed every time our Jeep pulled alongside another civilian vehicle. I was surprised that the road didn't look scarred and filled with bomb craters.

I thought about Kiki and the girls as neighborhoods of concrete-block homes dotted with palm trees rolled past. They all sat behind a wall separating the rest of Baghdad from the highway. The five-mile drive took just fifteen minutes.

As on most days, Iraqi insurgents lobbed mortars at the airport throughout the day, but none came close enough to us to cause much alarm.

Five hours after leaving the bureau, I found myself on a twin-engine, turboprop airplane spiraling to altitude above the Baghdad airport. The pilots had determined that the best way to avoid being shot down by insurgents was to stay directly above the protected airport compound until they were out of range of most small arms and shoulder-launched missiles.

That meant climbing to altitude in a continuous, tight circle.

The pilots performed a similar maneuver upon landing in Baghdad, except losing altitude happened much faster. Those who had experienced the Royal Jordanian landing called it "the death spiral."

As the plane gained altitude, I began to relax for the first time in more than a month.

A young Iraqi man was sitting next to me on the plane. His right arm was horribly mangled and was held together by a series of pins. They protruded from the bandages covering his wounds like poles from a circus tent.

The injury was fresh, and his arm looked to be still broken in several places. He was in obvious pain, but was also fascinated by the view out the window.

"Have you flown before?" I asked, already knowing the answer.

"I'm Iraqi. Never."

"Are you going to be okay?" I asked, pointing to his arm.

He managed a pained smile. "Yes, now I think."

"Where are you going?"

"To Germany. There are doctors there who can operate on my arm."

"How did that happen?"

"I am a cameraman for an American television." His English was serviceable, but not great. "I was tooking the pictures at a demonstration. These guys shot me."

"Who shot you?"

"These guys, I don't know these guys."

"So the network you work for is sending you to Germany for surgery. Why not to the U.S.?"

"It is not possible to get a visa. America does not want Iraqis."

Great, I thought to myself. *This guy gets shot up working for Americans. A major television network can't pull strings to get him into the United States for emergency surgery, and I think Rafraf can come over just to visit?*

It was a stark reminder that Rafraf had little chance of ever setting foot in America.

"Good luck with your surgery."

"Thank you," he answered sincerely.

He turned his attention back out the window and watched in awe as Baghdad got smaller and smaller.

SEVENTEEN

TEL AVIV

There should have been a list of things all correspondents must know before being sent to Israel. In no particular order, that list might have included:

- The names and political accomplishments of every member of the current and former Israeli government . . . dating back to Moses.
- The date, casualty count, and alleged reason for every act of violence for the last sixty years. Every new act of terror or retaliation seemed to be related to a previous grievous act of terror or retaliation, so a scorecard would be helpful.
- The name of every Palestinian leader, terrorist organization, alleged terrorist, potential terrorist, and falsely accused terrorist for the past sixty years. Assassinations happened quite frequently, so again, a scorecard.
- Decent places to eat.
- Places to avoid at all cost.
- Need-to-know information.

In early April 2004—one month after my departure from Baghdad—I learned what may be the most valuable piece of information every correspondent in Israel must know. I had just returned to my hotel following a five-mile run along the beach in Tel Aviv.

Shabbat does not mean "elevator."

People who live in cities with large Jewish populations already know *Shabbat* does not mean "elevator."

One only need know that *Shabbat* is the Hebrew word for "Sabbath" to figure out why the word appears directly above *elevator* at the Hilton Tel Aviv.

I had discovered, upon checking in at the hotel, that all of the signage was written in two languages. I immediately recognized the first language as English. Score one for the American.

The second language written on all of the signs at the Hilton Tel Aviv was Hebrew.

Exit, No Smoking, Restaurant, Uneven Surface, and other common signs were written in both languages and, for the most part, made perfect sense.

In fact, Shabbat Elevator was the first sign I noticed on the day I checked in. I was quite proud that I had learned my first Hebrew word.

I learned the true meaning of the word on that Saturday afternoon in April. Five miles seemed to fly by as I zigzagged through the masses enjoying the Mediterranean Sea. I returned to the hotel, soaked with sweat but invigorated by the run and the energy of the beach.

Ding!

I heard the doors open as I rounded the corner to the bank of elevators in the lobby. A family dressed in the traditional clothing of Orthodox Jews stepped onto the elevator. I hurried to catch it before the doors closed.

I smiled pleasantly to the family as I entered, then immediately pushed the button for the fourteenth floor.

Nothing.

"That's weird," I said to no one in particular. I noticed none of the lights were lit.

I pushed the button for fourteen again, then again. Nothing.

"Which floor are you going to?" I asked.

Nobody answered. I turned and saw what can best be described as a look of bemused horror on their faces. The eldest man in the family eyed me sternly. His wife wouldn't make eye contact at all.

"You think it's broken?" I asked. The doors were still open.

One of the children, a boy of about twelve years old, shook his head almost imperceptibly. His eyes were wide with . . . what?

More people stepped on the elevator. None of them made a move for the buttons.

"Which floor?" I asked. There was that look again.

I pushed the button for fourteen once more. I heard the faintest gasp from a woman behind me.

The doors had been open an awfully long time. I was now convinced that the contraption was broken when the elevator started making noise.

Bzzzzzzz!

This awful sound was surely the buzz of an elevator that was hopelessly broken.

The doors started to close, but the buzzing continued.

The last thing I wanted was to be trapped on the elevator with all of these silent people for the rest of the day.

At the last possible second, I jumped out of the elevator. I hoped the others would save themselves and follow me out, but none did.

The doors closed. The buzzing stopped and was replaced by a muffled, but recognizable sound.

Laughter.

Had I listened closer, I would probably have learned another new word.

The Hebrew word for "idiot."

I googled *Shabbat elevator* as soon as I got to my room. The Wikipedia entry said it all:

"A Sabbath elevator is an elevator which works in a special mode, stopping automatically on every floor, to allow for the Jewish law for abstaining from using electricity on Shabbat. An elevator may be marked with a sign noting that it is specially configured for Shabbat observance."

I was still laughing at myself in embarrassment when my cell phone rang. It was Rafraf.

"I think my brother can help me get a passport," she said excitedly.

"Your brother the police officer?"

"Yes. He works in the Green Zone now, and he knows people at the passport office. He says if I give him one hundred dollars, he can get the passport done right away."

"They charge one hundred dollars for a passport?"

"No, that's for him."

"So you have to bribe your own brother?"

"It's the Iraqi way," Rafraf said matter-of-factly. "I don't care if I pay him, as long as I get the passport. Have you heard anything about the visa?"

"That's going to take a while. We've written letters to the State Department, and we've got calls out all over Washington."

"Okay," Rafraf said, sounding dejected.

In the month since I'd left Baghdad, I had made exactly zero progress in securing Rafraf a visa.

"How is Atlanta?" Rafraf continued. "Is it still cold there?"

"It was warming up when I left, but I'm not in Atlanta. I'm in Tel Aviv. They sent me here the day before Easter to cover the bureau for a while."

I didn't mention to Rafraf the toll the near constant travel was taking on my family. It felt to me, and to them, that I had been home from Baghdad for only a few days when the demands of working for an international organization seemed to take over my life again.

I had taken a week of vacation after returning home from Iraq. Kiki and I drove the girls to Disney World for some quality time together, but I never managed to relax. Kiki noted more than once that I drove way too fast on the trip from Atlanta to Orlando. The fact that I was still carrying the stress of war with me seemed like a silly thing to mention, considering Rafraf was living with the war every day.

"Israel!" Rafraf practically shouted. "Why would you go there? It's so dangerous."

"It's actually pretty nice," I said, remembering my jog along the beach. "Nothing like Baghdad, that's for sure."

"But the Jews, you have to be careful."

It was becoming a predictable theme. How do you get past such a potent combination of fear and hatred for everything Jewish?

I knew the history, of course. Israel and its Arab neighbors had been violently at odds since the tiny nation was established in 1948. There had been wars, threats of war, skirmishes, terror attacks, assassinations, and mass murder for six decades. The rest of the world had also taken sides, and Arab nations clearly fell on the side opposing Israel.

"I'll be fine," I said.

In reality, I was concerned about my safety. The Israelis had assassinated the leader of Hamas, Abdel Aziz al-Rantissi, a week into my trip, and Hamas was calling for revenge. Israeli security forces went so far as to warn Western journalists that, for the first time in memory, Palestinian extremists were plotting to kidnap American reporters in Gaza.

"I'm supposed to go to Bethlehem in the West Bank later this week," I said. "It's basically off-limits to most people, so I'm looking forward to seeing it. I'm going to interview some Palestinian families about the peace process."

"Just be careful," Rafraf said again, before hanging up.

I couldn't get past the irony that she was worried about me. Even with the recent wave of violence, Israel was paradise compared to Baghdad. That Rafraf considered the Israelis the biggest threat to my safety was telling.

* * *

A FEW DAYS LATER RAFRAF'S cell phone rang at seven o'clock in the morning. She knew it was the bureau. Who else would be calling so early?

The driver assigned to pick her up that day was sick, and it would be several hours before they could get someone else to her house to pick her up.

"No problem," Rafraf said, "I'll find a taxi."

It was a security risk to take a taxi. NBC drivers picked up Rafraf in the first place, in part, to limit the use of taxis. Cabdrivers might eventually figure out whom she worked for and that could lead to trouble.

But Rafraf had taken taxis for years. She had taken a taxi to the wedding office that day in February without incident. What would one more taxi ride hurt?

Rami walked her to the main highway and flagged a car for his big sister.

Taxis in Baghdad weren't specifically marked as they are in other cities. To hail a cab you stood on a street corner and looked as if you needed a ride. If a car pulled over to give you one, it was probably a taxi.

A blue sedan pulled up to the sidewalk, driven by a balding man in his early forties.

"Taxi?" Rami asked the man.

He nodded yes.

"Take her to Al Hamra hotel," Rami said. "It's just a few kilometers from here. Do you know it?"

"Yes." The man gestured with his hand down the road. "I go up there and turn left, I know it."

"Good." Rami paid the driver with Iraqi dinars, then opened the back door for his sister.

Rami watched as the car pulled away and merged into the morning traffic on the highway into the city center.

The driver should have stayed in the left lane, but he immediately moved to the far right. Rami sensed something was wrong, but he could do nothing.

"We're supposed to turn left here," Rafraf said to the driver.

"There's too much traffic that way," he said as he turned the car to the right.

"But that's the wrong way."

"I know a shortcut."

"No, turn around here. Make a U-turn."

"Okay." The driver's voice sounded agreeable, but his actions were anything but.

He floored the accelerator and began racing as fast as traffic would allow in the wrong direction.

The realization of what was happening hit Rafraf like a wave. She was being kidnapped! But why? Surely the insurgents hadn't been waiting near her house on the off chance that her ride wouldn't show up. Could they do that?

If she was being kidnapped for a ransom, that would be even worse. Her family couldn't pay, she'd be killed for sure.

She had to get out of the car, but how?

The driver must have read her mind because he hit the automatic door locks.

"What are you doing?" she screamed. "Take me to the hotel, you have to turn around!"

"Shut up," the driver yelled. Suddenly all attempts to seem friendly were gone. He looked back at her through the rearview mirror with hate-filled eyes.

Then slammed on his brakes!

Traffic, thought Rafraf. She reached for the door lock and pulled the knob. But before she could get the door open, the lock slammed down again.

The driver knew he had to keep moving or Rafraf would jump out of the car. With traffic blocking the intersection ahead, he turned abruptly right and roared down a side street.

Then, without warning, he hit Rafraf in the face with the back of his fist. It was a powerful blow, but he didn't connect well enough to knock her unconscious. She covered her face with her arms just as he swung his fist a second time.

"Shut up," he ordered, "or I'll kill you right now."

"No," she screamed. She tried to scratch the man's arm, but he withdrew it and put both hands back on the wheel.

The sedan couldn't continue down the side street. An intersection was ahead, and the driver would have to choose left or right.

Right would take them back toward her home. She knew he wouldn't turn that way. His only choice would be a left turn, and he'd have to slow down or he wouldn't make it. It might be her last chance to get out of the car.

Rafraf inched across the backseat toward the right passenger door. As predicted, the driver slammed on the brakes at the end of the road and made a hard left turn.

In one coordinated move, Rafraf unlocked the door, pulled the handle, and jumped headfirst out of the still moving car.

She wasn't prepared for the impact. The vehicle was going at least twenty miles per hour when she jumped out. The impact with the pavement took her breath away. Luckily, she tucked her head in and didn't knock herself out. She rolled once, then again, and scrambled, wobbling to her feet.

That's when she saw the other car. A red sedan had been behind them on the road. It stopped just as the driver of the blue sedan did the same.

Could this be more kidnappers in a chase car? She had no way of knowing for sure, but she didn't have a choice.

She saw the bald kidnapper open his door and step out of the car. She didn't wait to see if he had a gun.

"Help me!" she screamed through tears at the man in the red car. She ran toward him because it was her only choice.

It was the right choice.

"Get in," he shouted as he reached across and flung the passenger door open.

Rafraf jumped in.

The driver threw the car in reverse and floored the accelerator. The vehicle careened backward down the street with the driver barely in control.

Rafraf watched the driver of the blue sedan. Would he chase them?

He hesitated for a split second, weighing his options. Finally, he got back behind the wheel of his car and raced away in the opposite direction.

"What just happened?" the driver of the red car asked.

"You just saved my life," Rafraf answered.

IT WAS THE BEGINNING OF a treacherous spring and summer for Rafraf in Baghdad. The violence in her country grew by the day. The number of attacks, and the death toll, climbed into the thousands.

Within weeks of Don's departure from the country, a violent mob in Fallujah ambushed four American security contractors, beat them, and set them on fire. The men's bodies were hanged from a bridge leading into the city.

The U.S. marines responded with a massive assault on the city that killed hundreds of insurgent fighters and displaced tens of thousands of residents.

For Rafraf, the pace of work increased with the violence.

On a blistering hot day in April, she was sent with Sa'ad, the Iraqi cameraman, and an Iraqi soundman to cover a protest in Baghdad's Fardus Square. The square was frequently used for protests because of its location near the center of Baghdad. The world knew Fardus Square not by name, but by history. It was in the square that U.S. troops and Iraqis had torn down a giant statue of Saddam Hussein as American forces took control of Baghdad.

Now, thousands of Shiite demonstrators had gathered in the square. The mostly male protesters were supporters of anti-American cleric Muqtada al-Sadr. They were angry over the closure of a Sadr-controlled newspaper, and the arrest of one of the cleric's top aides.

The protesters—most wearing white robes—appeared to be unarmed. Rafraf and the camera crew headed toward the crowd to interview some of the men.

Then there were gunshots.

An Iraqi police officer, apparently trying to control the restless crowd, fired several warning shots into the air. It was a mistake.

Suddenly, the previously unarmed "peaceful demonstrators" pulled weapons from under their robes and began running and shooting.

U.S. and Iraqi troops, hearing the gunshots and seeing the armed men running toward them, opened fire. Rafraf was standing in the street, right in the middle of the cross fire.

Bullets flew in all directions. She could hear the supersonic rounds from American M16 rifles zipping and popping past her head. She crawled toward a metal streetlight pole and huddled behind it in the gutter.

Then Rafraf remembered her cell phone. She couldn't call for help. It wasn't as if someone from the bureau was going to walk through the gunfight and get her.

She couldn't even call Sa'ad because she was holding the cameraman's phone for him when the shooting started. On journalistic instinct, Sa'ad and the soundman had run toward the gunshots as Rafraf dove to the gutter, and she lost track of them.

She called the bureau and told them what was happening. They said the security team was on the way to help, and to stay hidden.

Rafraf hung up, then decided to make another call.

"This is Don," said the scratchy voice at the end of the line.

"It's Rafraf. Listen."

She held her cell phone slightly above her head, turning the mouthpiece toward the gunfire. The sound of automatic-weapons fire crossed the electronic connection.

"Did you hear that?" Rafraf asked after putting the phone back to her ear.

"Of course. Are you okay?"

Rafraf started crying. "No. I'm not okay."

"Where are you?"

"In the street," she cried, "hiding behind a pole. Please get me out of here."

"I'm trying."

Then the connection cut out.

I KNEW RAFRAF WAS DOING her part. She managed to get one of the first passports issued by the new Iraqi government, and she applied for a tourist visa from the United States.

"I'll have to go to Jordan to fill out paperwork and request an interview," she told me a couple of months after the demonstration in Fardus Square.

"Why Jordan?" I asked.

"Because I have to be interviewed by immigration officials at an American embassy. They won't do it in Baghdad. It has to be Jordan."

"Can you do that? You've never even left Iraq."

"Yes. Our producer in Amman says he needs me to help him work on a story there, to interview lawyers for Saddam's family. Since I'm to be there for work, he can get me into Jordan and put me in the hotel."

"Perfect. Paul Nassar and I have both written letters to go with your application. I'll be your official sponsor here, so make sure to get my home address down correctly on the forms."

"I know," she said, sounding confident. "And I have someone who I think can help me if the visa is denied."

"Who? Do I know him?"

"I shouldn't say his name over the phone. He has many contacts at the embassy. I'm only to call him if everything else fails."

"This is an American?" I asked skeptically. "Honestly, it sounds sort of fishy to me. Where did you meet this guy?"

"We did some work with him for a story. He said he could help me if I ever needed anything, so I called him."

"Well, hopefully you won't need to. When are you going to Jordan?"

"Next month," she said.

It was the first good news on the visa front since I had left Baghdad.

I had personally called immigration officials in Washington and had even asked some NBC producers with strong connections in government to do the same. The answer always came back the same.

"Not a chance," said one producer who had reached out to a source in the State Department. "They say there's no mechanism to get an Iraqi into the U.S. Apparently a bunch of military commanders have been trying the same thing with their translators, and they're getting the same answers."

"All right," I said, dejected. "I appreciate you trying."

A FEW WEEKS LATER, RAFRAF was on a Royal Jordanian turboprop from Baghdad International Airport to Amman.

Kamal had been against his daughter's leaving Iraq even for a few days. Rafraf talked him into letting her go by saying the trip was necessary for work. He was still against her work in the first place, but Rafraf had thus far won the battle of two strong wills.

She assured him that she would have her own room at the hotel in Jordan, and that people there would supervise her movements at all times. He reluctantly agreed.

In reality, Rafraf would have gone to Jordan even without her father's permission. She realized that for her life to go in the direction she wanted, she would have to make her own decisions.

But she also knew the trip would only be for a few days, and she would have to go back to her family. It would make matters much easier if she didn't have drama with her father after she returned. Life at home was miserable when he was angry.

Rafraf was nervous about flying. She squeezed the armrests of her seat tightly every time the plane bounced in the air. She imagined she was on a journey of mystery—bound for a land of luxury and exotic new people. She was leaving Iraq for the first time in her life.

"No new boyfriends," Don had teased her over the phone the day before she left. "You don't have time for that."

"What kind of girl do you think I am?" She laughed.

*   *   *

RAFRAF HAD LITTLE TIME FOR sightseeing during her brief stay in Jordan. She worked with the NBC producer on the interview with Saddam's lawyers, then turned her attention to the U.S. embassy.

"And what is the purpose of your planned trip to the United States?" an immigration official asked.

"To visit friends," Rafraf answered honestly.

The woman across the counter peered suspiciously at Rafraf over the top of her reading glasses. "There's no date. When are you planning to go?"

"As soon as I get the visa."

"Hmmm," the woman replied.

She reminded Rafraf of the Iraqi woman who had denied her a job translating for the American military because Rafraf's English wasn't good enough. Bureaucrats, she concluded, were the same no matter where they worked. All they cared about was exercising whatever bit of power they were given over somebody else's life.

The woman pushed a paper back across the counter to Rafraf. "I wouldn't get my hopes up if I were you. Here's the appointment for your interview with an immigration officer."

Rafraf looked at the date. "What does this say?" she asked, hoping she was reading it wrong.

"September twenty-first, 2004."

"More than two months from now?" Rafraf almost cried. She had expected to be able to do the interview during her trip to Jordan. Now she would have to go back to Baghdad, then figure out a way to come back.

"If I pass the interview, how soon would I get the visa?"

"If you are approved, it's just a matter of days, but again, don't get your hopes up."

I HONESTLY DIDN'T KNOW IF Rafraf would survive long enough to go back to Jordan for her visa interview.

By midsummer, Iraqis working with U.S. troops and American or other news organizations were being killed daily. Lists were being circulated throughout neighborhoods of known and suspected "collaborators," as the insurgents called them.

One of Rafraf's friends from the university, a young woman named Zina, had also found work with an American television network. Insurgents left a note on Zina's door warning her to quit collaborating with the Americans or die. She refused to quit and was shot to death at her doorstep the following week.

IN AUGUST, A MAN FROM Rafraf's neighborhood was kidnapped and held for ransom. His family paid for his return. The first thing he did after he was freed was speak to Rafraf's father.

"Rafraf's name is on the list," he told Kamal. "And not for ransom. They said they will kill her if she doesn't stop what she is doing."

Kamal waited outside for Rafraf to come home from the bureau that night.

"Why are you out here?" Rafraf said, joking. "Since when do I get special treatment?"

"We'll talk about it inside." Kamal explained the threat and told Rafraf that she had pushed her luck too far.

She had worked with the Americans for more than a year, and that was long enough.

"I won't quit," she said simply.

"But they know where you live," Kamal insisted. "You are in danger here, and so is everyone in this house."

"Then I'll live at the hotel. Or with my sister Sawsan."

"And put her in danger too?" Kamal spat.

"I won't put anybody else in danger. You won't have to worry about me anymore."

Sawsan was Rafraf's oldest sister. She had recently married and at thirty-two years old had been permitted to start her own home with her husband. Rafraf didn't want to put anybody else's life at risk, but she would also not quit her job at NBC.

She felt so close to finding a new life. The Americans offered at least a glimmer of hope. All Iraq held for her was nothingness.

Rafraf knew her father was right. She was putting herself and the people she loved in danger. But a growing sense of desperation told her she might never get another chance to start a new life.

Rafraf packed her things and moved the next day to the hotel. For her remaining time in Iraq, she would move between Al Hamra, her sister's home, and her own home as unpredictably as possible. NBC drivers had to use extreme caution to make sure they weren't followed when transporting Rafraf to or from her homes.

THANKFULLY, SHE HAD A DATE marked on her calendar to look forward to . . . September 21.

Rafraf had waited months for the day. All she needed to do was impress the immigration officer during one interview.

I always make good impressions, she thought to herself.

She was so hopeful that her visa would be approved, she took everything she could with her to Jordan for her interview. If things went as planned, she could be just a few days from boarding a plane for the United States.

"Don't let the Americans change you," her mother warned as they said their good-byes.

"I won't," Rafraf said.

"You must always remember who you are and where you come from," Jamila continued. "Do not indulge yourself in their culture. And know that I love you no matter what."

"I love you too, Mother," Rafraf said through tears.

Twenty-four hours later, Rafraf stood at the counter across from an immigration official at the U.S. embassy in Jordan.

She didn't like the look of the man standing across the counter from her. He was thin and balding with hazel eyes and a cold, flat stare.

The interview took just a few minutes. The questions, a matter of routine.

"How old are you?"

"Do you own property in Iraq?"

"Do you have a husband in Iraq, or children?"

The man's mind was already made up. He made a show of stamping her application.

DENIED.

"What does this mean?" Rafraf asked, though she already knew the answer.

"It means we will not grant you entry to the United States at this time," the skinny, balding man said. "You can reapply at a later date if your circumstances change."

I COULD BARELY UNDERSTAND WHAT she was saying. Rafraf called me from her hotel room in Amman, but she couldn't stop crying long enough to get the words out.

"They said no," she sobbed. She cried like a mother who had just lost a child. The grief coming through the earpiece of my cell phone broke my heart.

"They didn't even read the letters," she managed. "They don't care."

I feared for a moment she was going to jump out the window of her hotel.

"What about your friend?" I asked. "The guy with no name? He said he could help if everything else failed."

"Uh-huh."

"Can you call him?"

"I'll try."

I never met the man who had promised to help Rafraf. I didn't have much confidence that he could actually do what he said he would. More likely, I suspected he was one of thousands of men who simply said they could help in an effort to win favor with a pretty girl.

But suddenly Mr. No Name was Rafraf's only hope of getting to the United States.

Whoever he was, as events told, he was the real deal.

Rafraf called me back the next day. She was still in Jordan. "He got me another interview." A glimmer of hope was in her voice, but I could tell she was trying not to get too excited again.

"Seriously?" I said with obvious surprise. "When?"

"In two weeks. And he gave me the name of a man to ask for at the embassy."

"Why so long? Can you stay there for two more weeks?"

"For a visa, I'll stay here for a year." She laughed.

RAFRAF WOULD HAVE TO SPEND all her savings to stay in Amman until her interview date. But what choice did she have?

She moved to a cheap hotel for the first week and rented a furnished apartment for the second week.

She did her best to keep a positive attitude, but the waiting was terrible. She passed the time by visiting some of Amman's architectural attractions. She even found a place that offered camel rides, so she did that too.

When the time came for her second interview, she was terrified.

Please don't say something stupid, she told herself. If this didn't work, she was out of options.

Once again, she found herself standing in front of a counter with an immigration officer examining her paperwork. Rafraf tried her best not to fidget or break into a panicked sweat.

It was a different officer from the first time.

"I see you have already been denied entry," he began, "just two weeks ago."

"Yes."

"So what changed?"

Rafraf shrugged. "Now I have a name. I was told to come back and use his name."

When she said the name, the man looked up from his paperwork for the first time.

"Wait here for just a moment please," he said, then hurried away to a back room.

No more than a minute later, the immigration official walked back through the door toward Rafraf. She noticed he was smiling.

"Here you go." He handed her paperwork back across the counter.

APPROVED was stamped on the front of the form.

"You will need to go back to Iraq to await the visa. It's a formality I'm afraid we can't get around. You'll need to have the visa and your passport stamped in Baghdad before it's active. You'll receive everything you need in an e-mail within the week."

Rafraf could hardly believe it. She tried not to cry, but she felt the tears well up even as she grinned from ear to ear.

"Is that all?" Rafraf asked as she gathered her paperwork.

"No, there's one more thing. Enjoy your visit to America."

EIGHTEEN

ARRIVAL

The arrivals board at Atlanta's Hartsfield-Jackson International Airport had the flight listed as on time.

Ironic, I thought to myself. After a nearly eight-month battle with entrenched bureaucracy, closed doors, and heartache, Rafraf's flight from New York to Atlanta was on time.

The date was October 27, 2004.

I went to the airport by myself to pick her up. The girls were at school, and Kiki thought it would be best to let Rafraf adjust to one shock at a time. Simply arriving in Atlanta, Kiki said, would be enough change. The last thing Rafraf needed was to step off a plane after forty-eight hours of travel and try to make a good impression.

"I know how women are," Kiki told me. "She'll be glad it's just you at the airport." Kiki would wait at home.

I knew Atlanta's airport. Along with being one of the busiest in the world, it is also one of the easiest to navigate as a passenger. Arriving passengers simply walk from their gate toward the middle of their concourse, where they find a sign pointing them downstairs toward the trains.

Trains run underground, connecting the airport's five concourses to the main terminal and baggage claim.

When the train doors open underneath the main terminal, passengers, flight crews, and airport employees dash madly toward what must be one of the tallest groups of escalators in the world. The escalators travel from the depths of the tunnel more than one hundred feet below the surface, to the center of the main terminal, where they dump everyone in front of a car-rental agency.

The arrivals came in waves. A train would arrive, hundreds of new faces would rise to the top of the escalators, then disperse to points unknown. Several minutes would pass before the next train, and during that time the escalators carried nobody at all. Then, another train opened its doors, and like ants escaping from a mound, hundreds of people would pour from the escalators again.

Airport officials had roped off a waiting area for people to meet arriving passengers. I stood behind the ropes with hundreds of others, waiting to see Rafraf's head emerge from below.

One wave passed, then another.

I almost didn't recognize Rafraf when she finally emerged near the end of a wave of passengers.

The first thing I noticed emerging from the tunnel was the head scarf. It was pink, her favorite color. As usual, it was wrapped tightly around her head, concealing all her hair and revealing only her face. She wore a heavy sweater, and jeans that seemed at least a foot too long for her. She had a heavy backpack on her shoulders and, on her left arm, carried a large purse.

But the reason I almost didn't recognize her was the dog. Her right arm clutched a stuffed animal; its face was buried in her neck as if the dog were afraid to see what was waiting at the top of the escalator.

Rafraf looked tired and, I thought, a little bit frightened.

I waved when I finally saw her and smiled.

She tried to smile back, but seemed too exhausted or tense to actually pull it off.

I took her backpack and gave her a quick hug.

"How was the flight?"

"I slept."

"That's good. Follow me. We'll get your bags and get you home." It was small talk, but what else was there to say?

It occurred to me that Rafraf had left her real home with no idea how long she'd be gone, or what she was heading into. I was reminded again of how much courage it had taken for her to simply drop everything and leave.

We quickly found her suitcases on the baggage carousel and within minutes made it to my car in the parking garage.

As I loaded the bags, I felt a little self-conscious about my car. I had bought the Mercedes new just a year earlier. It had heated leather seats, a pristine paint job, and all-wheel drive. It occurred to me as I closed the trunk that the car alone cost more money than every member of Rafraf's family had earned in their entire lives.

I was paid well for my work, but I didn't consider myself rich by any stretch. The car was nowhere near being paid for, nor was my house. Like most Americans, I spent most of my paycheck every two weeks just supporting a lifestyle that was, in retrospect, extravagant compared to the lives of billions around the world.

"It's about forty minutes to the house," I said as we pulled out of the parking garage and waited in line at the payment booth.

"What's this?" She seemed concerned by the somewhat official-looking people sitting behind the glass. A gate, similar to the one that blocked the entrance to Al Hamra, blocked the exit of the parking garage. Drivers had to present a parking ticket and payment before the gate was raised, allowing them to pass.

"It's nothing," I said as we pulled to the booth.

I fetched my parking ticket from above the visor and handed it, along with $2, to the attendant. Without a word being exchanged, the gate lifted and we were on our way.

"You must have a system for everything here." Rafraf seemed almost awestruck at the efficiency of the parking operation.

"What do you mean?"

"You just give them money, and they let you out? Just like that? You didn't have to negotiate or find out who's in charge."

"I guess not." I had honestly never given airport parking a second thought.

I didn't know it, but for Rafraf the culture shock of life in the United States was already well under way.

"Are you hungry? Or thirsty?" I asked. "We could make a quick stop along the way if you are."

"I am thirsty. Maybe we could get some water."

RAFRAF WASN'T SURE IF THE thirst was from excitement or fear.

What am I doing here? she thought to herself as the Mercedes eased northbound on the freeway toward Don's house.

Everything that passed by her window was so strange. Two words flashed across her mind over and over: *expensive* and *new*.

And the trees! Some must have been more than one hundred feet tall. The landscape was so green it seemed almost unreal. Rafraf knew that Atlanta, unlike Baghdad, did not sit in the middle of a vast desert. But she never expected so many trees, and so much green.

She could see the side streets from the freeway. Traffic lights gleamed red, yellow, and green. She had, of course, seen such things before, but it had been so long since the lights in Iraq actually worked.

Don explained that rush hour hadn't yet begun in Atlanta, so everything moved in an orderly fashion. For the first fifteen minutes of their ride, the speedometer never dipped below seventy miles per hour.

"It won't last," he said. "The good news is there are no traffic circles."

The buildings in Atlanta were like nothing Rafraf had ever seen in person. Skyscrapers reached more than a thousand feet into the air. Many looked to be made entirely of mirrors. They shimmered in the late-afternoon sun as the car raced between the downtown portion of the city and the area known as midtown to the north.

Don wasn't content to ride in silence. He narrated along the way, filling Rafraf in on bits of information he thought she'd find useful.

"Atlanta," he explained, "has about four and a half million people. It has almost as many people as Baghdad."

"Uh-huh," Rafraf replied as if she already knew that. She didn't.

"The city is really considered the capital of the southern U.S. It actually is the capital of Georgia. That's the statehouse over there."

He was pointing at something, but Rafraf didn't see it. She was too busy looking up at the giant buildings towering overhead.

"We're going to hop off here, just for a quick drink. Are you sure you're not hungry?"

"No, but I would like some tea."

The Mercedes was already pulling off the freeway into a parking lot. A sign said Drive-Thru. Rafraf wondered why it was spelled wrong.

"They don't have the kind of tea you drink here, but you like Coke, right?"

What happened next proved everything Rafraf had ever suspected about how lazy Americans were.

Don pulled up to a giant board with a metal speaker mounted in front of it.

"Welcome to Chick-fil-A," said a voice from the speaker, "can I take your order?"

Don ordered a Coke for Rafraf, a Diet Coke for himself, and a large serving of something called waffle fries.

Less than a minute later they were back on the freeway, once again traveling northbound at seventy miles per hour.

Rafraf was shocked at how quickly food could be had in Atlanta, and how delicious waffle fries were.

*   *   *

A SHORT TIME LATER, THEY were off the freeway again and driving eastbound along Roswell Road in east Cobb County.

Soon, neighborhoods emerged with houses made of brick, stucco, wood, and stone. To Rafraf, they looked like cartoon homes from a Disney movie. Green lawns were dotted with trees that seemed to be exploding with color. The leaves were red, yellow, orange, and even purple.

Every house had a steeply pitched roof with shingles made of tile or asphalt.

"You can't sleep on the roof here," Don joked. "You'd just roll off."

"Why are they like that?" Rafraf asked.

"Because of the rain. It rains a lot here. And it usually snows at least a couple of times in the winter."

Rafraf had never seen snow. The thought of it gave her a chill. She wondered if it was from the imagined cold, or from fear of the unknown.

"That's the Avenue," Don said, pointing to a large collection of shops. "Great shopping there, and it's less than a mile from home so you can walk there if you want."

But Rafraf had stopped listening. She was being bombarded with so much information, so many new images, that it all just blended into a giant montage in her mind.

And then they were home.

"This is it," Don said as he pushed a button on his rearview mirror. As if by magic, one of the garage doors of a large, white house glided open. The Mercedes coasted into the garage, and the door closed behind them.

Rafraf suddenly felt an apprehension that she hadn't expected. Perhaps it was the finality of the garage door closing. The outside world—her real home, her country, her life—suddenly seemed to be sealed off behind her.

Rafraf noticed the other spot in the garage was empty. "Is your wife not home?"

"I guess not." Don looked at his watch. "She must be picking the girls up from school." He jumped out of the car and motioned for Rafraf to follow. "Don't worry about your bags right now. Let me show you the house and your room. I'll come down and get your stuff later."

It had been less than an hour since leaving the airport, and already Rafraf faced her first dilemma.

It was not appropriate, in fact it was expressly forbidden in the Koran, for Rafraf to be alone in a house with a man she was not related to.

Yes, she had bent that rule a time or two in the past, but suddenly it seemed that there might be a good reason for it.

Irrational thoughts raced through her mind. *Is this guy really even married? Maybe this is just an elaborate trick to sell me into slavery! What's really waiting inside that house?*

Don picked up on her reluctance. "It's okay, Rafraf. If you want, you can stay in the living room or hang out in the kitchen until Kiki comes home. Or I can just tell you where your room is and you can go find it."

Whatever was waiting inside the house, Rafraf decided it was time to face it. She grabbed her stuffed animal, stepped out of the car and into her new home.

The big house had three levels. The door from the garage opened onto a room off the kitchen with floors made of wood and its own fireplace.

The kitchen was big, with a center aisle for cooking. Adjoining the kitchen was a dining room, and a huge living area. That room had twenty-foot ceilings with wooden beams, a stone fireplace, a sofa, and stuffed chairs.

Don and Kiki's bedroom, and a room that housed a computer and a desk, were also on the main floor.

Suddenly, Don yelled for no apparent reason, "Suni!" Then he waited for a second.

Rafraf couldn't imagine why Don was yelling "Suni" in the house—Shiites and Sunnis were killing one another in Iraq. She decided not to ask.

"Must be with Kiki," Don mumbled to himself, then continued the tour.

Downstairs were three rooms: one for painting and doing crafts, a workout room full of fitness equipment, and a room that was set up like a movie theater with four huge reclining chairs, and the largest television Rafraf had ever seen.

"I put in the home theater after my first trip to Iraq," Don said. "I had money left over from my per diem. I wanted to give Kiki and the girls something for going through the stress. It's not really finished, but there's also a Sony PlayStation 2. I'm sure the girls will show you how to play Dance Dance Revolution."

Rafraf had no idea what per diem was and had never heard of a PlayStation 2, but she was too tired to ask. The last thing Don said caught her attention though.

"Dance Dance?" Rafraf asked.

"It's a dancing video game. You like to dance, right?"

Rafraf loved dancing. It was, she thought, the best thing about Iraqi weddings. She downplayed her enthusiasm. "Of course."

"Okay, back upstairs. Let's see your room."

From the basement floor they climbed two flights of stairs to the top floor.

Don had said he wasn't rich—*upper-middle class* was the term he used—but to Rafraf the house seemed extravagant. *Who needs all this?* kept running through her mind.

"There are three bedrooms up here," he said, first turning right at the top of the stairs. "The girls each have their own room. They share a bathroom between their rooms.

"And finally, to your room."

Rafraf followed Don back toward the stairs and across a hallway that overlooked the downstairs. At the end of the hall he opened the door to what was to become Rafraf's new home.

It was huge! A big bed had four pillows and a plush white comforter. A small desk sat next to a large window that overlooked the front lawn. The two closets had more than enough room for all of her clothes.

"And this is yours too." He opened another door at the far end of the room.

It was a full bathroom, bathtub with shower, and several drawers beneath the sink. Decorated in a nautical theme, it had a picture of a sailboat on the wall.

"Who do I share this with?" Rafraf asked. Her family home in Baghdad had only one functioning bathroom, shared by twelve people.

"Nobody," Don said simply. "The house has four bathrooms. This one is all yours."

Rafraf was overcome by both appreciation and guilt. How could this be fair? Her entire family, her brothers and sisters, were in Iraq living with practically nothing, and she was being given all this.

"Make yourself comfortable." Don left the room before Rafraf could say anything. "I'll be up in a second with your bags."

She sat on the bed and surveyed the room once more. For the first time she noticed the art on the wall. Stylized paintings of farm animals hung just above the bed. A picture of a pig was centered between ones of a horse and a cow.

Muslims don't eat pork. The Koran says swine is unclean and tells followers of Allah to avoid it. Rafraf couldn't imagine why anyone would put a picture of a pig on the wall.

The pig would have to go, she thought.

Someday.

KIKI AND THE GIRLS WERE excited and anxious about meeting Rafraf. Kiki had had a couple of brief conversations with her by telephone, just to assure her that it really was okay for her to move in. The girls had no idea what to think.

Rachael was twelve years old, Madison was three months shy of her tenth birthday. Both were confident and adaptable girls, but they were about to face the biggest change yet in their lives.

Rafraf was sitting by herself on a leather chair in the great room when the door from the garage burst open, and the house exploded into chaos.

"Suni!" she heard a woman's voice shout from within the garage. "Stay! Shiloh, stay!"

But the excitement and new smells were just too much. Three dogs burst through the door and ran immediately to the unfamiliar woman sitting on the leather chair. Their tails wagged, and they sniffed relentlessly at her legs.

He was giant! The one called Shiloh had long brown hair and feet the size of saucers. He must have weighed seventy pounds at least. Rafraf guessed the big dog would be at least as tall as her if he stood on his back legs.

She was frozen with fear. Don had mentioned something about dogs, but he had never said they would be in the house. In Baghdad, dogs were wild animals that roamed the streets scavenging for food. Rafraf had been chased by vicious dogs more times than she could re-member, and she was deathly afraid of them. Nobody she knew had a dog for a pet.

"Shiloh!" Kiki yelled again. The biggest dog knew she was serious this time. He removed his nose from Rafraf and padded back to Kiki across the room. She grabbed his collar, opened the back door, and released the dog into the backyard, where he immediately started chasing a squirrel.

A medium-size black dog sat in a corner and growled.

"Sorry about that. I'm Kiki." She crossed the room to Rafraf.

Rafraf stood and extended her hand to shake.

Kiki ignored the hand and gave Rafraf a big hug instead. "We're so glad you're finally here."

"Me too," Rafraf said tentatively. She was still shaken by the expe-rience with the dogs.

Kiki motioned for the girls to come forward and introduce them-selves. They put down their backpacks full of books and walked toward Rafraf.

"I'm Rachael," said the older girl, extending her hand as Rafraf had done. The two shook hands uncomfortably.

"And I'm Madison." The younger hid shyly next to her mother the way little girls often do.

For a moment the four evaluated each other.

Rafraf felt out of place. She looked so different from these people and felt self-conscious about her appearance.

She was afraid of the third dog named Suni. Every time he came within sniffing distance of her, she recoiled.

And the Teague women looked foreign to Rafraf.

Kiki was beautiful. She had short blond hair and spectacular blue eyes. She wore no makeup at all, but her face could easily have graced the cover of a fashion magazine. She was at least six inches taller than Rafraf, had the most perfect teeth she had ever seen, and carried herself with the confidence of an athlete. Rafraf knew Kiki was thirty-five years old, Don had told her that, but she could easily have passed for her late twenties.

"Sorry about the clothes," Kiki said, looking down at herself. She wore dirt-covered jeans and boots with spurs on them. "I've been training horses."

Rafraf secretly wondered if the horses were allowed in the house as well.

Her daughters were pretty too.

Rachael had curly blond hair, and the same blue eyes as her mother. She had braces, which were on full display because she hadn't stopped smiling since seeing Rafraf.

Madison's hair was darker, and straight. Her eyes were intense and deep blue. To Rafraf she seemed serious and thoughtful—much older than nine years old.

Rafraf wondered how she would ever fit in with such a family. One thing she had to get to the bottom of right away.

"I have a question," Rafraf announced with as much confidence as she could muster.

"Yes?" Kiki answered.

"That white dog, why do you call him Suni?"

It took Kiki a moment to understand the question. Then it seemed to dawn on her. She burst out laughing.

"His name is Tsunami," Kiki said when she had finally composed herself. "It's the Japanese word for a tidal wave! He's a Japanese breed, so we thought it would be cute. We call him Suni for short!"

"Oh, that's good," Rafraf said, relief written across her face.

NINETEEN

ADJUSTMENT

Dracula walked cheerily down the street in front of the Teague house in suburban Atlanta. On most nights, he wouldn't be so bold as to show himself in public, but this was his night.

An evil witch followed just a few steps behind Dracula. She wore a crooked, black witch hat, carried a straw broom in her left hand, and a plastic jack-o'-lantern in her right.

It was Halloween and the entire population of the Mallard Lake Subdivision were meeting for a costume party in the cul-de-sac just down the street from Don's house.

Rachael and Madison hurried excitedly to the front door. Both wore Halloween costumes that combined pieces bought from a party store and their own artistic flair.

Madison was a scarecrow and had a plastic bird perched on each shoulder. Rachael was a pirate, complete with a teenage crush on Johnny Depp.

"Let's go, Rafraf!" Rachael shouted. "The pizza is going to be gone before we even get there."

Upstairs, Rafraf was putting the finishing touches on her Halloween costume. She leaned closer to the mirror in her bathroom, taking a long look at herself.

Rafraf had been in the country for just a few days, but she was already undergoing a visible change. Maybe she was just imagining it, but it seemed her acne was clearing up.

That was the good news.

The decidedly bad news was that something strange was happening with her hair. It had been perfectly straight her entire life, but now it wasn't straight at all. *Frizzy* Rachael called it. Kiki said it had something to do with Atlanta's humid air.

"Great," Rafraf said in frustration to her reflection. One of her favorite head scarves hung at the ready on the towel rack behind her. It would easily cover up the frizzy issue, but Rafraf didn't reach for it. She felt a brief pang of guilt.

She swore to her mother that she would continue wearing her scarf in the United States. For the first few days in Atlanta, she wore it whenever she left the house, or if Don was home.

If she was home with just Kiki and the girls, she felt comfortable without the scarf. But the moment she heard the garage door signal Don's arrival, she would rush upstairs and put her scarf on before being seen again.

"Are you doing that because of your religion?" Kiki asked after watching the scarf drill for a few days.

"It's what I'm supposed to do. I'm not allowed to show my hair to a man who's not my husband or my family."

"But what about your brothers or cousins? When you're at home in Baghdad, can they see your hair?"

"Of course."

"This is your home. I know you're probably wearing the scarf around Don out of respect for me, but you don't have to. We're your family."

"Are you sure?" Rafraf asked hopefully. She actually hated wearing the scarf in the house. It made her head hot and her face look fat.

"Yes."

The next morning, Rafraf came downstairs for breakfast without her scarf.

Rafraf had always considered her hair her best feature. It was jet-black and hadn't been cut since she was a child. Her long hair cascaded down past her shoulders, past the small of her back.

Don acted as if he didn't notice. Rafraf assumed he didn't want to make her feel self-conscious about her appearance.

"Good morning, Rafraf." He went right back to reading the paper as if nothing were different at all.

"I THINK PEOPLE HERE HATE me," Rafraf had said to Don the day before Halloween.

"Why do you think that?" he asked.

"Because they stare at me, everywhere I go, they stare at me."

"Well, they don't hate you. But people in this part of Atlanta don't see many women wear the scarf. If anything, they're just curious, or even afraid of you. After September eleventh, people are afraid."

"I think they can tell I'm Iraqi so they hate me."

"I've got news for you, Rafraf. Most Americans don't give Iraqis—or anybody else for that matter—a second thought. This country is made up of people from all over the world. Sure, some are racists, like in any country, but I can't imagine anyone here hating you because of where you're from."

"But your country went to war with Iraq. You must hate us."

"That's not why countries go to war," Don said.

"Of course it is. Iraqis hate Iranians so we went to war with them. We also hate Kuwaitis and went to war with them. And it's not just us. Jews hate Arabs, so they fight the Palestinians. Bosnians hate Serbs, so they went to war."

"So who do you hate?"

"Jews," she said flatly. "Everybody hates Jews."

"Okay, stop! Even if you do hate Jews, you can't say things like that here. And you're going to have to get over the whole hate thing. Americans don't hate."

To Rafraf, it seemed a naïve thing to say. She may not have known everything about the United States, but she knew they had slaves just a few generations ago. She also knew that black people were legally treated as second-class citizens until the sixties. How could he possibly think Americans don't hate? She decided not to press the point.

"You think people are afraid of me because of the scarf?" she asked, getting back to the original subject.

"That's most of it, but they also look at you because you're pretty. Kiki has been stared at her whole life. Sometimes she likes it, but it usually drives her crazy."

"Do you think I should stop wearing it?" Rafraf asked hopefully.

"It's not up to me. If you stop wearing the scarf, nobody will know you're a Muslim and especially not an Iraqi. They'll probably think you're Mexican."

He paused and looked at Rafraf seriously. "Please don't tell me you hate Mexicans too."

"I have nothing against Mexicans," she answered.

"Anyway, the scarf decision is yours to make, and yours only."

"I know," she said glumly.

It would have been much easier for Rafraf if Don had told her to take off the scarf. Then she could justify the decision. She could say that she was following the rules of her new home, and it would be disrespectful not to do so.

She thought back to the conversation she had had with her mother when she was a child. Jamila told her she must wear the scarf for life, and Rafraf had promised she would. If someone forbade her from wearing it, she could convince her mother she had no choice. But Don wasn't doing that. He was leaving the decision up to her.

Rafraf saw coming to America as an opportunity to redefine who she was. She could still hold true to her beliefs, but with different boundaries. Millions of Muslim women around the world chose not to wear the scarf and were still faithful to Allah. Some in Baghdad did so too.

Shedding the scarf, Rafraf concluded, would displease her mother but would not be a sin.

"By the way, I found the information about the nearest mosque," Don continued. "It's not that far away. I'll take you there whenever you want. There's also a place called the Islamic Community Center of Atlanta that I can take you to. You can meet people you're comfortable with."

"I'll let you know."

But in reality, Rafraf was in no hurry. Her immediate priority was to find a way to fit in with Americans, not to hide from this new culture by immersing herself in her old one. The Halloween party gave her a safe way to take a step in that direction.

"COMING," RAFRAF SAID AS SHE bounded down the stairs and caught up with Rachael and Madison at the front door.

Her costume consisted of a green-and-blue polo shirt with horizontal stripes. She wore bell-bottom blue jeans, and white tennis shoes with no socks.

The most remarkable thing about her costume, though, was her hair. It was pulled back into a ponytail, held tight by a pink band.

By the time Rafraf made it to the front door, Don and Kiki were there too. Neither of them wore costumes.

"What are you supposed to be?" Don asked.

"Can't you tell?" Rafraf did a slow spin so Kiki and Don could see the whole "costume."

"I give up," Don said.

"She's an American girl," Kiki said, smiling, "jeans, sneakers, and a ponytail."

They all laughed and joined the procession of ghouls and goblins heading toward the party.

For the first time in her adult life, Rafraf walked down a public street with her hair uncovered.

It's just a costume, she told herself. *It doesn't mean anything.*

* * *

RAFRAF HAD EATEN TWO BITES of the pizza before I spotted it.

"Stop," I practically shouted, snatching the slice out of her hand. "That's pepperoni."

"It's good," Rafraf said.

"It's pork."

The look of horror that crossed Rafraf's face was almost comical. For a moment I feared she would throw up.

"Why would there be pork on pizza?"

"Because it's awesome," I said. "Most Americans don't have a problem eating pigs. Bacon is particularly delicious." I thought I was being funny, but she didn't seem to appreciate my porcine proclivity. "I should have warned you about the pepperoni, but I thought you knew. I'll get you a slice of cheese pizza."

The pepperoni incident aside, I was surprised at how quickly Rafraf seemed to be adjusting to her new surroundings. At least, she acted as if she were adjusting.

Rafraf had gone grocery shopping with Kiki earlier in the week and had also been to a couple of clothing stores nearby. I half expected her to return from those trips looking starry-eyed and speaking of the magic of American consumerism. She didn't.

She seemed, in fact, numb to the whole experience. I wondered what was really going on inside her head.

"Have you noticed she sleeps with the lights on?" Kiki asked with a tinge of concern in her voice. We were watching as our neighbors clamored around Rafraf. She was the star of the party.

"Yeah," I said, "I wonder what she's afraid of."

"She's been having bad dreams. She tells me about them in the morning after she wakes up. It's really bizarre stuff with demons and all sorts of scary creatures chasing her."

"I wonder if she has post-traumatic stress disorder. Considering everything she's been through, it wouldn't surprise me."

Kiki was already convinced Rafraf was suffering from PTSD. "She

scared the heck out of me the first morning she was here. I came
downstairs and she was just sitting in the leather recliner holding her
stuffed dog."

"She didn't sleep in her bed?" I asked.

"She said she's afraid of the dark. And she's used to sleeping with
her sister next to her. She told me she's not afraid in the living room
because it feels like there could be people around her."

"That's not good."

It didn't help, I thought, that Rafraf was still living on Baghdad
time. It should have taken just a few days to adjust to the eight-hour
time difference, but Rafraf's body clock was still set to Iraq.

"Do you know what time she goes to bed at night?" Kiki asked me.

"No."

"Four o'clock in the morning. She spends all night on the Internet. There's a Baghdad radio station online. She e-mails requests, then
waits up to hear them play her songs and say her name on the radio."

"And how do you know this?"

"Rafraf talks," Kiki said as if exhausted by listening. "A lot. She
wakes up at about noon and finds me wherever I am in the house and
just starts talking. It's nonstop."

"That's funny, she hardly seems to talk at all when I'm around."

"You'll get your turn," Kiki said. "I can tell she misses her mom.
When I would go home and visit my family after we were first married, I did the same thing. I followed my mom everywhere and chat-
ted away. If it helps Rafraf feel better to talk, I don't mind listening."

"I guess we need to get her out of the house more," I said.

Was "getting her out of the house" what Rafraf really needed? Kiki
and I had no idea. Prior to her arrival in Atlanta, the entire idea of
having her live with us had been theoretical. Neither of us had fully
expected it to happen, and we hadn't thought through the emotional
and psychological impact the move would have on Rafraf.

Rafraf was a grown woman, twenty-three years old. It was
common, perhaps even the norm, for American women of the same
age to live by themselves, work, and have control of their lives.

But Rafraf's upbringing didn't prepare her for such control. She had never been more than a few miles from the authority of her parents, and the safety that came with it. She was well prepared to live in the society that had shaped her; she wasn't at all prepared to live in America.

"It's only been four days. I just wanted to give her time to adjust."

"Have a look," Kiki said. The Iraqi in her American-girl costume was laughing and scarfing down cheese pizza as if it were going out of style. "I think she's adjusting."

A better statement would have been "she looks like she's adjusting."

Rafraf quickly became one of the girls, and when Kiki went to vote in the presidential election on November 2, 2004, all of the girls went along to watch.

"I took Rafraf with me to vote today," my wife told me that evening.

"What did she think?"

"It's hard to tell; she plays it cool."

"Did you tell her who you voted for?"

"Yes, and I told her why."

"Hmmm, and what'd she say?"

"Nothing."

TWENTY

TICKING CLOCK

W e had three months to figure out how to keep Rafraf in America. Her visa to visit the United States was valid for ninety days.

By some estimates, more than 10 million illegal immigrants were in the United States in 2004. Many of them were people who originally entered the United States, as Rafraf had, on tourist visas. But when the dates on their visas ran out, many of those "tourists" stayed, melting into the shadows of America.

That wouldn't be an option for Rafraf. At least, not if I had any say in the matter. I wouldn't be a part of allowing somebody to break American laws by overstaying a visa. Particularly since I was her official sponsor in the United States.

But how could we keep her in the country beyond three months?

The answer came from one of my best friends at the network, correspondent Kerry Sanders. Kerry knew Rafraf from a tour he had done in Baghdad, and he had the same high opinion of her that I had. He was enthusiastic about bringing Rafraf to the United States and pledged to do everything within his power to help.

"I could talk to the University of South Florida," he told me a few months prior to Rafraf's arrival in the United States. "Rafraf has a bachelor's degree already, right?"

"Yes," I said, "she just finished her degree from Baghdad University."

"That's perfect. I'll talk to the school and see what we can work out."

Kerry was a graduate of USF. The school, located in Tampa, had more than thirty-five thousand students, including many from foreign countries. As one of the university's most famous alumni, Kerry was confident USF would work with him to help Rafraf gain admittance.

Kerry and I had worked together during the initial months of the Iraq War. His energy and craftiness earned him two of the most appropriate nicknames I had ever heard.

Our bureau chief Heather called him Lawrence of Absurdia. That had something to do with Kerry's constant flow of story ideas, and fearless conquering of the brutal desert. He could smile and keep working—even enthusiastically—in the harshest conditions.

My favorite nickname for Kerry—issued shortly after he somehow managed to commandeer an NBC satellite dish for his personal use, then talked his way into an embed with the marines—was the Electric Ferret.

Being embedded with troops meant living and traveling with the unit no matter what they did or where they went. With thousands of journalists covering the war, it took months of negotiations and paperwork to set up an official embed. Kerry did it in days.

For Rafraf, Kerry worked out an elaborate plan that, if all things came together, would allow her two years in the United States to earn a master's degree in political science. The university would admit Rafraf based on her degree from Baghdad University, as long as she could pass the Graduate Record Examination (the GRE), and an English-proficiency test.

But just getting accepted to an American university doesn't guarantee a student visa for foreign students. To receive a visa, foreign students must also prove they have the ability to pay for tuition and living expenses.

"Rafraf can't pay for lunch," I told Kerry, "much less graduate school!" She'd saved a few hundred dollars from her work in Iraq, but the rest of the money had been spent on living expenses for her family. As a tourist in the United States, Rafraf was also prohibited from working. I had hoped the university would give Rafraf a full scholarship.

"We'll have to pay for it then," Kerry said. "Are you in?"

"How much are we talking about?"

I was willing to spend money helping Rafraf—but paying for college? I had two daughters that were growing more expensive by the day. I was already beginning to worry about how I was going to pay for their college, and it was still years away.

"Sixty thousand dollars," Kerry said bluntly. "That's if she can finish it all in two years."

I had to sit down. "I don't have that kind of money."

"I don't either, but I've got a way around it."

The solution, Kerry explained, was to create a fellowship at the University of South Florida. Rafraf would have to apply and compete for the fellowship, but if the university granted it to her, we could fund it with donations and ask others to chip in.

"Immigration officials will grant a student visa to a foreigner who has won a fellowship to study in the U.S.," Kerry added.

"Interesting."

"There's more. Contributing to a fellowship is a tax-deductible donation. So we can raise money from people and they can get a write-off."

"That's brilliant," I said.

It was especially brilliant because we couldn't count on the network to financially support Rafraf. Dozens of other Iraqis had worked for NBC over the years. Some had put their lives on the line as many times as Rafraf, if not more. How could the network give to one, and not the others? The logic was absolutely fair.

What was special about Rafraf? I didn't know the answer, beyond that I felt called to protect her. We had developed a friendship—a bond that was sealed by the close call at the bombed school—but there was more to it than that. God had something planned for Rafraf. I had no idea what it was.

I tried to find a way to work Lawrence of Absurdia and the Electric Ferret into a single nickname that would do justice to the plan Kerry had come up with. Nothing worked.

Kerry and I became the official sponsors of the fellowship and agreed to raise the required money to pay for the recipient's education.

All we needed was $60,000.

"We can do it," Kerry said confidently, "trust me."

Kerry and I agreed we would each put $4,000 into the fellowship to get the ball rolling. Then we went to work begging.

I asked everyone I knew who had worked with Rafraf to contribute to the fund . . . even $100 would go a long way. I also got money from neighbors, my sister, my agent, and Kiki's parents. Anyone with a job was fair game. I carried preaddressed, postage-paid envelopes with me wherever I went. I was amazed at how many people who had never even met Rafraf were willing to give to help her go to school in the United States.

Rachel Levin, one of the producers from Iraq, offered to help as well. She didn't have much of her own money to give, but she knew a woman in San Francisco who might be willing to help.

"Can Rafraf write a short letter explaining why she's here?" Rachel asked.

"Sure," I said.

I never read the letter Rafraf wrote, but whatever she said, it worked. The woman in San Francisco sent a check for $10,000.

While I focused my efforts on raising money from friends, relatives, and people who actually knew Rafraf, Kerry set his sights much higher.

Kerry hit up practically every major star at NBC News, along with correspondents and anchors from other networks. The money poured in. Within months, the majority of the fellowship was funded.

BUT EVEN WITH KERRY'S PLAN coming together, it might still all fall apart. Before USF would admit Rafraf to graduate school, she had to achieve an acceptable score on the GRE.

The GRE is a standardized test that measures every aspect of a student's undergraduate knowledge.

"How on earth," I asked myself, "can a person who thinks the president of the United States can freely round up and kill his political opponents get past the GRE?"

I knew Rafraf was extremely smart, but I wondered what else Baghdad University either didn't teach her or got wrong.

I went back to the Internet and found a company called Kaplan, which offered intensive study courses for passing college entrance exams.

Kaplan had a course in Atlanta beginning in December. It consisted of nine three-hour classroom sessions over one month. The Web site claimed the course would help students raise their scores on the GRE, but offered no guarantee of an acceptable grade.

The fee? $1,100 that I didn't have.

But I had become good at begging for money in recent weeks, so I picked up the phone and called Kaplan's corporate offices.

I explained who Rafraf was, why she was in the United States, and what so many people were trying to do for her. I also explained to the corporate PR person on the other end of the line that there would be no publicity for the company for helping.

"It would be a violation of NBC's corporate policy," I said to the man from Kaplan, "to receive any financial benefit in exchange for coverage of a story. So even if the network were to someday do a story on Rafraf, we could never mention that you helped."

I had made a call to NBC's legal department prior to contacting

Kaplan just to make sure I was on solid legal and ethical ground asking for something for nothing. They told me that since Rafraf was no longer an employee of NBC, it was fine.

"So you're asking for us to waive the eleven-hundred-dollar tuition?" the man responded.

"With nothing in return, except knowing you helped someone who really needs it."

I expected the PR man would have to make calls and get back to me. I was wrong.

"Done," he said. "She'll need books and other supplies. We'll cover those too."

"Seriously?"

"Absolutely. We're glad we can help."

I was floored. Nothing about getting Rafraf into the United States had been easy. I knew keeping her in the country beyond the limits of her tourist visa would be a difficult, if not insurmountable task.

I had reasoned, after first asking Kiki about helping Rafraf, that if God really wanted it to happen, he would open doors. Now, doors were flying open.

RAFRAF KNEW SHE NEEDED THE GRE preparation course, but she also knew she had to get out of the house.

She spent most of the month of November locked in her room, living on Baghdad time. She cried as she wrote poems in Arabic about her family and her lost country. She missed it all more than she ever imagined she would.

Shortly before arriving in the United States, Rafraf purchased her own laptop computer. That computer, with the help of Don's wireless Internet connection, had become her link back to Iraq and the life she had known for twenty-three years.

She e-mailed her poems to her favorite radio station in Baghdad. She stayed up all night e-mailing people back home, and listening to the radio station over the tinny-sounding Internet connection. The

DJ would often play her requests, and on a couple of occasions he even read her poems over the air.

Sometimes her brother Rami, or even her mother, would go to an Internet café that had videoconference capabilities. Rafraf had discovered an unused webcam in a junk drawer in Don's kitchen and hooked it up on her own computer.

She always put her scarf on before chatting on camera with anyone back home.

The Halloween party had been a trial. Rafraf had initially felt self-conscious about being seen without the scarf, but that led to a sense of freedom. Two days after the party, she packed all of her scarves away in a drawer and never wore them again—except when chatting with her family in a videoconference.

She would tell her mother someday why she'd stopped wearing the scarf, but she wasn't ready just yet.

Her life, Rafraf knew, was out of phase. She tried to blame in on jet lag, but the real reason she stayed up all night, then slept all day, was fear.

It wasn't a physical fear. Rafraf was no longer worried that people would try to hurt her. Instead she feared whom she was about to become. She could feel herself changing, but into what? Her electronic ties to Baghdad were a lifeline to herself.

"This has to stop," Kiki told her one afternoon. Rafraf had just woken up and come downstairs.

"I know," Rafraf said. "But I don't know anybody."

"You won't if you never leave your room, and you have to start sleeping at normal times."

"I know."

"Do you like cooking?"

Rafraf's face lit up. "Yes, do you?"

"No."

Rafraf's face fell.

"But I could really use some help in that area," Kiki said. "Could you make some traditional Iraqi meals? It would help me out a lot, and I know the girls would love it."

"Really?" Rafraf jumped up and opened the cupboard with the spices. "Do you have the yellow spice and the one that is like a lemon?"

Rafraf happily dug through all the cooking supplies in the house and started a list of what she would need.

The girls both pulled up chairs and watched, asking lots of questions. To Rafraf, it seemed they had never seen anyone actually cook a meal before. She explained in great detail how each thing is made and what she would be doing if she were at home.

Once the food was cooking in the pots, Rafraf gave Kiki, Rachael, and Madison the first of what would become many belly-dancing lessons.

TWENTY-ONE

BOYS

The first week of December 2004 was cold in Atlanta. It was more than simply sweater weather, it was ski-jacket-and-gloves weather.

I came home from work on Friday, looking forward to an easy weekend at home. Such things were never guaranteed with my job, but I wasn't the on-call correspondent for the weekend, so short of a disaster or a terrorist attack, the chances were good that my phone wasn't going to ring.

I walked into the kitchen at about seven thirty, looking forward to a relaxing evening in my warm, cozy home.

Rafraf clearly had other plans for herself.

She was standing in the kitchen when I walked in. She wore a short black dress and high-heeled shoes with open toes. Her hair was up off her shoulders, revealing her neck and dangly earrings. She had clearly spent hours on her makeup.

Kiki was standing in the kitchen too. She did not look happy. I recognized "the look" as soon as I recovered from the shock of the black dress.

"I'm missing something," I said in that way men say when they know they're in huge trouble but don't know why.

"Oh, just wait," Kiki said. "I'll let you deal with this."

That's when Kiki turned and stormed out of the room, leaving me with Rafraf.

"Do you know where the Taco Mac restaurant is?" she began.

"Uh, yeah. It's just a couple of miles from here."

She flashed a mischievous smile. "Can you take me there at eight o'clock?"

"I suppose. Why?"

"Because I'm meeting a boy for dinner." By *boy,* she obviously meant *man,* but this was no time to quibble about semantics.

I was dumbfounded. "Wearing that?"

"Don't I look good?" She once again flashed that smile.

"That's not the point. You've hardly even been out of the house. How did you end up getting a date for dinner?"

Her answer would forever be burned into my memory.

"MySpace," she said simply.

"You're going on a date with a guy who asked you out on MySpace?" I practically shouted. "Since when are you on MySpace? Do you even know this guy?"

"He looks nice. And Kiki said I should meet new people. Plus it's not a date, it's just friends."

"You're not dressed for friends. You're dressed for a date."

Kiki and I, of course, expected that Rafraf would want to find a boyfriend. She was an adult and entitled to make her own decisions. But we had also expected her to seek someone from a culture more like her own; it was part of the reason I kept suggesting she go to the Islamic Community Center.

I thought other Muslims living in America could help Rafraf find balance; they could teach her to live within our culture while remaining true to her religion and traditions.

Kiki and I weren't Rafraf's parents, but we were trying to offer guidance that would allow her to make good decisions. Our preparation for Rafraf's transition into American culture, we now realized, had been woefully incomplete.

The sudden date, the short dress, all of it seemed to come out of nowhere.

"We have to have a talk," I said.

We sat down at the kitchen table.

I wasn't at all sure what to say, but something had to be said. What did Rafraf really know about men, or sex for that matter? I honestly didn't know and didn't want to know, but suddenly there was no avoiding the topic.

"How old is this guy?" I began.

"Chris, his name is Chris, and he's twenty-five."

I squirmed uncomfortably in my chair. "Look, I don't know about dating in Iraq, especially since dating isn't really allowed in Iraq. But this is America. Even if this Chris is a really nice guy, there's a pretty good chance that he's expecting more from this date than you are."

"Meaning what?"

I didn't want to discuss this.

"Meaning he may not expect sex on the first date, but he will pretty soon. Especially if you go dressed like that."

"But we're just friends. It's not even a date."

"I know you're saying that. Look, I know this sounds really sexist of me. I'm not one of those guys who thinks a woman is asking for sex just because she wears something sexy. But the reality is a lot of guys do think that way. You don't know this Chris at all."

"I don't think he's that way," she said sincerely.

"Don't you have something longer you can wear, and with sleeves?"

"I want to wear this," she said. "It's not that short." Clearly she had made up her mind about the "not-date date" with Chris. "And whatever he thinks is his problem, not mine."

FIFTEEN MINUTES LATER, RAFRAF and I pulled into the parking lot of the Taco Mac restaurant. She was still wearing the dress and heels, though I had convinced her to put a sweater over her shoulders.

"Stay here," I said. "I'm gonna meet this guy first. I'll come back and get you if it's okay."

"Okay, thank you."

The Taco Mac was basically a sports bar that served Mexican food. It was a bit nicer than the fast-foodish name implied, but it certainly was not fancy.

I did not know what Chris looked like. I walked in the front door figuring he would be easy to spot . . . either the biggest loser or the biggest dork in the place. Fortunately, he was neither.

A guy was sitting by himself at a table near the bar. He was about five feet ten, medium build, and with short, sand-colored hair. He looked to be about the right age, so I headed straight for him. He wore a long-sleeve shirt and khaki cargo shorts, despite the cold weather.

"Are you Chris?" I said, sitting down at the empty seat across the table from him.

A look of alarm crossed his face. That was understandable. At six feet one and 220 pounds, I was already bigger than most people. And I was trying to look even bigger and more imposing with this particular guy.

"Yes," he said, clearly confused.

"I'm Rafraf's friend Don. She lives with my family."

"Nice to meet you." He extended his hand. He had a confident handshake.

"Do you have any idea what you're doing?" I began somewhat bluntly. "Do you know anything about Rafraf or where she's from?"

"She's Middle Eastern or something. I don't even know what she looks like. Her picture on MySpace only shows her eyes."

"Well, she's fresh off the plane from Baghdad, never left Iraq in her entire life until now."

"Seriously?"

Clearly Rafraf was being somewhat evasive with her online persona.

"Seriously," I said. "And whatever you think is going to happen tonight, you should know it's not. Rafraf is a Muslim. She has completely different cultural traditions and standards than we do. And she hasn't even begun to figure out how she fits in with all this."

"I see," he said sincerely.

"I'm not sure you do. You're the first American guy she's ever been out with. There's a lot of responsibility on you."

"Okay, I appreciate that you would tell me all this."

Surely this was already the strangest date Chris had ever been on.

"You seem like a nice guy," I said, "so sorry about the vetting. But I have a responsibility to Rafraf's family to look out for her."

"I totally get that, no problem."

I HEADED OUT TO THE parking lot to get Rafraf, only to find that she was already on her way to the door.

"He seems okay," I said. "Whatever you do, don't leave the restaurant with him, just in case. Call me when you're ready and I'll come get you."

"Okay," she said, "and thanks again."

Chris really did seem like an okay guy, but I wasn't happy about leaving Rafraf with him. I felt that I had been put in an impossible situation. I wasn't her father. Could I have refused to allow the date? Would she have changed clothes if I had demanded that she do so? I didn't know the answers to those questions.

I watched her walk through the glass doors of the restaurant.

From Chris's table near the bar, he could see the front doors too. She recognized Chris from his MySpace picture, smiled, and headed his way.

He almost fell out of his chair.

*   *   *

I GOT AN EARFUL WHEN I got home

"I just want to go on record as saying I am totally uncomfortable with this. We would never let our girls find a guy on the Internet and then go meet him. If she is part of the family, then those rules should apply to her too."

"You're right."

"And you need to understand, she's not just any girl and you're not just any guy. She's a young Iraqi woman and you are a TV correspondent. There are people out there who would consider you perfect targets."

She was right.

"We need to make it very clear that she is never, ever to bring anyone to this house that she met on the Internet!"

After being married to Kiki for twelve years, I knew better than to add my two cents now. I also knew she was fiercely protective of the people she loved and I could tell she loved Rafraf.

"I'll make sure it doesn't happen," I said.

Kiki was mad, but she also seemed disappointed. She, Rafraf, and the girls had become close over the preceding weeks; the relationship was sealed within hours of meeting, when Rafraf told a joke.

"If a blonde and a brunette fall off a building," Rafraf had asked, "who would hit the ground first?"

"Wait, you know blonde jokes?" Kiki said. "Are there even blondes in Iraq?"

"Not many real blondes," Rafraf said, "though I do have a blond cousin. But everyone knows blonde jokes. So who hit the ground first?"

"Who?" Kiki played along.

"The brunette," Rafraf said, laughing, "because the blonde would have to stop and ask directions."

It was funny, because Rafraf thought it was funny. Kiki, Rafraf, and the girls laughed until their cheeks hurt.

Later, Rachael and Madison taught Rafraf how to play Dance Dance Revolution on the PlayStation, which they did for hours on end. In exchange, Rafraf gave the girls and Kiki yet another belly-dancing lesson. They danced around the living room, with Arabic music blaring on the stereo.

CHRIS TURNED OUT TO BE a nice guy. Rafraf liked him, but not romantically. They had a couple of dates before both determined that their relationship would be strictly platonic.

Plus, Rafraf realized, many more fish were in the sea.

The GRE prep course was filled with students who were about Rafraf's age. Women and men in their midtwenties were all thrown together for several hours, two nights a week.

Rafraf made a few female friends, but she also enjoyed the attention she got from the men.

She had always enjoyed such attention, though in Iraq it would get her in a great deal of trouble. It even cost her an entire year of college.

IT WAS THE SPRINGTIME OF Rafraf's sophomore year at Baghdad University. She and her older sister Laila were bickering. Laila was jealous about something and had made Rafraf's life miserable for weeks. Laila was a senior at the time, though Rafraf did her best to avoid seeing her at school.

Rafraf, as usual, had a boyfriend whom she kept secret from her family. But Laila spotted them together one day in May and immediately made the connection.

"Oh, no," Rafraf said to the boy. "That was my sister."

"Do you think she saw us?" he said, fear rising in his voice.

"I know she did. We're sitting together in the cafeteria. We might as well have been wearing a sign."

Rafraf grabbed her things and bolted for the door.

"Where are you going?"

"Home," she yelled over her shoulder. "I have to try to stop her before she tells my father."

She raced home, but it was too late! She opened the front door and could see Laila already talking to her father in the kitchen.

"Rafraf!" he shouted.

She didn't answer. She bolted upstairs and locked herself in a large storage room.

Seconds later her father pounded on the door. "Open this door now."

"No," Rafraf said through tears. "You'll beat me."

"I'll break the door down if you don't open it. I promise I won't hit you, just open the door."

Rafraf opened the door just a crack. Her father pushed it open the rest of the way, then grabbed her by the hair.

"No," she screamed through tears. "Please don't hit me."

"You are not going back to school, or to work, or leaving this house ever again. You will stay in this room until I say you can leave. I don't want to see you or hear you."

He slammed the door closed and left Rafraf crying on the floor.

She stayed in the room for four months.

When her father was out of the house, she was allowed out just long enough to go to the bathroom. When he was home, she had to hold it. Food was brought to her and shoved through the door as if she were a prisoner on death row.

Her imprisonment came at the hottest time of the year. Her house had no air-conditioning, and it seemed all the summer heat rose and enveloped the sweltering room.

Day after day, Rafraf would lie on the hard floor like a dog, her face close to the crack under the door hoping to catch a breeze.

"All this over having lunch with a boy," she told herself. "It's not right."

She missed all of her finals at the university and as a result lost a whole year's worth of work. She was finally let out of the storage room and the house just as fall classes were beginning.

Somehow, Jamila had talked Kamal into allowing Rafraf to return to school. She had to repeat her entire sophomore year.

* * *

IN ATLANTA, THE OLD RULES didn't apply. Rafraf was free to talk to whomever she wanted, whenever she wanted. But where was the balance? There had to be a middle ground.

Kiki and I were particularly concerned about Rafraf's clothing.

"I'm no different than anybody else here," Rafraf said. "American women dress this way, so why can't I?"

She was right, of course. Rafraf's clothes weren't any more revealing than those of most other American women in their twenties. It just felt to Kiki and me that the wardrobe transition should have happened more slowly.

I had to admit defeat at Rafraf's logic, and Kiki decided it was time to step up and give it a go.

"Look, we don't have the same kind of rules here that you had. You are free to make your own choices, but with that freedom comes responsibility. You are responsible for the consequences of your choices."

Rafraf looked a bit confused.

"What you do and how you dress has an effect on people, and I'm concerned that you are sending mixed messages that will eventually get you in trouble. Like my dad always said to me, 'You're writing checks your body can't cash.'"

Rafraf's head bowed a little; rebelling against the old rules was one thing, disappointing Kiki was another. Despite being so similar in personality, Rafraf treated Kiki with great respect and, whether she agreed with her or not, always listened when she spoke.

Kiki and I discussed the situation later that night. "She's like a boy-crazy sixteen-year-old," Kiki said. "I'm worried about her. I'm not at all sure she's emotionally equipped for what she's doing."

Rachael, our oldest daughter, was not old enough to date. Kiki and I had only just begun discussing what parameters we would set for her as a teenager when, or if, we decided she was responsible and mature enough to date. There would be no dates without supervision, no going to a boy's house if his parents weren't home, or bringing one to our house if we weren't home. No older boys. No staying out past eleven o'clock. We had plenty of rules for a sixteen- or seventeen-year-old daughter.

For a grown woman, we had only advice.

"I'm worried about her too," I said, "but surely it's just a phase. She's been so sheltered her whole life."

"Well, she needs to slow down. She's dating three guys at the same time."

"She says it's not dating, they're all just friends . . . but still."

"Well, she sure likes the attention," Kiki said. "Where does she even meet these guys?"

"She's a dude magnet. She meets them in her night class, or they are friends of girls she meets at class. Anyway, she's going to Florida in a couple of days. Maybe spending the week with Kerry and his wife will give her a new perspective."

"Let's hope so, for her sake."

TWENTY-TWO

THE CHRISTMAS

The Kroger grocery store in Roswell, Georgia, was as new and modern as any grocery store in the country. Tucked into a hillside near an upscale community of townhomes, the store's stone facade welcomed shoppers into a shopping experience like nothing Rafraf had ever seen in Baghdad. By late December, she had been grocery shopping with Kiki several times and was always struck by the abundance of seemingly everything in America.

Unlike the bustling outdoor markets of Iraq, the inside of the Kroger store was quiet, with classical music drifting above the soft hum of refrigeration units. The lighting was warm and inviting, the aisles were wide, and the selection of food was unbelievable.

"Why do you call it stinky Kroger?" Rafraf asked Kiki as she and the girls headed to the grocery store.

"Everybody calls it stinky Kroger," Rachael answered.

Madison just laughed in the backseat of Kiki's SUV.

"You'll see," Kiki answered. She pulled into a parking space, and the four hopped out of the SUV.

The smell hit Rafraf immediately. It was awful.

Madison covered her nose and laughed. "That's why they call it stinky Kroger," she managed.

"It smells like my street back home," Rafraf said. "What is it?"

"A sewage treatment plant," Kiki said. "You can't see it from here, but it's right behind the store. Whenever the wind blows from the south, which is most of the time, it smells like that."

"I guess sewage smells the same all over the world." Rafraf shrugged. "At least we have that in common."

Thankfully, the inside of the store never smelled bad. No doubt the work of an elaborate air-filter system.

The store had a large indoor balcony about twenty feet above the main entrance. From the balcony, acoustics were surprisingly good, and someone decided it would be a great place to perform live music.

It was an odd location for a Christmas concert, but that was the real reason the Teague family converged on stinky Kroger that night.

Madison, who had a beautiful singing voice, was part of the Timber Ridge Elementary School choir, and they had spent months rehearsing for the stinky-Kroger performance.

Don left the bureau in midtown Atlanta early and made it to the store just in time for the first song.

"We wish you a merry Christmas," the children sang with enthusiasm. All across the store, shoppers looked up toward the singing children on the balcony.

For Rafraf, it was a pleasant if oddly surreal experience. She stood with the Teagues and a dozen or so other parents, listening to children sing Christmas carols in a grocery store that—at least on the out-side—smelled like home.

"Are you someone's sister?" one of the mothers asked Rafraf.

"No, I'm living with Madison Teague's family."

"That's nice. Where are you from?"

"Iraq," Don chimed in. "She's been here for a couple of months now."

The children finished their first song, then slowed the pace.

"Silent night, holy night" drifted across the store.

"Oh," the woman said, clearly surprised. "Well, I hope you enjoy your first Christmas in America."

"Actually," Don said, "it's going to be her first Hanukkah. She's heading to Florida tomorrow to spend a week with a friend of ours. He's Jewish."

"Oh," the woman said again. "Well then, happy Hanukkah."

But Rafraf didn't hear her. Didn't hear anything, in fact, after the words "he's Jewish" entered her ears. The room started spinning around her and the color drained from her face.

She was terrified, and furious.

Don saw it instantly. "You didn't know Kerry is Jewish?"

"Of course not. How can I go tomorrow?"

"You can go," Don said flatly. "Kerry Sanders has done more for you than anyone! He's raised money and convinced his school to help you! Rachel Levin raised more than ten thousand dollars for you. She's been making phone calls and writing letters for months to try to sort out your visa. Did you know she's Jewish too?"

Rafraf was floored. As far as she knew, she'd never even seen a Jew in person, much less talked to one. As a child she watched Arab television shows and movies that depicted Jews as monsters.

Now Don was telling her that two people she had worked with every day, and even considered friends, were Jewish? It couldn't be.

"Why didn't they say anything?" she asked.

"Are you kidding?" Don asked. "In many Arab countries it's a crime for a Jew to set foot on their soil, much less spend months working and living there. The last thing they want to do is advertise."

"I don't know about this," she said.

"We'll talk about it later." Don turned his attention back to the balcony. The conversation was clearly dampening his Christmas spirit.

LATER THAT NIGHT, RAFRAF FOUND Kiki in the kitchen and told her of the situation. Don wasn't home. He had been called back to the bureau to work on a story for the *Today* show the following morning.

"Have I ever told you about Mr. John?" Rafraf asked.

"Don mentioned something about it once," Kiki said. "He's like the bogeyman, right?"

"Yes. All my life I was told to fear him, that he was going to hurt me." Rafraf sat down, struggling to put her thoughts and emotions into words. "But he's not trying to hurt me, he's trying to help me."

Kiki smiled, but didn't say anything.

"And now," Rafraf continued, "I find out that Kerry Sanders is Jewish, and he's trying to help me too. It makes me wonder." There was something more, but Rafraf was afraid to say it.

"Wonder what?" Kiki prodded.

"If they lied to me about those things," Rafraf said, "then I wonder what else they lied to me about."

Rafraf thought back to Baghdad and her first experience with the Internet. Reading news about the war—about how the rest of the world viewed her country—had been so painful. Now she was feeling that pain all over again, and she wasn't sure exactly why.

"So what are you going to do?" Kiki asked, though Rafraf suspected she already knew the answer.

"I'm going to Florida."

DESPITE RAFRAF'S INITIAL WORRIES, KERRY and his wife, Deborah, did not have sinister intentions toward her. They were, in contrast, eager to welcome her into their home.

And much to Rafraf's delight, they did actually celebrate what Rafraf called "the Christmas."

Rafraf had seen the Christmas in movies and always thought it looked warm and inviting. Plus, she loved giving presents. She saw the Christmas the way many Americans do, not so much as a religious holiday, but as a time to appreciate friends and family.

Like many American couples, Kerry and Deborah came from different religious backgrounds. Deborah was raised Christian, but Kerry came from a mixture of religious faiths.

His father was, indeed, Jewish. Kerry had spent his childhood going to various churches and synagogues with his father. But Kerry's mother was a Christian, and so his family celebrated Christmas as well. As an adult, Kerry considered himself a Christian by faith, and a Jew by heritage. That kind of arrangement seemed to work for a lot of American families.

Rafraf enjoyed a great week with Kerry and Deborah. Enjoyed it so much that she extended her stay in Florida for an additional three weeks. She escaped the cold of northern Georgia. She learned that she could open her mind to areas she once thought impossible.

She went with Kerry to Tampa to visit USF, and he walked her through filling out the required paperwork for admittance as an international student.

She also bought her first bikini, which she wore to the beach immediately.

KIKI AND I DISCUSSED RELIGION in great detail before Rafraf arrived in the United States. As Christians, we both believe that faith in God, and belief that Jesus Christ died for our salvation, holds the key to life.

It is possible, we know, to succeed in the world without Christianity or any faith at all for that matter. Billions of people have found wealth, power, love, and happiness without believing what we believe.

But Kiki and I had been walking with God long enough to truly understand that things don't matter; people matter. We believe that every human heart is longing for God, not for his sake but for ours.

When I told Rafraf about God talking to me, I wanted her to understand that I felt loved by God. I hear God in my heart; that still, small voice that guides me. Kiki hears God a lot too. She didn't understand who Jesus really was until she was twenty-nine, but her heart had always been searching.

We both believe what we do on earth matters, but what's most important is what happens next. Where does your soul go? For us the answer is in accepting Jesus. He is the way to God and he paid a price we could never afford. He loved us so much that he came down to walk with us, show us love and mercy and demonstrated through the cross that he had victory over death and that he wanted us to be with him forever in heaven. All we had to do was believe and accept the gift.

"For God so loved the world that he gave his one and only Son, that whoever believes in him shall not perish but have eternal life. For God did not send his Son into the world to condemn the world, but to save the world through him. Whoever believes in him is not condemned, but whoever does not believe stands condemned already because he has not believed in the name of God's one and only Son."*

The "good news" is that the gift of salvation is that simple . . . accept the gift that God gave the world through Jesus.

The bad news is that Christians are human, just as guilty of hypocrisy and treachery as they are capable of love and compassion. Over the centuries, some have tried to spread the gospel at the tip of a sword or at the end of a gun.

The message is not delivered with much tact by many. People aren't usually drawn to God by someone hitting them over the head with a Bible and saying, "Believe what I believe or burn in hell."

Indeed, I suspect one of the biggest problem many nonbelievers have with Christianity is Christians.

Kiki and I agreed that our responsibility toward Rafraf was to help her. That was what we believed God had called us to do. By loving her, we would demonstrate God's love and, in that way, try to be the best examples of Christians we could be.

"Our job is to be a light of the world," Kiki said, referring to Jesus' words in the book of Matthew, "a city on the hill that can't be hidden."

---

* John 3:16–18, NIV.

If Rafraf had specific questions about our faith, then we would gladly answer them—but we trusted God would lead Rafraf on her own spiritual path, and we didn't want to get in his way.

IN THE MEANTIME, RAFRAF WAS in serious need of yet another miracle. As the end of January neared, her visa situation began to look bleak.

Most of the details of Kerry Sanders's fellowship plan had come together. We had the money in hand to fund the first year of graduate school. Rafraf, to my amazement, received a passing score on the GRE, and the University of South Florida was going to admit her for the fall semester.

But Rafraf's visa was set to expire January 29.

"That's no problem," the coordinator for international graduate students at USF told me over the phone. "If her visa expires, she just has to go back home and reapply for her I-20 student visa."

"She can't go home," I said. "There are people trying to kill her there."

"She has to go home. The government won't issue an I-20 to somebody who's already in the U.S. Somebody should have told you that."

"Nobody ever said that. Isn't there some way around that rule?"

"Not that I've ever seen" was the predictable reply.

We were sure Rafraf was about to be in an impossible situation. Her tourist visa was set to expire in just days, but her application for a student visa had no chance of being approved before it did.

"What can I do?" Rafraf had called me on the phone from Kerry's house. She was on the verge of panic.

"I honestly don't know," I said, "but something will work out. The hard part was getting you out of Iraq in the first place. God wouldn't put you through all that to send you back now."

"But you can't know that."

"Have faith, Rafraf."

*   *   *

IT WAS KERRY WHO DISCOVERED the mistake. Rafraf was packing to head back to Atlanta the next day, and probably back to Baghdad a few days after that. She was dejected.

"What's this stamp?" Kerry asked. He was holding Rafraf's Iraqi passport open and pointing to one of the pages.

"That's my visa," she said, "or what's left of it."

"So the date here is the date your visa expires?"

"Yes, January twenty-ninth."

"So why does it say April twenty-ninth?" he asked, cocking a suspicious eyebrow.

"Let me see that." Rafraf grabbed the passport and looked at the page.

"It does say April twenty-ninth," she said in obvious disbelief. "But I know they only gave me a three-month visa. They told me that from the beginning."

"Let's go," Kerry said. "We're going to take your passport to the airport and ask the immigration officials there what this means."

An hour later, a U.S. immigration officer at Fort Lauderdale airport confirmed what seemed too good to be true.

Somewhere between Amman, Jordan, and Atlanta, Rafraf's three-month visa had magically transformed into a six-month visa.

"Somebody at JFK must have liked you," the officer said.

"I don't understand," Rafraf answered.

"That's where they stamped the date, when you cleared customs in New York. They stamp the arrival date, and the date you have to leave, April twenty-ninth. You never looked at it until now?"

"I guess not," she said.

"Well, like I said, somebody there must have liked you, because they extended your visa by three months." The officer handed the passport back to Rafraf. "Enjoy your stay in the U.S."

Was it divine intervention? Rafraf supposed anything was possible, but on the drive home from the airport she figured out the most likely answer.

Rafraf's flight to the United States from Amman had, as the immigration agent said, landed at John F. Kennedy International Airport in New York. All arriving passengers first cleared customs there before switching to other flights within the United States.

Most of the people on Rafraf's flight had cleared customs with no problem, but about a half dozen passengers were held for further questioning. Rafraf was among those detained, and as she looked at the other passengers with her, she knew why.

All were of Arabic descent. None of them was traveling with spouses or children. All of them, like her, had boarded the plane alone.

They waited in a room full of empty desks waiting to be interviewed. To Rafraf, it seemed they had waited long enough.

She got up, walked out of the room, and stopped the first man she saw wearing a badge. The look on his face and slump of his shoulders spoke of a long day at work.

"You were told not to leave the room," he said abruptly.

"How long are you going to keep us in there? It has been two hours, and nobody even comes in to talk to us."

"We're getting to it."

She feared the worst, that something was wrong with her paperwork and the man would send her back to Jordan.

"Why do you speak such good English?" he asked suspiciously.

"Because I learned in school."

"A lot of people take English in school," he snapped. "They don't sound like you."

"I studied hard," Rafraf replied with her slight British accent. "I work as a translator for NBC in Baghdad."

"Oh, lucky you. Now go back and sit down."

A few minutes later, the officer entered the room with another man. They began trying to interview the first of the passengers. He spoke no English, and neither of the immigration officers spoke Arabic.

"If you wish, I can translate for you," Rafraf offered.

"Aren't you in a hurry?" the immigration officer asked. "Everyone else seems to be."

"It's okay. I have twelve hours before my flight to Atlanta."

"Good," the man said, "because none of these other people speak English either."

Nothing was particularly difficult about the questions immigration officials needed to ask. But Rafraf was proud that she could translate for each of the passengers so well. Yes, they all spoke Arabic, but some were from Lebanon, others from Egypt, Jordan, and Syria.

Rafraf had learned the accents and nuances of each of the countries, so much so that no matter whom she was talking to, they always thought she was of the same nationality they were.

Within an hour, all of the interviews were complete, and Rafraf gathered her things to leave the customs area.

The last bit of unfinished business was her visa.

"Here you go," the immigration officer she had first met said. He stamped her passport and handed it back to her with a smile.

"Thank you," Rafraf said. "Is there anything else?"

"Yes, enjoy your stay in the U.S."

She never looked at the date the man had stamped. She clutched her passport and her dog and stepped into America for the first time.

Only three months later did she learn how appreciative the man at JFK had been. Apparently an hour of work had earned her three extra months in the country.

TWENTY-THREE

BALANCE

Rafraf returned from Florida at the end of January. She was optimistic about the new year, and where her life was heading in 2005.

She had more boys chasing after her than she knew what to do with, and she had even found some girlfriends she enjoyed hanging out with.

Still, one thing in Rafraf's new life was seriously lacking . . . transportation. Rafraf had never driven a car in her entire life. Don said his insurance wouldn't cover her as a driver, and no way was he putting her behind the wheel of his Mercedes. Plus, even if she knew how to drive, she couldn't get a license with just a tourist visa.

"Can you teach me to ride a bicycle?" Rafraf asked Don one Saturday morning in February.

"Are you serious?"

"Yes. I can ride to the store or to see friends. And I never learned, so I always wanted to anyway."

"Sure. I taught Rachael and Madison, I guess I can teach you too."

It's unclear what Don expected to happen next, but he clearly didn't expect Rafraf to come downstairs ten minutes later and announce she was ready.

"For what?" Don asked.

"My lesson." Rafraf had changed into jeans, a sweater, and sneakers.

"You mean like right now?"

"Yes, of course," Rafraf said, smiling.

TEACHING A CHILD TO RIDE a bicycle was relatively easy, at least it was for me.

I taught both my girls how to ride their bicycles on the same day. Rachael was six and Madison was four. The trick, I determined, was to first teach them the concept of balance. Until a person "felt" balance and learned to stay within its bounds, there was no way to stay upright on a bicycle.

But bicycles are intimidating. Even a child's bike seems huge to a four-year-old. I remembered being terrified as a child as my dad pushed me down the sidewalk on my first bike.

"Don't let go," I cried.

Of course he did let go. What choice did he have?

"You're doing it," he said proudly.

At which point I panicked, crashed, bloodied my knee, and cried even more. So instead of starting my girls on bicycles, I first put them on Razor scooters.

It takes the same sense of balance to ride a Razor scooter, which has two small wheels in line, as to ride a bicycle. But the deck of the scooter is only three inches from the ground, so the fear of trusting balance is almost nonexistent.

Give most children a scooter and they will happily be riding it, and balancing, within minutes of their first attempt.

So that's how I taught both the girls to ride their bikes on the same day. I gave them Razor scooters, helmets, and pads, then had them ride around on the driveway for a few hours.

Later that afternoon I took the girls to a vacant lot with a slight downhill slope. One at a time I put them each on a bike, pushed them for about five feet, then let them go.

Both of them rode down the hill in perfect balance on their first attempt. I thought I was a genius . . . until I realized I hadn't taught either of them how to use the brake.

But I couldn't find the Razor scooters on that Saturday in February. Did we get rid of them at a garage sale? Probably.

So Rafraf would have to learn balance on Kiki's mountain bike. I lowered the seat as much as possible, and we went to the flattest part of the street we could find.

"I'm not wearing that," she said as I handed her Madison's bike helmet. "It will mess up my hair."

"It could mess up your head if you don't," I said. Reluctantly she put on the helmet.

Then I did one of the strangest things I had ever done. I pushed a grown woman down the street on a bicycle, urging her to find her balance.

"Stop leaning," I said. "I can't let go if you keep leaning on me."

"I'm not leaning. You can let go."

I did.

She crashed.

"Don't lean this time," I said, pushing her again, "find your balance."

"Let go."

I did.

She crashed again.

And again, and again, and again.

"I have to learn this," she said. "Even children can ride a bicycle."

"Do you understand what I mean when I say *balance*?"

"No," she said honestly.

It was true of more than just bicycles.

* * *

TO ME, IT SEEMED RAFRAF was rushing into her new life. She was definitely rushing dating.

"You can be honest with me," I said one day. "Are you trying to find a husband? Is that what's going on?"

Rafraf was well aware that marrying a U.S. citizen would make all her visa troubles go away almost instantly. She would be granted permanent-resident status and put on a fast track to citizenship, all with a simple "I do."

"That's the last thing I want," Rafraf said. "If I wanted to be married, I already could be. Two boys have already asked me."

"You've been here less than four months! And you've had two marriage proposals?"

"I think one of them was just trying to help me. But I don't need that kind of help."

Actually, I thought but didn't say, *you need more help than that.*

It had become painfully clear over the past few months that Rafraf's upbringing in Iraq had done little to prepare her for a life of independence in America.

She was a product of her family and her culture's traditions and expectations. A woman was expected to live with her parents until she found a husband. After the wedding, a couple was expected to live with the husband's parents for years before having a home of their own. Those were the expectations Rafraf was raised to meet.

As a result, Rafraf was—to borrow a phrase—extremely high maintenance, despite her streak of independence. In America she needed help with practically everything, and constant reassurance. Kiki and I were more than ready to help her, but at times doing so required a large measure of patience.

When I was traveling on a story, I could count on several calls from Rafraf per day. They always came at the most inopportune times.

"It's Rafraf," she would say. "I have to talk to you about something."

Being a man, I had learned that when a woman began any conversation with a variation of "we need to talk," it was never a good thing. At times Rafraf would forewarn of a conversation for days before actually getting to the topic.

"When you get back from the tornado, I need to ask you something," she would say. Or, "I have to talk to you later."

Maybe that was how all conversations began in Iraq, but in America it scared the heck out of me.

What can possibly be so bad that she needs three days of preparation to build up to it? I would think to myself.

But when she finally got around to whatever was on her mind, it was usually some mundane issue such as filling out paperwork, or registering for classes at school, or picking a major. I had to remind myself that simple things for me were completely new for Rafraf.

She leaned on me, on and off the bicycle.

TWENTY-FOUR

BREAD AND OTHER TREATS

The pain had begun in January. At first it was a dull ache that came and went, but by February it was intolerable. Rafraf's stomach hurt, and she didn't know why. She didn't want to bother Don and Kiki by telling them about it. She thought maybe she just needed good food from home.

She needed bread.

American bread made no sense at all to Rafraf.

"Real bread" wasn't full of air, shaped into sliced loaves, and wrapped in plastic. It was supposed to be flat, warm, and just a little crisp around the edges.

Rafraf had taken bread for granted her entire life. It was so simple, she baked it with her mother every day and ate it at every meal. When times were good, she would sometimes have it with butter or yogurt, but even dry the bread was delicious and comforting.

Lack of good bread, as it turned out, was not Rafraf's problem. The stomach pains were caused by something much more serious.

"WE'RE AT THE HOSPITAL," KIKI said over the cell phone. "Rafraf's going in for emergency surgery."

"What happened?" I asked. "Is she okay?" I was on the road, traveling back home after a three-day shoot.

"She will be after they take her appendix out. It ruptured yesterday, but she was too afraid to say anything. The doctors said if she had waited any longer to get to the hospital, she could have died."

Kiki stayed with Rafraf through the surgery.

I made it to the hospital to visit Rafraf the next morning. She was loaded with painkillers and barely able to talk.

"I need to call home," she said through the fog of the drugs. "But you have to dial because my hands don't work."

"Sure," I offered. Rafraf had an international calling card in her purse. I punched in the endless string of numbers; a few seconds later a phone was answered in Baghdad.

It wasn't Rafraf's mother, but her brother Malik, who was one year younger than Rafraf.

"This is Don Teague. I'm going to hand the phone to Rafraf."

I didn't actually hand her the phone, but held it next to her ear. She spoke with her brother for a minute or two, then looked back at me.

"He wants to talk to you," she said weakly.

I held the phone to my ear and tried to sound reassuring when I spoke.

"Hello, it's Don again. Rafraf is going to be fine."

Malik's English was not good at all, but considering I spoke no Arabic, it was the only option.

"Thank you," he said, "for taking Rafraf."

"Of course." I wondered if he meant taking her to the hospital, taking care of her in general, or taking her out of Iraq.

"She need a family to look for her."

"You don't need to worry about her."

"Okay. Good-bye."

I hung up and looked at Rafraf. "Your mother's not home?"

"No. She's at the hospital with my sister."

It was, I later discovered, a miracle of bad timing. One of Rafraf's sisters had her appendix rupture on exactly the same day. Seven thousand miles separated them, but they were both suffering the same medical crisis at the same time.

Rafraf, however, was lucky. She was immediately taken in to surgery. Her sister had to wait.

The hospital in Baghdad was full the day her sister arrived with her ruptured appendix. A market had been bombed earlier that day, and all of the operating rooms were full. There wasn't even a bed or a room for her sister to stay in overnight, so she was sent home and told to try again the next day.

Her sister lived, but had to endure much more pain and a longer recovery than otherwise necessary.

Rafraf came home after a successful surgery and two days in the hospital.

EVEN AS SHE RECOVERED FROM surgery, Rafraf's craving for the taste of home grew. She missed Iraqi bread almost as much as she missed her mother.

"They'll have it at Whole Foods," Kiki suggested. "They have everything there."

So a few weeks later, Kiki and Rafraf made a special trip to the specialty grocery store to try to find bread for Rafraf. They found plenty of flat breads from around the world, but nothing tasted like home.

"Can't you make some?" Kiki suggested. "You should know the recipe by heart."

"Of course," Rafraf said, "but you don't have the right oven."

True Iraqi bread didn't lie flat on a pan. It was baked vertically, on the sidewalls of the large clay oven in Rafraf's backyard. The flames, stoked by real wood and charcoal, carefully licked the top of the bread, browning it just enough to add texture. It tasted best right out of the oven.

Sometimes Rafraf even dreamed of the bread, which she was convinced she would never taste again.

But Whole Foods had other ingredients Rafraf recognized. After almost four months of eating pizza, macaroni and cheese, and Chick-fil-A, she decided she would introduce Rachael and Madison to another Iraqi treat.

Kiki was in Texas sorting out the details of the family's upcoming move. NBC News was transferring Don from the Atlanta bureau to the Dallas bureau in May. Kiki had a lot of work to do.

But before she left, she took Rafraf to buy all the ingredients she needed. Rafraf had in mind a type of puff pastry that she cooked for special occasions back home. Its preparation was relatively easy—flour, sugar, eggs, and spices such as cinnamon. The mixture was kneaded into a smooth dough, rolled into balls, and deep-fried in oil. The result was similar to what Americans called doughnuts, but Rafraf knew her pastries would be much better.

She happily prepared her specialty on a cool Thursday evening in March.

MY CELL PHONE RANG DURING the *Nightly News.* I was at the bureau waiting for my story to air.

"Do we have any of that burn-cream stuff?" Rachael asked over the line.

"Are you okay?" I wasn't that alarmed because Rachael sounded completely calm.

"Yeah. Rafraf just burned her hand and I was wondering if we had burn cream."

"How? Is she okay?"

"Yeah, I guess. She just got hot water on it or steam or something."

"Oh, all right," I said. "We don't have any burn cream that I know of. Have her run cold water on her hand. I'm sure it'll be fine. I'll call back on the way home from work. If she still thinks she needs something, I'll stop and pick something up."

"Okay, Daddy," Rachael said, and promptly hung up.

In about twenty minutes, I called back. I was in my car on the way home.

Rachael answered the phone.

"Hey, Goob," I said, "just wondering if Rafraf still needs me to pick up something for her hand."

"I don't know."

"Well, let me talk to her."

"She can't really talk, all she does is moan."

Horrified, I suddenly realized the injury was worse than I thought. "Where is your sister?"

"She's still in the closet. She ran in there when Rafraf fell on the floor and started screaming."

"Wait," I said, trying to get a grip on what had actually happened. "I thought you said she burned herself with hot water?"

"Well, it was water or maybe that cooking-oil stuff. It sort of blew up while she was making doughnuts."

"Stay near the phone," I insisted, "I'll call you right back."

I hung up, then called Kiki in Texas. "Do you know what's happening at home?"

"Rachael said Rafraf burned herself with steam," Kiki said. "I'm sure she's fine."

"She's not fine. I think maybe she's unconscious, and Madison is hiding in the closet."

"Where are you?" Kiki asked, now equally alarmed.

"Stuck in traffic downtown. I'm gonna call 911."

"Okay. I'll call our neighbor Karen too. She's a nurse."

"Okay, good plan."

I hung up and called 911, kicking myself for not taking Rachael more seriously the first time she called. I had no idea Rafraf had been deep-frying anything.

Kiki had told me a story years earlier about her cousin being horribly burned as a child by oil from a fondue pot. Kiki's aunt and uncle were using it on the kitchen table, with the power cord plugged into the wall.

The four-year-old cousin ran past the table and tripped over the power cord. The cord pulled the fondue pot over, dumping frying oil all over the child's head. She was horribly burned and spent months in the hospital undergoing skin grafts.

I had resolved that we would *never* deep-fry anything in the house. If I had known Rafraf was doing so, I would have made her stop. I certainly wouldn't have allowed the children to be in the kitchen.

BY THE TIME I ARRIVED at the house, the place was crawling with people. The fire department had shown up in force. An engine truck, ambulance, and police car were all parked in front of the house with their lights flashing. It must have been a slow night in east Cobb County.

Rafraf was lying on the sofa in the living room. The paramedics were preparing to put her on a stretcher for the ride to the hospital. Her right arm was wrapped in white gauze bandages.

I pulled one of the paramedics aside immediately.

"She's burned pretty badly," he said. "Third-degree on her hand and arm, and some second-degree spots on her chest and face where the oil hit her."

"Like surgery and skin-grafts burned?" I asked.

"I don't think so, but she should definitely get checked out at the hospital."

"Are you taking her, or should I?"

"We were going to," he said. "But she doesn't need to be in an ambulance. If you're planning to go to the hospital, you can take her."

"Okay, I'll take her right away. Thanks for all the help."

I sent the girls home with our neighbor and immediately drove Rafraf to the emergency room.

The paramedics had treated her burns as much as possible, but she was still in excruciating pain. She rocked back and forth in her seat and moaned all the way to the hospital without saying a word.

*   *   *

RAFRAF HAD BEEN HURT PLENTY of times in her life. She'd suffered her share of bloody lips, knots, and bruises, but had never had so much as an aspirin to dull the pain, much less any sort of pharmacological painkiller.

Such drugs were difficult to come by in Iraq. The Gulf War of 1991 left much of the country's medical infrastructure damaged. Iraqis blamed the United Nations–imposed sanctions that followed the Gulf War for widespread disease and death. Medicine, while not directly affected by the sanctions, was in constant short supply. Even families who could afford drugs were often unable to obtain them. Pain was something to be endured . . . not managed.

But within minutes of her arrival at the hospital emergency room, Rafraf's pain went away.

Don told her they might make her wait before seeing a doctor, but they rushed her into her own room as soon as they saw her.

A nice man came in and gave her some pills, and within a couple of minutes she felt great. Better than great, actually. She felt *awesome!*

A few minutes later, a female nurse popped her head in the room.

"Please stop singing," she said. She was so serious.

"Who's singing?" Rafraf asked.

"You are. Loudly."

"Oh, I guess I am." Rafraf grinned. She didn't see what the problem was with a little singing, but she would try her best not to do it anymore.

A minute later, Don walked into the room. He looked serious too. "They need me to ask you some questions. It's kind of embarrassing. The doctor usually asks, but he's worried about cultural differences. He thought a family member should ask, so I guess that's me."

But Don didn't ask her anything right away. He just stood there looking confused and uncomfortable.

"What are you waiting for?" Rafraf asked.

"Um, I was hoping you'd stop singing."

She did, and he started asking questions. Rafraf didn't see what the big deal was.

"Do you have any known allergies?" Don began. "Anything that you're allergic to like penicillin?"

"Nope. . . . Have I ever told you about my sister?"

"You can tell me later. Are you taking any prescription drugs? Do you drink alcohol? Do you smoke? Any past medical history they should be aware of?"

"Nope, nope, nope, nope," she said, shaking her head like a child. She let out a long sigh. "I love my little Rami. I miss him so much."

"Is there any chance at all that you could be pregnant?" Now Don really did look uncomfortable.

"Hmmm, let me think about that."

"Seriously?"

"Of course not," Rafraf said, laughing. "What kind of girl do you think I am?"

Don asked a few more awkward questions, including something about what time of the month it was.

Then she got really sleepy. "Do you think they'd mind if I lay down on this bed?"

"I think you're supposed to."

"Good."

It was such a nice place for a nap.

THANKFULLY, RAFRAF SURVIVED HER ATTEMPT at pastry making without the need for surgery.

The damage wasn't caused from the oil exploding, but from a pastry.

She later explained that one of the puffs had grown much too large while sitting in the hot oil, inflating like a balloon. Rafraf was trying to remove the balloonish pastry from the oil when it popped, splattering oil everywhere.

She had reflexively covered her face with her arm, which was lucky. Her hand and arm were severely burned by the flying oil, but only a drop or two hit her face and chest.

The scars, doctors assured her, would heal. I told her the days of frying pastries in the house were over.

She was still enjoying the warm glow of painkillers as I drove her home from the hospital.

"I guess now I'll have two hospitals sending me bills," she said cheerily.

"I guess you will. I'm just glad you're okay."

A few minutes passed in silence.

"You know what I really want?" she finally said with a hint of sadness. "Some bread. And my mom."

A single tear rolled slowly down her cheek. It reminded me of Rafraf herself . . . alone and falling with no way to turn back.

TWENTY-FIVE

SUNDAYS

The Teague family went through the same drill every Sunday morning.

First, I would get up and make coffee.

Second, I made a huge batch of pancakes.

Third, I woke everybody else up and we ate pancakes.

Finally, we would all simultaneously realize that we were late for church and rush out of the house as if it were on fire.

One might guess we would alter our routine in an effort to make it to church on time, but we never did. Instead, we started going to a closer church that started half an hour later.

The Roswell Assembly of God wasn't technically our church. Neither Kiki nor I had ever been to an Assembly of God church. But we weren't hung up on denomination or church doctrine. If we felt a connection to the congregation and learned from what the pastor had to say, that was good enough for us. While we believed that Christ was indeed the way to God, we believed that Christians don't all have to worship in exactly the same way.

That said, I was never really comfortable in a charismatic church. It wasn't how I was raised, so I quickly fell out of my comfort zone with such things as dancing in the aisle.

"Who does that on a Sunday morning?" I would say.

"You need to lighten up a little," Kiki would reply.

The actual reason we started going to the Assembly of God church, aside from our poor planning, was because Rachael's best friend went there.

Rachael had such powerful faith. She felt so close to God, but she was also at the age when kids started drifting away from him. We hoped going to church with her best friend would help her continue to grow in that faith.

It never occurred to us to invite Rafraf to church. We would rush out of the house on Sunday mornings, leaving her alone without giving it a second thought.

A couple of weeks after the burn incident, we were going through our usual Sunday-morning rush to get to church on time. As we gathered our stuff downstairs, I noticed Rafraf watching us from the top of the stairs. She was just standing there looking as if she had something on her mind.

"We're going to church," I said, "we should be back in a couple of hours."

"Okay." She sounded down.

I looked at Kiki, who was thinking the same thing I was. She shrugged her shoulders.

"You can come with us if you want," I offered. "But it's totally up to you."

Rafraf's face lit into a smile. "Give me five minutes to get ready," she said, then rushed into her room.

RAFRAF HAD NEVER BEEN INSIDE an American church, though she had seen them in movies.

I tried to tell her what to expect before we got there: "You don't have to be a Christian to go to a church. But Assembly of God churches are really into evangelism, so I can't guarantee someone won't ask about your religion. You don't have to do anything though, you're welcome to just be there and be a part of the congregation."

"I understand," she said.

"You should know there's also a band."

Rafraf smiled again.

THROUGHOUT HER ADULT LIFE, RAFRAF tended to think of her head scarf as something symbolic. But after she stopped wearing the scarf, she began to feel that her connection to Allah was slipping away. He began to feel distant.

That was the last thing she wanted.

Rafraf had an independent and rebellious streak, but she wasn't trying to rebel against Allah. She had lived her life knowing what was right or wrong based on what the Koran told her. No, she didn't always do what was right, but she wasn't turning her back on Allah. She wanted to please Allah, or at least she thought she did.

She fasted in November, during the entire month of Ramadan. She tried to think only pure thoughts during Ramadan, and she even prayed several times a day, something she rarely did back home in Baghdad.

She would never knowingly eat pork. That was out of the question.

Alcohol? She couldn't imagine why anyone would touch the stuff, but she never would.

Sex before marriage? Out of the question.

But why was it a sin to just talk to a man or be alone with him for dinner? She had struggled in that area her entire life.

Surely there was a way to balance her new environment with her desire to please Allah.

That's why she wanted to go to church. Not to look for Jesus, but to be around people with a heart for Allah. That they called him God seemed of little consequence.

Yes, Don had offered on numerous occasions to take her to the mosque or the Islamic Community Center, but Rafraf didn't want to go. She worried she would be judged, if not condemned, by others who would say she had turned her back on where she was from. That her mother had warned her about doing so only made her guilt worse.

Don and Kiki treated her like an adult and didn't seem to judge her.

They would occasionally tell her they didn't approve of her actions, such as staying up all night, or wearing inappropriate clothes, or dating what Don called a "loser." But they also said her choices were ultimately hers to make.

And they never yelled at her. For the first couple of months, she thought it was because they were hiding something.

"Why don't you yell at me?" she asked Kiki one day.

"Do you want us to yell at you?"

"Well," Rafraf continued hesitantly, "I know I've messed up. If I was home, I would be beaten, or at least yelled at. That's how my parents punished misbehavior. But you and Don never do that. It makes me think you're really mad, but trying to hide it."

"I suppose there are people who do that here too," Kiki said. "But we don't do that. If we're mad about something you did, trust me, we'll tell you. But we're not going to yell at you."

"Okay," said Rafraf, relieved.

"But if you want," Kiki joked, "we could set up a daily beating whether you need it or not."

"No thanks." Rafraf laughed. "I think I can get by without that."

But she couldn't get by without feeling some connection with Allah. That's why she wanted to go to church.

RAFRAF FELT AT HOME THE moment she walked into Don and Kiki's church. She had expected to be the only person there with dark skin. In most of east Cobb County, Rafraf felt like a novelty in a sea of fair-haired Caucasians.

But white people were barely half of the two hundred or so people who made up the congregation.

She spotted several families who were obviously immigrants from such places as Africa, Korea, Mexico, and South America. There was no separation of races as she had expected from watching movies. Everyone was mixed in together, and they all looked happy to be there.

The music was good too. It wasn't the robed choir she had originally expected to see. It was a band, with guitars, drums, a piano, and a lead singer with funky hair.

Don had explained to her in the car that there were plenty of more traditional churches in America. That many people grew up with those traditions and felt most comfortable there. But in recent years, a growing number of churches had begun offering "contemporary services." She had had no idea what he meant at the time. Now she did.

She sang and clapped her hands with the music. She listened to the pastor's message and laughed at his jokes. She didn't really know what he was talking about most of the time, but none of it made her mad or feel bad about herself. He mostly told stories about Jesus and explained how people could learn by hearing what Jesus did—and said.

Nobody tried to convert her or even asked about her religious background.

All in all, she had a good day.

That evening, while Kiki and I were watching TV, I asked her about church.

"How do you think it went?"

"Good."

Oh boy, a one-word answer. Those were rarely good. There was a long silence as I pondered my next move. Then Kiki spoke up.

"She said the most amazing thing while we were leaving church. I asked her what she thought of it and she smiled really big and said, 'I needed to be where God was and he was there.'"

I looked over at her sitting in the chair next to me and paused the DVR. I could tell she was wrestling with what to say next. She looked back at me.

"When she said that, I could see how much she loved God and how her heart was searching for him, and I saw him loving her. He loves her so much. God showed me he loves people right where they are and reminded me how he loved me when I didn't know him."

I could tell something had changed in Kiki's heart. All this time I thought we were helping Rafraf, but it turned out God had plans for us too.

TWENTY-SIX

ROOMMATES

Marine Corps lance corporal Mary Katherine Mason came home from Iraq on a stretcher. It was not the way the twenty-year-old's war was supposed to end.

Before heading to Iraq in January 2003, she figured she'd either come home a hero, or in a body bag. Getting injured never entered into the equation.

Mary Katherine was a truck driver, and not just any truck driver, but a fuel-truck driver who resupplied frontline combat units. She knew that the difference between life and death could boil down to simply being on the wrong stretch of road at the wrong time. She accepted that. That she could deal with.

But the mangled mess that used to be her left ankle . . . how could she deal with that?

And the way she hurt it . . . falling off the top of her truck. It still bothered her to think about it, particularly since it wasn't her fault that she fell off the truck.

It could have been worse. She could have fallen on her head. Instead, her left ankle absorbed the impact of the fall, though not well. It was now held together by titanium screws. And after two surgeries and rehab, it still throbbed with pain.

She didn't even get a Purple Heart to go with the pain; those are reserved for service members who are shot or take shrapnel from a bomb, not people who fall off the top of a truck.

Sure, she was on the battlefield, just a few miles from the site of an ambush that led to the deaths of eleven American soldiers, and the highly publicized capture of several others—including Jessica Lynch.

Mary Katherine was refueling combat troops from an infantry unit when she fell off the stupid truck. It happened in the middle of a vicious sandstorm as the battle for Nasiriyah raged around them. She was standing on top of the truck's tank, doing exactly what she was supposed to be doing, when the truck suddenly lurched forward and she fell off. No Purple Heart, no TV news stories, just a stretcher and a long ride out of the desert.

She felt horrible guilt for leaving her unit in battle. Her best friends in the world—people she would fight and die for—would have to go on without her.

Instead of going to Baghdad, Mary Katherine went home to Florida.

Her destroyed ankle made it impossible for her to stay on active duty with the Marine Corps, so instead she would finish her college education at the University of South Florida.

Her junior year of college began in August 2005.

Mary Katherine arrived at the dorm dragging her Marine Corps duffel bag, and her destroyed left ankle. She immediately set out decorating her dorm room. A Marine Corps flag hung on the wall, military certificates and athletic trophies from high school went on shelves.

She brought back one souvenir from the war that also came with her to the dorm. She'd picked up a beautiful, multicolored rug from a shop in Kuwait. It made a great doormat and added a splash of color to the otherwise stark dorm room.

Mary Katherine was excited about the new school year. She had been assigned a new roommate, with a funny name that she couldn't remember. She wanted the room to look great by the time her new roommate arrived.

She surveyed her handiwork.

Marine Corps flag. Check.

Fancy doormat. Check.

Can-do attitude. Check.

RAFRAF WAS IN OVER HER head and she knew it. Who was she to think she could cut it at an American university? Her whole fantasy of staying in the United States was based on something she knew she wasn't capable of; she had to maintain at least a B average, taking a full load of graduate courses, or she would immediately be sent back home.

"There's no way I can do that," she told Don. "I don't know any of the things they teach in American schools. How am I supposed to even pass in graduate school?"

"It's easier in grad school," Don assured her. "The professors assume you're smart because you've already made it through a bachelor's degree. Plus, you're taking political science, that's totally subjective. You can fake your way through that."

Rafraf didn't know what *subjective* meant, but saying so would only prove what she already knew. She was in over her head.

Don had an annoying habit of saying things were going to be okay, when Rafraf knew they weren't.

"You have to have faith," he said more often than she could remember. "You've been singled out for something good. You're not here to fail, you're here to succeed."

He had said the same thing about the bicycle. Rafraf was convinced she would never figure out how to ride the thing. She crashed more times than she could remember and always got back on expecting to crash again. She was right. Every time Don let go, she fell.

But one day, after weeks of trying, she didn't fall. Don let go, and she just kept on going—even pedaling! She went all the way to the end of the street before she realized she didn't know how to use the brakes.

"I told you you could do it," Don said while helping her up from the pavement. "You can do anything you put your mind to, you've just got to believe."

Rafraf wanted to believe that about graduate school, but circumstances had made it so difficult. Beyond her doubts about her academic ability, she was also getting enormous pressure from her family.

Rafraf had made sure to always wear her scarf before video-conferencing with her mother. For ten months, she kept up the appearance that she was wearing her scarf whenever she left the house. She lied repeatedly to her mother hoping to avoid the inevitable tears if Jamila learned the truth. But somehow, her mother found out.

"I told you not to forget your culture or turn against Allah," Jamila said over the phone, "and look at what you've done."

"But, Mother," Rafraf pleaded, "you don't understand how hard it is here."

"I don't care. I told you when you were twelve years old that the decision to wear the scarf could never be changed. It's an insult to Allah. You are never to call this house again. You have no family, and I have no daughter named Rafraf."

With that, the line clicked off.

Rafraf was crushed.

But once again, Don started up with his annoying optimism: "She'll get over it."

"No, she won't," Rafraf managed to say between sobs. "You don't know my mother."

"But I know you, and your mom does too. She loves you. She'll figure it all out in her own time."

Rafraf knew that would never happen, but decided not to argue. She would focus instead on her next failure . . . graduate school.

A semester lasted four and a half months, so assuming she failed all of her classes, she had that long until her world came crashing down. Rafraf decided she would make the best of it.

AS RAFRAF WALKED THE HALLWAY looking for her assigned dorm room, her anxiety graduated to fear. She almost had to laugh.

People have tried to shoot me and blow me up, she thought. *Whatever this is like, it can't be that bad.*

She found her room and knocked on the door. A few seconds later, a giant opened it.

The woman stood just over six feet tall. She was pretty, with sandy brown hair, hazel eyes, and an amused look on her face.

"I'm Mary Katherine," she said, extending her hand. "You must be my new roommate."

Rafraf introduced herself and the young women shook hands.

"Is something wrong?" Mary Katherine asked. It took only one look at Rafraf's face to see something was indeed wrong.

"Are you a soldier?" Rafraf asked, though she already knew the answer. SEMPER FIDELIS was written on a crimson flag hanging on the back wall of the room. The flag brought back a terrible vision of tanks and Darth Vader troops rolling past her house.

"Not a soldier, a marine," Mary Katherine corrected as she limped into the room. "My unit is back in Iraq, but I'm injured so I can't be there."

"Is that where you got hurt?"

"Yeah, right after the war started. I hated coming home and leaving the rest of my marines. I never even made it to Baghdad. I really wanted to see Baghdad." She looked at Rafraf seriously. "How about you? Where are you from? I'm guessing Cuba or maybe Spain?"

Rafraf wondered if she was at the center of a cosmic joke.

"Baghdad," Rafraf said simply, "I'm Iraqi."

"Oh, crap. I need a beer. Do you want one?"

"I don't drink alcohol, I'm Muslim."

"Right. I guess I should have known that. Anything else I should know before I continue offending you?"

"Do you know what that is?" Rafraf pointed to the colorful rug in front of the door.

"The doormat? I got that in Kuwait," Mary Katherine said proudly.

"It's a prayer rug," Rafraf said simply. "It's sacred. You're supposed to pray to Allah on it, not wipe your feet on it."

"Oh, crap. I had no idea. I was raised Methodist. I'm sorry."

"It's okay." Rafraf smiled.

"We can still be roommates, right? I never had a problem with Iraqis or anything. The war isn't about that."

"People keeping saying that, but if there's no reason to go to war, why is there a war?"

"I don't know. Maybe we can figure that out."

"Maybe we can."

MARY KATHERINE FOUND HER NEW roommate fascinating. The two young women spent long nights in those first few weeks of school learning about each other's life, family, and religion.

Mary Katherine was particularly interested in learning about Islam. "What's Allah like?" she asked during one of their late-night sessions.

"He's like a judge," Rafraf explained. "He judges everything we do."

"Is there a heaven for Muslims?"

"Yes, and a hell."

"How do you go to heaven?"

"Well, it's not easy," Rafraf began. "Allah keeps track of everything you do in your life, the good and the bad. We believe that there's like an angel on each shoulder. The angel on the right is good, and the angel on the left is bad. Those angels are who keep the score."

"And when you die?"

"When you die, the angels lay out your life before Allah. If the good outweighs the bad, you go to heaven. If the bad outweighs the good, you go to hell. If they're the same, you go to a mountain and wait for Allah so you can plead your case."

Mary Katherine had already learned enough about Rafraf's life to know her new roommate had a rebellious streak. "So what about you, Rafraf? Why do you break the rules?"

"Because it's too late for me," Rafraf said sadly. "My mother told me all the time when I was growing up that I was sinning, and I would go to hell. By now, there's no way for me to catch up. The scale is tipped to the left."

"But you don't break all the rules. You're not running around sleeping with guys, and you don't drink alcohol or eat pork."

"Because I know those things are wrong. I may be going to hell, but at least I know right from wrong."

"Do you know what Christians believe?" Mary Katherine was not in the habit of speaking about her faith to others. In fact, Mary Katherine couldn't remember *ever* asking such a question to anyone. But considering the subject was religion, and Rafraf had just laid out her beliefs, it seemed like a fair question to ask.

"Don and Kiki are Christian," Rafraf answered. "I've been to their church. They believe Jesus is more than just a prophet, that he's God and he died and rose again."

"Do you know why he died?"

"Because the Jews killed him."

"Technically, it was the Romans," Mary Katherine said, "but that's not why he died. He died to pay the price for our sins. For all that stuff that stacked up on your left shoulder. He paid for it so you don't have to."

"But what must you do in return? Nothing is free."

"You just have to believe and accept it."

"What about your sins?" Rafraf said. "You drink and do other things against God. What about that?"

"If you ask for forgiveness, God forgives you. Yes, you're supposed to try to not sin, but nobody can. That's why Jesus paid the price."

"Well, you have your way, and we have ours," Rafraf said. "We'll know who's right someday."

With that, the new roommates moved on to other topics. Mary Katherine invited Rafraf to go to church with her a couple of times during the school year, but Rafraf never accepted the invitations. They didn't have to believe the same things to be friends.

But while the young women differed in areas of religion, they agreed on one thing.

Men.

Mary Katherine had never known a woman as popular with men as Rafraf. She was truly a guy magnet.

Within seconds of walking into a party or a nightclub, Rafraf would be surrounded by men. Mary Katherine wondered if the Iraqi had the same effect on men back home. She suspected that if she did, life would be difficult for her indeed.

But this was Tampa, not Baghdad. Mary Katherine made it a point to always invite Rafraf when she and her friends went out. With Rafraf around, there would never be a shortage of men to dance with.

RAFRAF'S MOVE TO TAMPA CAME at about the same time my family moved to Dallas. Jim Cummins, the NBC News correspondent based in Dallas for nearly twenty years, was retiring, and I was to be his replacement.

Kiki and the girls were thrilled to be moving to Texas. It's where my TV news career began, and Kiki had always considered it her adopted home state. We bought some land, built a house with a barn for the horses, and set about planting new roots.

At least, they did.

I, as usual, spent most of my time on the road. The 2005 hurricane season was a nightmare for millions along the Gulf Coast, and I was right in the middle of it.

I spent three weeks in New Orleans covering Hurricane Katrina, and another two weeks covering Hurricane Rita in southeast Texas. The hurricanes were tragedies, but for me at least they provided one bit of respite.

For almost six weeks, I had no cell phone coverage at all. That meant that for the first time in nearly two years, Rafraf couldn't call on me to solve minor problems.

We all loved Rafraf. The girls thought of her as a big sister. Kiki considered Rafraf a friend as well as a member of the family. I was never able to define my relationship with Rafraf. I didn't think of her as a daughter, though at times I felt my role was as a father. A little sister? Perhaps, but that doesn't seem to fit either.

In short, you don't choose family members. They are assigned to you at birth; either yours or theirs. But Kiki and I chose to make Rafraf a part of our family because she was in need.

Still, there was so much drama with Rafraf! We could count on a daily crisis involving bureaucracy, confidence, school enrollment, her mother, finances, or boyfriends. She was always embroiled in some horrible circumstance that seemed to threaten life itself. Living with Rafraf was exhausting.

So as bad as the aftermath of a hurricane or other natural disaster was, it did offer a break from the daily phone calls from Florida that almost always seemed to involve worry.

The separation from our family, and my phone, would do Rafraf good.

ABOUT MIDWAY THROUGH RAFRAF'S FIRST semester at USF, it dawned on her. She was actually doing well in her classes. She wasn't an A student by any stretch, but with enough hard work she decided that maybe she could get the B's she needed to stay in school. The only problem was finding time to do her schoolwork, or even to go to class.

With the freedom to do whatever she wanted for the first time in her life, Rafraf decided to do . . . everything.

Armed with a valid student visa, Rafraf was allowed to work a part-time job while in school. She found one, as many college students do, at Starbucks.

Funny, she thought, *I don't even like coffee, and now I'm making it for people.*

She also decided that it was time to learn to drive and convinced one of her new friends to give her driving lessons in his car.

It didn't go well.

Rafraf sat behind the wheel of Sean's Ford Focus feeling more confident than ever.

"Just put it in gear and go slowly around the parking lot," Sean instructed. Rafraf had met Sean in one of her government classes, and they immediately became friends. He was one of the few male friends she had who didn't hit on her constantly. She liked that.

"I know," Rafraf said.

After a few tries, she managed the timing of the manual transmission, and the car lurched forward.

"Second gear now," Sean urged as the rpm of the engine began to climb. She awkwardly shifted from first to second, let out the clutch, and the Ford picked up even more speed.

It was Sunday, and the huge parking lot was practically empty.

"You're doing great," Sean coached as the car accelerated toward the end of the parking lot. "Just slow it down to turn, and remember to put the clutch in so it doesn't stall."

"What?" Rafraf said, looking at Sean.

"Stall. Don't stall the car."

But Rafraf didn't understand. She looked at Sean to try to get a better idea of what he was saying, taking her eyes off the course in front of her. "I don't understand what you're saying."

"Tree, stop or you're going to hit a tree."

The car was accelerating rapidly toward the tree-lined sidewalk at the end of the parking lot.

"But you said *stall,*" Rafraf repeated, still looking at Sean.

"*Tree*," he said with greater urgency. "*Stop!*"

But Rafraf didn't put her foot on the brake or turn the wheel or even look where the car was going. She just kept looking at Sean, wondering why he was talking about trees.

"*Stop!*" Sean shouted. He grabbed the handle of the emergency brake and pulled it as hard as he could. But it was too late. The small car bounced hard as the front tires hit the curb protecting the sidewalk. A half second later, the car slammed into a giant oak tree.

"Oh, that tree," Rafraf said. "Why didn't you say so?"

"You just crashed my car," Sean said, trying to sound calm. "I only have liability insurance."

Rafraf didn't know what that meant, but by the look on Sean's face, she guessed it wasn't good. She suddenly felt stupid again. She tried not to start crying, but she couldn't help herself.

"I'm sorry," she pleaded. "I don't actually know how to drive."

Sean laughed in spite of the situation. "Obviously. It's okay, Rafraf, you didn't hit the tree that hard. I'm sure the car is fine."

"Then can we try again?"

"I don't think so."

Rafraf and Sean remained friends, but he never let her drive his car again. She did convince some other friends to give her lessons, and within weeks she was ready for her driving test.

She failed. It may have been the shortest driving test in history. The instructor failed her before she even backed out of the parking spot.

"That lady was mean," Rafraf told Don on the phone later that day. "She said I tried to back up with the parking brake on. I don't even know what that is."

"They'll let you take it again in a few weeks, right?" Don asked.

"Yes. Hopefully I'll get a different instructor who's not so mean."

Two weeks later, she took the test again with a different instructor.

She failed for not looking over her shoulder while backing out of the parking spot. Still, it was progress . . . the second-shortest driving test in history.

"Why don't you just give it some time," Don told her over the phone. "The buses on campus can't be that bad."

"I don't have a choice," Rafraf said sadly. "I'm not allowed to take the test again for at least a month. If I fail it again, I'll have to wait a year before trying again."

"Well, don't worry about it. You're coming home for Thanksgiving in a few weeks. Just concentrate on your schoolwork, and maybe we can work on driving when you come to Texas."

"What's it like there?" Rafraf had seen pictures of the new house, but had never been there.

"It's hot and dry and mostly flat. You should feel right at home."

"Do I have a room?"

"Of course. You're part of the family. You always have a room."

"Good." Rafraf smiled.

"Oh, I almost forgot. Congratulations."

"For what?"

"Your one-year anniversary in the U.S.," Don said cheerily. "I told you things would work out. You just have to believe."

NEW LIFE

Rafraf walked confidently down four steps and continued until she was standing waist deep in the water. She smiled at Kiki and me, then turned her attention to those who had gathered in the sanctuary.

In her left hand she clutched a copy of the New Testament translated into Arabic and English.

"I'd like to read a passage from Romans twelve." She opened her Bible and spoke with a strong voice. " 'Do not conform any longer to the pattern of this world, but be transformed by the renewing of your mind. Then you will be able to test and approve what God's will is—his good, pleasing, and perfect will.'"

The date was October 5, 2008. It had been almost four years since Rafraf had left her family and her life behind in Iraq.

THE RAFRAF WHO STOOD BEFORE me was in many ways a different person from the frightened young woman who had carried her stuffed animal up the escalator at the Atlanta airport. She was secure in her identity, and confident of her place in the world.

Three years had passed since Rafraf entered graduate school at the University of South Florida.

In what I still consider to be a comical move on God's part, Rafraf spent her first year of college—her first period of real independence—sharing a dorm room with a veteran of the Iraq War.

She and Mary Katherine became close friends. They laughed, cried, studied, and celebrated life in that unique way that only college students seem to do.

And Rafraf made other friends in Florida. Her close circle included young women and men from all over the world: American, Egyptian, Iranian, Syrian, and—most surprising of all—Israeli.

She dated, but not in the frantic way she had in Atlanta. It seemed to me that she was realizing that her value as a person wasn't determined by what men thought of how she looked. She found meaningful relationships and she found love.

Rafraf finally did learn to drive, which was not nearly as easy as it should have been.

When Rafraf came home for Thanksgiving week in Texas, I started giving her driving lessons. She was doing great . . . until Thanksgiving morning. It's a morning the clerk at the mini-mart near our house will never forget—the morning Kiki's SUV, with Rafraf behind the wheel, destroyed the ice machine in front of the store. Nobody was hurt, but I learned that ice machines cost about $2,500 to replace.

Rafraf is a better driver today; she has her own car—with an I LOVE IRAQ bumper sticker—and her driver's license. She passed the test on her third try.

IN MANY WAYS, THE LAST few years have been even more trying for Rafraf, and us, than her first year in the United States.

The biggest source of stress was Rafraf's visa, which remained tied to her performance at school. The strain of working two jobs, taking a full load of classes, and maintaining a B average was a constant burden.

Rafraf completed all of her required classes in 2007, but allowed her grade point average to slip just below the required level. She needed an A in an elective to raise her overall average, but got sick midway through her final semester and had to withdraw from school. The withdrawal resulted in a crisis, with the government set to pull her visa and send her back to Iraq.

But once again, God intervened. An immigration lawyer took Rafraf's case, for free, and eventually got Rafraf a hearing in front of an immigration officer with the power to grant her political asylum. Ellen Gorman, ironically, was referred to Rafraf through Gulfcoast Jewish Family Services.

Rafraf told her story to the immigration officer who would decide her case.

"Is there anything that hasn't happened to you?" the officer asked. She was laughing when she said it, but it was a sympathetic laugh.

"I think that's everything," Rafraf said, unsure if she was supposed to answer.

In April 2008, Rafraf was granted political asylum in the United States. She's on track to become a U.S. citizen in a few years.

As of the writing of this book, Rafraf is back at the University of South Florida, raising her GPA and beginning to write her master's thesis.

RAFRAF'S MOTHER FORGAVE HER FOR abandoning the scarf, but relations with her family remained strained. They would become more difficult with the decision Rafraf was about to make.

Kiki and I had made every effort to encourage Rafraf to stay connected with her culture and to follow her religious traditions. We continued to believe that we should leave Rafraf's spiritual life as a matter between her and God. It was often painful to watch her struggle.

Still, Kiki and I feel that Rafraf's journey has been a blessing for our family. We all love her dearly. We set out to help someone else, but our lives were made better.

Rachael and Madison gained a big sister who taught them about a world they could never have imagined.

Kiki learned that she was more compassionate and patient than she thought she was.

I learned to trust God in a way I had never before done. I saw his will, his love, and his plans revealed in unmistakable ways. I learned that saying yes when God calls can lead us in directions we would never plan for ourselves.

I learned that my wife is infinitely smarter than me, though deep down I probably knew that all along.

Finally, I learned that faith takes courage.

IN THE SUMMER OF 2008, Rafraf started having dreams—vivid dreams that she couldn't ignore no matter how hard she tried.

Something was chasing her. Something not human. Something not of this world.

Rafraf escaped by running into a building. When she emerged on the other side, she found herself standing at the edge of a cliff. There was no place left to run—a deep chasm fell away beneath her.

She noticed Kiki and I were standing at her side, along with a woman she didn't recognize. The woman hugged Rafraf and smiled.

"She's not here getting married," Kiki said.

The woman started to cry.

"Why are you crying?" Rafraf asked.

"You only come here when you get married, or you die," the woman said. "I'm crying because you're dying and you won't make it to the other side."

"What's over there?" Rafraf asked, looking across the chasm.

"God," the woman said.

"I can still make it," Rafraf pleaded, "tell me what to do."

The woman tried to tell her, but Rafraf didn't understand what she was saying.

Rafraf never learned the answer. In her dream, she died. When she awoke, she vowed to find the answer for herself.

RAFRAF CLOSED THE BIBLE, AND smiled at those who had gathered in front of her. There were a few dozen people in the room. She knew them all from a year of Sundays.

The water around her felt warm.

She looked toward the pastor, a young man named Jordan leading his first congregation in a small Dallas church called Mercy Place.

Rafraf nodded that she was ready.

"I'm doing this," she said, "because life is too short to live apart from God."

ACKNOWLEDGMENTS

This book, like Rafraf's story, would not have been possible without the hard work and encouragement of countless people.

Special thanks go to my wife, Kiki. Without her faith in God, trust in me, and willingness to open her home to a stranger, this story would still be untold. Thank you also to my daughters, Rachael and Madison, who bring more joy into my life than I could ever express.

Dozens of my colleagues played critical roles in Rafraf's journey. My friend Kerry Sanders proved invaluable and endlessly upbeat. Kevin Sites, who now calls Rafraf his little sister, gave generously of his time and effort. More people than I can name gave money, and they all did so enthusiastically. I am grateful to all.

My literary agent, Wes Yoder, and manager, Garrett Hicks, helped a guy who clearly knew nothing about writing a book begin the process. My editor, Cindy Lambert of Howard Books, provided constant encouragement and patiently helped guide the story.

I would like to thank Rafraf's parents, brothers, and sisters for raising a confident young woman. I would especially like to thank her mother for having the courage to let her daughter pursue a new life.

I sincerely thank the men and women of the U.S. military for sacrificing so much for all of us.

Thank you, Rafraf, for your friendship.

Above all, I want to thank God for loving me . . . and for faulty detonators.

Printed in the United States
By Bookmasters